Bush Flying

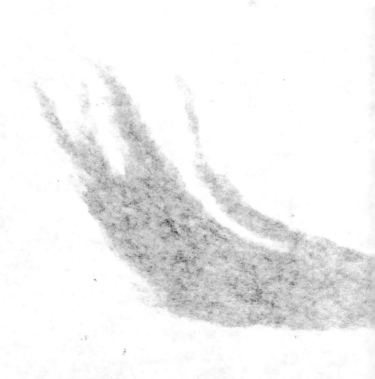

Bush Flying

The Romance of the North

Robert S. Grant

hancock

house

ISBN 0-88839-350-4
Copyright © 1995 Robert S. Grant

Cataloging in Publication Data
Grant, Robert S.
    Bush flying
ISBN 0-88839-350-4

    1. Grant, Robert S. 2. Bush pilots—Canada—Biography.
    I. Title
TL540.G72A3 1995 629.13'092 C95-910635-9

Editor: DM Communications
Cover photo: Robert S. Grant
Production: Myron Shutty, Sandi Miller, and Nancy Kerr

Published simultaneously in Canada and the United States by

HANCOCK HOUSE PUBLISHERS LTD.
19313 Zero Avenue, Surrey, B.C. V4P 1M7
(604) 538-1114   Fax (604) 538-2262

HANCOCK HOUSE PUBLISHERS
1431 Harrison Avenue, Blaine, WA 98230-5005
(604) 538-1114   Fax (604) 538-2262

Contents

1 Plastic Pen

As the tiny, fabric-covered airplane left the runway, a four-year-old boy on board began kicking and screaming. Desperately, his mother tried comforting him but the higher they went, the more he shrieked. Abruptly, the pilot stood the airplane on a wing tip and sharply banked around. With a horrific thud, the airplane plunked back onto the runway so hard that its black tires nearly burst.

The child-like reaction was hardly surprising. I was that child and, in 1946, the three-seat Piper PA-12 Super Cruiser belonged to a rental company called Central Airways at Island Airport in Toronto, Ontario. My father, the pilot, was disappointed, and he stomped away to wait in a nearby office while my mother gently wiped the tears from my face. The brief flight had been an attempt to introduce his firstborn to the so-called wonderful world of aviation.

Around the age of eight, I wandered into a hobby store in Belleville, on Lake Ontario's Bay of Quinte. From the shop's ceiling hung dozens of model airplanes. There were yellow ones, blue ones, some with checkered tails, and others with bright red sun bursts on their wings. Intrigued, I saved my meager allowance for weeks and bought a plastic airplane kit.

After assembling the model, I clipped photographs of things

with wings and perforated my bedroom walls with hundreds of thumbtacks. Over time, and with the help of a complete collection of bubble gum cards featuring airplanes from every nation, I developed a knowledge that partially redeemed me in my father's eyes. Few boys my age could identify airplanes as well.

A move to Madoc, twenty-six miles north of Belleville, brought my family closer to Peterborough where Chemong Airways based a half-dozen floatplanes for rentals and flight training. Older now, I began riding regularly as a dubious passenger with my father in two-seat Aeronca Champions and Chiefs. Slowly, I started acquiring an understanding of the passion he felt for airplanes.

My grandparents lived in Chapleau, 185 miles northwest of Sudbury. Each summer, they invited me to stay with them. In this quiet French-English railway community, I developed a genuine admiration for the forests and waters surrounding the town, especially a river flowing along the edge of town called the Kebsquasheshing River. It provided everyone with beaches and drinking water, and a place for fishing and canoeing. A pair of commercial air services sent their seaplanes out each morning into the nearby bush country.

Sometimes a bright yellow floatplane called a Noorduyn Norseman taxied away from the dock of Theriault Air Services. The engine's huge exhaust stacks emitted rumbling sounds, like the steam engines passing through Chapleau. Later, I learned that the Norseman was the first Canadian airplane designed strictly for bush flying and it flew its maiden flight in 1935.

From a bridge above the railway tracks, I watched the pugnosed freighter taxi the river's length until it became little more than a speck beyond the Ontario Department of Lands and Forests air base. Eagerly, I waited for the pilot to check the Norseman's 600-horsepower engine. On windless days, I heard the click of water rudders striking the backs of the oil-dotted Edo seaplane floats. That metallic sound marked the beginning of one of the greatest shows in northern Ontario.

The engine's rumble changed to a high-pitched, ear-shattering roar as the throttle went to full takeoff position. Around a bend, the yellow dot would become an airplane again, with brightly colored wings slanted back and blue-ringed nose pointed upward. White, foaming water enveloped the tail and sunlight flashed on the elevators as the pilot tried to ease his heavily loaded craft into the air.

Eventually, he raised one float, then the other, like a barrel in a ballet, and the Norseman slipped clear of the river. As it drew nearer, children on the beaches stopped playing, mothers put down their magazines and, if a train happened to be in town, passengers pressed their faces against the window panes.

Occasionally, the roar ceased seconds after the Norseman passed the sandy beach. It returned to the dock, its exhaust snarling like a hungry black bear as silvery ripples followed the floats. When the engine stopped, we sometimes heard the pilot yell, "The damn thing won't get off the water." To the consternation of the paying passengers, packsacks, fishing rods, or grocery boxes would come flying out the rear cabin door.

The pilot climbed back into his cockpit, slammed the door and repeated the takeoff procedure. Usually he made it into the air on the second run.

We respected the precisely-honed judgment of these hardy individuals but always wondered how they knew exactly what weight to unload. Over the years, I learned, that such people went largely unrecognized in Canada's aviation industry. Those who manipulated the giant airliners or military jets received the accolades; not the Norsemen "drivers" who shunted fuel drums, loaded drill rods, or shuffled bags of gold ore everyday. It didn't matter to us on that Chapleau beach whether pilots wore gold braid or scuffed bush boots.

My entry into the hands-on world of aviation resulted from my first summer job as a section-hand laborer on the Canadian Pacific Railway. A scrawny, pimply-faced sixteen-year-old at the end of August in 1959, my $200 CPR savings of amounted to more money than I had ever seen. At home—the family had moved back to Belleville—I needed something on which to spend what seemed like a teenage fortune. My father intended to ensure my earnings wouldn't be wasted—so he drove me to meet Murray Clapp, chief instructor at the Prince Edward Flying Club in Picton south of Belleville.

Flying lessons began on a 65-horsepower trainer called an Aeronca Champion, registered CF-JUQ. At $12 per hour with an instructor, my savings soon disappeared. Luckily in 1960, a job wasn't too hard to find, and work as a clerk-typist and packer in a tomato cannery plant enabled me to fly alone for the first time in August. Instructor Tony Jacobs guided me through the steps to acquire a private pilot license at the age of seventeen.

After high school, several jobs led me to General Motors Corp. in Oshawa and I promptly bought a Piper J-3 Cub for $1,400 in 1963. Built in 1946, it had been modified to clipped wings and had a plywood instrument panel with a John Deere water temperature indicator in place of an oil pressure guage. After a year of flying CF-RCX, I returned to Picton for a commercial license course from ex-Nordair pilot Conrad Racine.

Despite a successful flight test in December 1964, chances of employment as a professional pilot were slim. To enhance my skills, I obtained an instructor rating at the Oshawa Flying Club. Before the course on 90-horsepower Aeronca Tri-Champions ended, the club offered full-time work. Not sorry to leave the world of time cards and time clocks behind, I resigned from "the Motors" and began earning $150 per month and $2 per flying hour—half my previous salary.

During the first summer of teaching people to fly, I found the work more enjoyable than anything I had imagined. Air cadets, senior citizens, pregnant women, and other student pilots from all walks of life kept the job exciting. One bad weather day, a club member suggested I enter university and only fly during summers. A meeting with a guidance teacher led me to Waterloo Lutheran University which accepted me in September 1965 as an adult student majoring in biology. Near the end of my first term, when not probing gastric pouches and gonads of scyphozoans, I sent applications to air services across Canada. At least four summers ahead presented opportunities to experience areas outside of southern Ontario. In April, 1966, a letter bearing a stylized blue caribou logo arrived in Waterloo.

2   Joyce's Sleeper

Caribou Air Charter Ltd.'s ostentatious letterhead alone would have enticed me to Kelowna in British Columbia's colorful Okanagan Valley. Intrigued with the mountain province, I accepted a position as fire patrol pilot. On a cool April morning, I left Kitchener behind and boarded a westbound Trans Canada Air Lines Douglas DC-8. At Calgary, runway sweepers barely managed to clear away the freshly fallen snow before a Canadian Pacific Airlines Douglas DC-6 rumbled into a parking place beside the jet.

After I quickly scampered up the boarding stairs of the "Six" and heard the clunk of its massive doors, I began to anticipate the new experiences, sights and sounds that lay ahead.

Soon, sharp-peaked mountains appeared beneath a thin cloud layer as the gigantic airplane descended toward Kelowna. On final descent, I couldn't see the runway and feared the pilots were landing on the side of a hill. At last, multi-hued cone markers flashed by the wing's trailing edge, and we touched down hard on Kelowna's asphalt surface.

The few passengers who disembarked the DC-6 quickly disappeared into taxis and drove away. Near by, Caribou Air Charter's office flanked a metal-sided hangar and beside it, I spotted several Piper PA-18s and a Piper PA-12 tied down with thick yellow ropes. Two men worked on one and another tightened the landing gear bolts of a round-nosed Cessna 195. The clink-clink of wrenches against metal were the only sounds I could hear after the DC-6 roared by on its final leg to Vancouver.

Inside the hangar, I introduced myself to the owner. Over the telephone, he had promised my salary would begin the moment I arrived in Kelowna. Denying having said so, he now insisted my pay would commence only after my assignment to Dawson Creek, 365 miles north of his office. Having borrowed airfare and with only a few dollars left, I felt exasperated, but there was nothing I could do.

"You know, I admire young men like you who go out on their own and get instructor's ratings," he said. "Tell you what; you do some flight training for me until it's time to go to Dawson Creek and I'll let you sleep in a trailer here at the airport."

The trailer's previous occupants left the place clean, but the structure lacked heating and spring nights in the Okanagan Valley were often cold. Another pilot in a similar situation moved in three days later. Caribou Air Charter had assigned Dick to work from Smithers with a Piper PA-18. Shortly thereafter, he accepted an offer from Canadian Pacific Air Lines and left. A decent type, I thought, until I noticed several personal items missing after he departed. I never saw him again.

Cooking facilities didn't exist in the trailer. For meals, I hitch-hiked to Kelowna and Vernon. Without heat, I developed a terrible wracking cold and for days, could barely leave the trailer or speak without bursting into fits of painful, nonstop coughing. Despite a lack of medication, I survived what I was later convinced had been pneumonia. Welcome to British Columbia.

My first flight took place six days after my arrival. A newly licensed pilot decided to rent the company's Luscombe 8E and fly seventy miles north to Anglemont on the edge of Shuswap Lake. Once there, he carried out an unauthorized landing and flew into the steeply rising, one-way airstrip hard enough to collapse the left landing gear. Miraculously, he didn't bend the propeller. Caribou Air Charter's owner flew me in the company's Cessna 195 to the site where we lifted the damaged Luscombe up to insert a bolt in the undercarriage. After a brief inspection my employer deemed it safe enough for flight.

11

"Take it to Kelowna. I'll meet you there," he snapped.

Luscombes, slim, all-metal airplanes designed in the 1930s, had developed a reputation for being sensitive on landings. This one, had spent the last twenty-four hours on its side and showed no indication of fuel in the gas tanks. I removed the wing gas caps and thought I heard some swirling inside. The owner seemed unconcerned, so, awed by his authority and lacking the confidence with which I taught in Oshawa, I started the engine.

Aware of the airstrip's short length and strong possibility of wind shear at the threshold, I taxied uphill to the extreme end and wheeled around. As the throttle reached its full open position, I found it difficult to keep the Luscombe in a straight line with the tiny rudder pedals. The airplane also became airborne at a slower speed than I'd expected and now began my first trip into the Rocky Mountains' Monashee Range. With an unknown quantity of gasoline aboard, I pointed the nose across another hill, picked up Shuswap Lake and reached for a map.

To my surprise, there wasn't a shred of paper aboard resembling a map. At best, I hoped to remember enough landmarks from the flight to Anglemont to find my way to Kelowna. Soon, Shuswap Lake led to a Canadian Pacific Railway line and beside the tracks, a well-traveled highway pointed southward. My fear that the engine might quit or I might become lost with nowhere to land made the minutes pass slowly.

Finally, an elongated body of water took shape to my right and I recognized it as Okanagan Lake. Moments later, Kelowna's airport became visible. Now, I thought, if the engine stops, at least I'd be close to base. The highway didn't look like inviting, since steep hillsides spread out from every edge, and hydro poles and telephone lines crossed the pavement regularly.

That trip turned out to be one of the longest, most terrifying of my career, and at the end, I had the tricky Luscombe landing to anticipate. Luckily, all went well. After several days of teaching students on the Luscombe, I overcame my misgivings about the aircraft.

As the weather warmed, renewed fire patrol contracts for the British Columbia Forestry Service led to my training checkout and familiarization with the Piper PA-18 Super Cub. Originally flown in the late 1940s, the Super Cubs became known for an ability to adapt to unusual circumstances. One Canadian Arctic company fitted them with oversized, low-pressure tires and landed them routinely near the North Pole. Some towed banners in the United States and Canada, a few hauled overloads of wild rice from shallow, short lakes, and others did well as trainers on wheels, skis, or floats. Caribou Air Charter pilots appreciated the Super Cubs' four-hour range and slow speeds. As fire patrol/aerial detection airplanes, they handled beautifully.

As the last snow flake disappeared from northeastern British Columbia, where my employer expected me to spend the summer of 1966, the province's Forest Service called. They demanded a pilot and airplane immediately in Dawson Creek. From this frontier town on Mile Zero of the Alaska Highway, I would patrol millions of acres of ranger districts. Having read every word I could find on the area's geography, I expected some fantastic scenery.

Aware of my southern Ontario background, the people at Caribou Air Charter wisely decided not to allow me to undertake the long Kelowna-Dawson Creek flight on my own. In mountain pilot parlance, they considered me a "flatlander," i.e., anyone ill-fated enough to be born east of the Rocky Mountains. Robert Bluett, one of the Okanagan's most experienced pilots, drew the assignment of accompanying me in Super Cub CF-ONN and intended to make sure I did not get lost.

We left Kelowna and its blooming fruit orchards early in the morning, shortly after the usual fog from Okanagan Lake burned off. Cruising past 8,000 foot peaks, we crossed the Columbia River and continued northeast toward a gravel airstrip at the Mica Creek dam site. The valleys, glaciers and steep cliff faces looked threatening as we plodded along at eighty-five miles per hour in our minuscule airplane pulled by a collection of parts called a Lycoming engine.

At Mica Creek we pumped some 80/87 octane from a fuel drum cache into our wing tanks, and took off again. On this leg, the clouds became broken and their nearness made the whole vista breathtaking from the Super Cub's cockpit. We tracked northwest now but snow showers forced us into a valley where solid squalls blocked our way.

Bluett took over, advanced the throttle to its limit and climbed the PA-18 for a very long time. Mount Robson, an awesome apparition 12,972 feet above sea level, loomed on our right as we continued upward, avoiding giant puffs of cumulus. We leveled at 17,000 feet and waited for a glimpse of level ground. Despite the height and our time aloft in thin air, neither of us felt any ill effects by the time we cleared the "Rocks." For me the surroundings of sky, rock and cloud resembled a mystical aerial world.

We spotted Grande Prairie in Alberta and altered course for Dawson Creek. After six hours and thirty minutes in the air since leaving Kelowna, we landed at Dawson, my base for the next three months. Caribou Air Charter's owner left instructions with Bluett to stay as long as necessary to ensure I could navigate and work amiably with the British Columbia Forestry Service staff.

Bluett stayed more than a week, even though I had taught basic air navigation back in Oshawa I could barely find my way around. Aerial detection maps lacked contours and consisted only of blue and white colors on scales of ten statute miles to one inch. In desperation, Bluett "laid it on the line." Either I map read and kept myself out of trouble or I went home to Ontario. His approach worked—after one last long fire patrol to Fort Nelson and back to Dawson Creek, he caught the first airliner out for Kelowna.

Most fire patrols took me to Fort Nelson 300 miles further up the Alaska Highway. Flight requests came in daily and salary started at $450 per month, with an additional $4.50 for every hour in the air. Departures took place at 10:00 A.M. every morning for runs east to the Alberta border, north to the Northwest Territories and then parallel to the point where British Columbia, the Northwest Territories and the Yukon Territory intersected. After a cruise along the Liard Plateau, where caribou were common and black bears trundled along creeks and rivers, the Super Cub's route crossed the Alaska Highway.

At the end of most days, CF-ONN's logbook showed up to ten hours in three ranger districts. As pilot/observer, I flew alone, but sometimes office radio operator Ann Dickey or supervisor Terry Matthews rode along. Occasionally, fire fighters accompanied me to look at blazes they had controlled.

One fire fighter developed a particular interest in a sleeper that had lain dormant after three days of heavy rain. Called the "Joyce" fire, I'd reported it and suggested the name—in honor of my sister—to the British Columbia Forest Service. A tiny smoke at first, it exploded into a fury that nearly claimed the fire fighter's life.

Other passengers enjoyed the scenery from time to time, but no one repeated the trip. Piper Super Cubs were noisy and uncomfortable. In the 1960s, the British Columbia Forest Service depended on fire towers and communicated with the tower men through several kinds of radios. Within a week or two, I recognized every voice in the ranger districts.

As a young boy, I enjoyed flipping through geographical atlases and learning the names of countries, water bodies, oceans and continents. In Chapleau, I added to my knowledge by exploring a hidden cache of adult magazines collected by an eccentric bachelor uncle.

The moment my Uncle Ernie left for work in the CPR railway car barns, I would sneak into his closet and pore through them. In one called *True Adventure*, I ran across an exciting feature story entitled, "Headless Valley of the Yukon." The tale described a tropical valley where mysterious men removed the heads of anyone foolish enough to enter. Supposedly draped in greenery, salt springs and waterfalls, the Nahanni Valley attracted many investigators and explorers.

During my first patrols, I noticed the Nahanni lay not far from a standard detection route. Visiting the legendary valley became an obsession. Every time I cruised along the Yukon border, I couldn't resist slipping a wing across the imaginary line, venturing a little further each time.

Finally, I discovered an airstrip not far across the Yukon border, less than sixty miles from the infamous Nahanni River. Abandoned long ago by a mineral exploration company, its gray length looked inviting. It wasn't terribly overgrown with weeds or trees, and several metal storage sheds stood on one side with various pieces of derelict machinery on the other. Looking the surface over, I could see rain from the day before hadn't affected the gravel, it appeared dry and solid. The length seemed more than adequate for a Piper Super Cub.

After an inspection run and a radio call to inform the Forest Service their detection airplane would be off the air, I landed. Instead of taxiing to the side of the runway, I parked at the extreme easterly end and faced into position for immediate take-off, before shutting down. Memories of stories read in the shadowed closet came flashing back and visions of headless men loping from the nearby poplar-aspen forest came to mind. I wondered if an undiscovered tribe of savage Indians really existed.

When the propeller stopped, it seemed as if someone had pulled a plug and all sound drained into the center of the earth. The contrast between the black rubber tires crunching across the marble-sized runway stones and the overwhelming silence when I opened the two-part door was incredibly eerie. Barely a whisper of wind shook the tall pink fire weeds. Fluffs of dandelion-like fuzz rustled as I walked by, scattering little clouds around my legs as if I alone brought the first breeze to this place.

I knew that no real demonic beings could be interested in any part of my humble carcass, especially my head. Nevertheless, I felt nervous about straying far from the safety of the Super Cub. Unable to forget that the Nahanni lay close by, I tentatively took more steps toward one of the tin sheds. So far, the wind kept still. Strange, I thought. Less than an hour before, gusty breezes raised white caps on sheltered ponds along the patrol route.

Reaching for the door handle of the shed, a gentle rustling in the aspens caught my attention. A gust of wind materialized from nowhere and slammed the door against the tin siding. The resounding clang of metal on metal vibrated through the air like a shriner's cymbal. No longer so fearless, I sprinted back to the Super Cub. As I reached it a rabbit that had crept behind the balloon tires, bolted, scattering gravel in its wake. I landed in the cockpit so heavily, the belly sagged. Seconds later, full takeoff power put me back into the air and out of reach of the Nahanni Valley head hunters.

By midsummer, the job became routine. Nevertheless, the scenery of northeastern British Columbia remained fascinating. In late August, fire patrol requests became less frequent, but occasionally the Forest Service dispatched huge Consolidated Canso water bombers to smokes I reported. In thick dry timber, these mammoth airplanes could do little to stop some of the fiercest forest fires I'd ever seen.

Unchecked, the blazes rolled through the province's magnificent bush country, destroying everything. The battles against them became epics of organization. The British Columbia Forest Service excelled in managing hundreds of men and dozens of airplanes and helicopters.

With plenty of spare time between patrols, I provided part-time flight training for the Fort Nelson Flying Club in a Cessna 150. Northern British Columbia had no flight instructors, and the extra flying hours all proved enjoyable. At the end of August, fire patrols decreased to short ones every three or four days.

My workmate in Dawson Creek, who flew a Super Cub on floats from a 5,000-foot "water alighting area" beside the main runway, covered ranger districts south of Dawson. For reasons I never knew, he informed Caribou Air Charter's headquarters in Kelowna that I used my off-duty hours to teach flying. The company owner issued a surly ultimatum to which I responded with an immediate resignation in late August. Years later, I spoke with the pilot sent to Dawson Creek to ferry the Super Cab back to Kelowna. No one told him about CF-ONN's thirst for oil. As a result, the engine quit halfway home but he landed safely on a bush road.

Fort Nelson turned out to be a pleasant community in which to spend several weeks before returning to my study of holozoic multicellular organisms and free-swimming trochophores. With a group of keen flight students, the days passed quickly until a stranger offered a ride to Saskatoon, Saskatchewan in his half-ton truck. From there, he suggested taking a bus to Kitchener. Eventually I arrived back at the men's residence at Waterloo Lutheran University. Barely a week went by in the next seven months, that thoughts didn't cross my mind on where next summer's job would take me.

17

3 Melba's Toast

The university term passed slowly. After months of waiting for responses for summer employment, the moment finally arrived. In early 1967, Jack Lamb of Thomas Lamb Airways Ltd. offered work in The Pas, Manitoba. The company's impressive letterhead carried a silhouette of a de Havilland Twin Otter and the motto, "Don't Ask Us Where We Fly; Tell Us Where You Want to Go."

Most pilots with interest in north-country bush flying knew Lamb Airways. It was formed in 1935 by Tom Lamb, the son of a Yorkshire schoolteacher, to haul fish to Winnipeg. Almost every aviation publication and major newspaper carried stories on the famous family. In fact, a clipping from a *Toronto Star*, had decorated my walls back in Belleville. Thomas Lamb's six sons all flew or worked in maintenance for the airline. Together, they became a legend in Canada.

When university ended in April, I traveled to Winnipeg. After a restless evening in the St. Regis Hotel, I climbed into a Transair Douglas DC-4 for The Pas, 281 miles northwest of Winnipeg.

When I stepped onto the snow-covered airport ramp, I saw no one resembling the famous Lamb family. A taxi driver nearby laughed when I asked if he knew anyone from Lamb Airways. He pointed to a white, two-door Chevrolet hard-top idling in the parking lot. I carefully walked across the slippery surface, lugging my flight bags.

Inside, a dark-haired man wearing a blue baseball cap sat on the right front seat. On the driver's side, a pudgy, red-cheeked individual watched me walk around the front of his car to the left window. This, the taxi driver had told me, was Dennis Lamb.

I approached the car and tapped on the glass. Dennis Lamb rolled down the window no more than two inches.

"Yeah?"

"I've been hired by your company to fly a Cessna 180. Could you give me a ride to the office?" I asked.

He rolled the window shut. I watched him open a center panel between the two front seats and extract a tall bottle half filled with dark amber liquid. He raised it to his lips, passed it to his colleague as they conferred between sips for several minutes. At last, Lamb with a wordless jerk of his head, gestured for me to get into the car.

I enjoyed the warmth of the sleek, red leather, lounge-like seats, glad for shelter from the frosty Manitoba wind blasts that shook the light posts. Lamb uncapped the bottle again and offered it to me. On the label, I read "Canadian Club" and in it, no ginger ale or cola softened the sharpness of undiluted rye whisky. Anxious to establish a favorable, one-of-the-boys impression, I took a long, deep swallow.

Still numbed from the cold, it took nearly half a minute before the alcohol burned through the lining of my throat and filtered down into my stomach. I began coughing, but tried desperately to contain myself, jerking spasmodically through my tightly sealed mouth. My eyes watered heavily and salty tears dribbled down my cheeks.

"Thanks," I chirped and handed the bottle back, Lamb removed it from my trembling hands and downed a thirty-second, nonstop gulp. Wiping his swollen lips, he passed it to his companion, an airplane maintenance engineer. He, too, took an equally long draught. My turn again.

God, I thought.

Officially, no one had hired me yet. With this in mind, I decided that no matter what the consequences, this airline owner wouldn't consider me a wimp. Placing both hands on the bottle I began swallowing, taking a second or two to surface for air. The acid-like pains no longer ravaged my interior and to my surprise, I began giggling. Quickly, I stopped and straightened up. Pilots of the frozen north did not giggle—they belched.

Before long, not an amber drop remained in the bottom of the glorious bottle, as Lamb placed the gear shift lever to "D" and drove to The Pas. A small, single-storied storefront building on the main street represented the company office. Almost completely incapacitated now, I stood outside with my baggage as Dennis Lamb drove away and left me standing in the snow.

Convinced I'd tasted the milk of paradise, instead of a few dregs from a fingerprinted bottle, I spent ten minutes contemplating the round and shiny door knob. Frostbite began touching my ears and fingertips, so I staggered inside the office and presented myself to a gracious sandy-haired woman in her midthirties.

The thought that no one placed me on a payroll yet helped pierce my fog and I straightened up. Before my eyes, a collection of artifacts behind protective glass plates riveted my attention. Ancient ship cannon, several yellowed Eskimo carvings and an assortment of whaling mementos brought me back to reality. Lamb Airways really represented the Arctic I desperately wanted to experience. Flying for them or any organization that delved into the barrenlands entailed more responsibility than I'd ever known. This, as someone once said, was "for real."

Grace handed over several forms to complete and didn't seem surprised at my condition or the reeking alcohol on my breath. In a few minutes, I became a Lamb Airways' pilot. That evening, another Lamb brother said with modesty, "We wrote the book on Arctic flying."

My first day with the famous bush airline didn't end once Grace relieved her ballpoint pen from between my trembling fingers. She telephoned the seaplane base at Grace Lake and asked for someone to pick me up.

Soon, a panorama of colorful airplanes filled the windshield of the truck that carried me to the base. A trio of bright red de Havilland Otters on skis parked by the edge of a small airstrip, with huge snow banks piled high along each side. Each of the ten-passenger giants had a wide, white speed line running from the front cowling to the tail.

On the frozen lake, a Beaver in the same eyecatching scheme rocked in the breeze. Beside it, three bare metal Cessna 180s sat, one with its left-hand door open, as someone jammed cardboard boxes inside. Across Grace Lake, deep snow-machine ruts extended to the far shore. A single row of tiny spruce trees designated a ski-strip and acted as warnings to snowmobilers for look up.

A neat brick building on the lake shore served as coffee room for pilots. Knocking gently, I waited. No one answered so I let myself in and sat down. Five pilots and several mechanics sipped coffee and picked titbits from a boiling pot on an electric stove. No one introduced himself or looked my way, so I listened. Dennis Lamb led the conversation.

The talk concerned hauling Indians throughout northern Manitoba, Eskimos in the Arctic and civil servants south to Winnipeg. As they chattered, I realized that fate had placed me in the presence of an august group of pilots, the same mettle of men I'd watched flog the mighty Noorduyn Norseman from Chapleau's Kebsquasheshing River. They knew the fabled tundra, had flown its breadth, smelled its salty shores and landed where few white men or *Kablunas* trod. They enjoyed their work and I hoped that I would become one of them. The hell with biology.

Interrupting my reverie, Dennis Lamb reached for the pot on the stove. He placed something in his mouth and talked on, discussing a recent incident in which one of his brothers flipped a twin-engine airplane upside down on a runway at Rankin Inlet. Another brother, Greg, noticing my curiosity, suggested I help myself to a snack.

Inside the pot, a greasy, dishwater-gray scum coated the rim and dripped over the sides in slimy rivulets. In the center, a small animal sat on its haunches while waves of bubbling liquid boiled over its ears and face. Not averse to eating wild rabbit, I reached for it, but suddenly realized the creature was not of the order *lagamorpha*. Two orange incisors protruded from between the tiny lips as the eyes boiled away to opaque, cream-colored cavities.

Holy God, I thought, it's a complete muskrat.

The pelt had been harvested, but the pathetic rodent had retained its long, sensitive moustache hairs. Nauseated, I turned away, collided with a chair and nearly retched upon the linoleum.

No one flew that day because of dark overcast cloud and strong gusting winds. Dennis dropped me back in The Pas where I checked into a downtown hotel. The clerk agreed to rent the cheapest room and threw a well-worn key ring across the counter top.

For $40 a month, I had a drapeless cubicle with an unfrosted light bulb dangling from a brown cord in the center of the ceiling. No sink, no toilet and no heat but previous owners had thought-fully jammed a tarnished brass bed against the garish blue wall-paper.

Sheets came with the room, but yellow urine stains colored them from one end to the other. In the middle, I noticed a particu-larly heavy accumulation deposited by some long-gone bed wet-ter.

On what the hotel considered a pillow, dried blood radiated in concentric circles. When anyone entered the community bath-room next door, the sound of cloth sliding over flesh carried through the walls. Sometimes, the clunk of a wooden seat upon a porcelain rim came next. Disgusting, personal noises followed and each time when they started, I clamped both hands painfully over my ears. Usually, the thundering vibration of a toilet flush followed. The slam of a door confirmed their exits and another slam announced the entrance of the latest refugee from the bar below.

My neighbor turned out to be a scabby-lipped, red-haired woman with a propensity to entertain customers late into the evening. Quarter-size cockroaches under the checkered floor tiles marked a lesson in the real-life world of northern flying.

The "Attic" became home for thirty-two days.

Next morning, I hitch-hiked back to Grace Lake's seaplane base where Dennis Lamb waited impatiently. A Cessna 180 trip had been booked and he planned a checkout flight for me. The 230-horsepower airplane would soon become the most powerful type in my logbook. Four seats, all metal and with a controllable pitch propeller, it responded instantly to the throttle and carried remarkable loads, despite its small size. After a few circuits and bumps across the snow-machine ruts, Lamb Airways considered me safe enough for a forty-mile hop to the Cree Indian reserve of Moose Lake.

Moose Lake happened to be the village in which Tom Lamb's father originally operated a trading post. Trips between the community and The Pas took place as many as five or six times per day. In winter, airplanes landed on the ice in front of the village. During open-water seasons several wooden docks were built to park floatplanes. At freeze-up and breakup, a short gravel airstrip within walking distance of the houses sufficed.

On the map, the thirty-four-mile route didn't look particularly difficult. Large lakes and river bends along the way would prove invaluable as navigational landmarks. As I preflighted Cessna 180 CF-SLH, a loaded half-ton truck approached the hangar. Two men stepped out and began transferring groceries into the airplane. Minutes later, a taxi cab arrived with two elderly Indian women laden with shopping bags bulging with potato chips, soft drinks and candy.

Accustomed to light Super Cub loads, I watched one of the Lamb brothers cram the Cessna 180 almost to the ceiling. Thinking he'd planned a second trip for the Indian women, I squirmed into the pilot's seat.

"Waitaminute. Don't start that thing yet," he said. "You've got two riding with you to Moose Lake."

He took their cases, jammed them between cartons of Carnation condensed milk and ordered the parka-clad ladies aboard. One stretched out horizontally on the load and the other wiggled into the right seat, where she sat on a case of soft drinks. The Lambs owned the airline and knew that jobs weren't plentiful. Ignoring any precepts of airmanship and overloading, I started the engine and taxied away. After a horrendously long takeoff run, the airplane slammed into a compacted snow drift and staggered airborne.

Eighteen minutes later, I bumped through the frozen drifts at Moose Lake, a collection of multi-colored boxes that served as homes for the locals. Moose Lake was the first such settlement

I'd encountered. Later, I visited hundreds of villages, all showing remarkable similarities. In most, little effort was made toward sanitation or garbage collection.

No one from the retail trading post came to the airplane to accept the freight and the two elderly ladies wandered away. Conscious of my lowly status as new kid on the Lamb Airways' block, I carried the boxes through the slush and up the shoreline to the store. As the last case of cans slammed down against the wooden steps, the owner came outside and kicked it through the doorway into the building.

The return to The Pas would be a snap. After all, I'd flown the route and looked forward to enjoying the Manitoba swampland scenery. Overly assured, I watched the "pushups," or small clumps of earth thrown up by muskrats in the marsh grasses, pass underneath the Cessna 180. Evidence of these little rodents dotted every lake side and muskeg bog.

Far below the horizon's edge, a lake reflected the afternoon sunlight. Assuming it to be Grace Lake's seaplane base, I saw no more need for the maps and tossed them over my shoulder toward the tail. Both instrument panel fuel gauges read empty but this mattered little. In a few minutes the dock boy could refill the tanks.

Coming closer to the gigantic frozen lake ahead of the airplane, it dawned on me that its size precluded the likelihood that it could be the skiplane base. I'd placed myself in a ticklish situation, with the maps out of reach in the rear of the fuel-gulping Cessna 180.

The aircraft carried few functioning radios. Company high-frequency, or HF, offered the only slim chance of contacting anyone who might provide direction. I called the base repeatedly, but got nothing more than a twinge of static. Resigned to landing on an unfamiliar patch of ice and waiting for a humiliating rescue, I began replacing the microphone in its cradle when a very bored voice responded.

After explaining my predicament, the air waves across cloudy Manitoba became silent again. Minutes later, the voice returned and in a disgusted, my-God-how-stupid-can-you-get tone asked for a description of the terrain.

V   It took nearly ten minutes to broadcast the shape of the lake over which I circled with CF-SLH. Throttled back to barely enough power to stay in the air, I waited. Occasionally, someone's finger depressed the microphone button and short snatches of laughter carried above the static in the Cessna 180's overhead speaker. Finally, a pilot came on the air and suggested a south-westerly heading.

Within minutes, I spotted Lamb Airways' aluminum hangar and landed quickly. Beside the dock, I pulled the mixture control to shut the engine off, as several pilots converged from the hangar and office cottage. No one said a word, but ill-concealed smirks told me all I needed to know. After sneaking away from the airplane and parking myself in the bathroom for thirty minutes, I came outside to find that everyone had left for The Pas. No one waited to offer me a ride. I walked to town.

That evening, I visited the bar on the floor beneath my room. Not feeling pleased with myself for the day's fiasco, the chance of encountering someone from Lamb Airways almost kept me upstairs, but I took an empty seat regardless. Lacking anything else to do, observing the local "wildlife" helped me pass the time. The noisy hotel was a favorite haunt for both Indian and non-Indian residents.

Friday night in The Pas coincided with payday for forest workers and railway men living in town. Welfare checks also flowed freely every two weeks. Before long, all chairs and tables in the bar became occupied and waitresses scoured the hotel rooms for more. Several pilots new to Lamb Airways joined me. Luckily, word of my stupidity had not reached them yet.

In the steamy bar room, patrons crowded so tightly together that shoulders of scruffy-jeaned strangers rubbed against each other. Rank, sweaty smells, unwashed bodies, and skunky beer seemed to bother no one. A pressure on my right made me turn and look directly into the eyes of a vivacious Cree girl. She held a tall glass of beer blended with tomato juice and slowly tipped it to her lips. Many native people who came to The Pas from outlying settlements enjoyed "Red-eye." Her companions, mostly male, held similar glasses, although one took gulps from a green bottle wrapped in a paper bag.

A happy group, I thought, and turned back to my new pilot friends. On the far side, we watched two inebriated locals fling empty glasses at each other, with shattered slivers dotting the tables before the bouncer reached them.

Again, something brushed against my shoulder but this time, the pressure lasted only an instant. Thinking it might be the pretty Cree girl, I swivelled my chair but saw no sign of her.

Her friends sat open-mouthed, their bottles stopped in mid air. A flash of white and a swish of black caught my eye and I looked down. Two struggling feminine figures on the floor pummeled each other, the sounds of flesh striking flesh overshadowing the din in the bar. No one separated them and fists flew back and forth like lightning flashes.

We learned that another young woman had become overwhelmingly jealous when my shoulder mate giggled at one of the Indian men. Entering the bar unseen, the newcomer had galloped across the floor, through the maze of furniture, people and purses to throw herself on her rival. The chair went over backwards and the ensuing battle resembled an alley cat fight. Tufts of black hair flew everywhere; one girl's blouse ripped and buttons clattered on the wooden floor as the other ripped away a brassiere strap. In retaliation, her blouseless opponent raked long, pointed fingernails across the other's forehead. Undaunted, they scraped, punched, gouged, kicked, and spit as they rolled under nearby tables, knocking bottled drinks and french fries everywhere.

The bouncer waded through the crowd and reached down. He plunged his colossal paw deep into the tangled mass of my shoulder mate's long black hair and snapped her head sharply backwards. With his left hand, he grabbed the other woman by what remained of her clothing. Both women kept trying to tear each other to pieces. Expressionless, the bouncer carried them outside and returned empty-handed.

I noticed that few people, other than the pilots with whom I shared the table, paid much attention. With the two women removed from the bar room, the bouncer tended to another fracas several tables away. As chairs and baseball hats flew across the room, we continued experimenting with several kinds of drinks native to Manitoba.

The following morning, I was the only pilot who arrived in time for work at Grace Lake.

During my first few days with the company, it became clear my policy toward airsickness was naive. By not mentioning the dreaded affliction to my passengers, I believed if no one thought about it, nauseating messes wouldn't hit the floor of my Cessna 180.

At Moose Lake, three women vomited before we taxied a hundred yards. After that, any passenger placing their derrieres inside my pristine flying machine received a personal cookie jar or paper bag before takeoff. The system worked, but occasionally the timid victims hid their containers under the seats where I discovered them two or three days later. Once I mailed a bag and its decomposing contents to a repeat offender. From that day, he always left the airplane carrying his dampened paper package with him.

Once, a nurse called for an airplane in Norway House to bring back a pregnant woman. With full fuel and no passengers or doctor aboard, I cruised at maximum airspeed and landed at the settlement not far from the northeast corner of Lake Winnipeg. After an hour's wait, the medical van drove to the lakeside and several people carried a stretcher from its side door.

The nurse stood beside the Cessna 180 as I released my front passenger seat and slid it onto the ice to make more room. A young Cree boy promptly sat on it to watch two uniformed Royal Canadian Mounted Police constables lift his mother from the stretcher and place her on the floor.

"Just her? Somebody's got to go with me," I pleaded.

The woman was pregnant for sure, but not for long, judging by the whimpering, squirming and occasional spasmodic flicks of her arms and legs. The Norway House nurse didn't want to make the trip to The Pas for she knew, as I did, the already marginal weather would probably drop below limits. Light snow began covering the wings after my arrival and besides, all nursing station staff had been invited to a dance in the log-walled community hall that evening.

With the RCMP glaring at me and the pretty blonde nurse carefully making little snow piles with her feet, I saw no alternative. I closed the airplane door, hoping my seat would still be there for pickup on the next trip to Norway House. At least the country back to the base was flat without towers, transmission lines or steep hills.

Fifteen minutes after takeoff, wet snow stuck in clumps to the wings, struts and skis. With engine power back and one notch of flap applied, we flew at low altitude, keeping close to the shorelines of the big lakes. One pilot had killed himself the previous winter while trying to cross a lake in a snowstorm and I intended not to follow his example.

The lady's head slapped against the bottom of the instrument panel each time we struck a patch of turbulence. Every few minutes her eyes opened. Her mouth would move and twist and her eyes would close again. Both feet lashed out from time to time, jamming my sleeping bag into a corner, while her right hand clenched the flap handle and the other flailed against the door.

At last, the muskrat marsh and dirty, gray ice of Grace Lake slid by underneath the skis. A touch of rudder skidded us closer to the spruce trees placed for whiteouts like this one. Power back, the Cessna 180 contacted the drifts, skidded a few yards but smacked a snow-machine trail and slammed back into the air. Down again a second later, we stayed.

The ambulance—a rusty station wagon—waited by the hangar, its driver standing behind a lowered back door. Two people dressed in white leaned against the vehicle as I taxied toward them in a cloud of spray and slush. My passenger, her whimpers audible now above the idling engine, tried to struggle up. She had no intention of allowing her baby to be born on the dirty floor of an airplane.

Someone flung the door open and two men grabbed her, dragged her outside and threw the unfortunate, suffering woman into the ambulance, slammed all doors and drove away. Part-way along the air base road, brake lights flashed on and the station wagon stopped. The attendants got out quickly and ran around to the back. Thirty-five minutes later, they continued into The Pas.

During my next trip to Norway House, I learned the population of Manitoba had increased by one and someone had stolen my seat.

At the time of my sojourn in The Pas, many pilots couldn't find employment, especially with bush airlines. A species of aviator, known as the "Air Canada Pilot's Son," rarely failed to climb into the carrier's Vickers Viscounts or Douglas DC-9s as soon as they collected a commercial pilot licence. This meant to us in the lower strata that we did exactly what employers ordered. Many loads exceeded legal limits, but operators made it clear in not-so-subtle ways that the load went or we did.

One morning at Grace Lake, as I scraped wing frost from Cessna 180 on wheel/skis, a taxi cab pulled into the base. The company mechanics kept working frantically, since all other airplanes were undergoing changeover from skis to floats for spring breakup. I knew if the people in the cab needed transportation, they'd have to ride with me. I counted enough heads to indicate at least two trips would be needed wherever they went. Any spring flights departed from the 2,800-foot gravel airstrip behind the hangar.

"Hey, you!" someone yelled from the office. I strolled over to Connie Lamb who stood with his hands on his hips.

"You got yourself a trip to Nelson House," he said. "Gas that thing up; it's about 176 miles north."

"Who's doing the second one?" I asked.

"What second one?" Connie took off his baseball cap and ran a hand through his long red hair. Beside him, his wife's white poodle cocked its head as the famous Lamb brother walked away, muttering something uncomplimentary about pilots from southern Canada. The dog followed, but not before urinating on the gas hose.

Someone helped me load the Cessna 180. Three corpulent women adorned wearing plaid handkerchiefs around their heads, squeezed into the rear bench seat. In the front, I found an elderly, man with two metal canes upright between his knees. Squirming into the pilot's seat, I realized each woman bottle-fed a small baby. A skinny girl about eleven years old smiled uncomfortably as she knelt on the floor between front and rear seats.

Some space remained. Connie slid four iron-sheeted suitcases between and under the passengers, then jammed another against the rear bulkhead. He removed groceries from cardboard boxes and inserted loaves of bread and tin cans into every crack and crevasse in the airplane. Now, no one could move. Seat belts, of course, were out of the question.

With nine in an airplane designed for four and full gasoline tanks, we barely cleared the scrub at the end of the airstrip. The run to Nelson House would last less than two hours. Surprisingly, only the young girl threw up. Unable to grasp the concept of an airsickness bag, she coated the knees of the women and filled her mother's rubber boots. The babies screamed during the entire trip. The elderly man, who I took to be a former village chief, said nothing. He stared straight ahead from the moment we left the gravel.

Having learned well, the map stayed on my lap every minute. Eventually, we spotted the long white length of Footprint Lake. Knowing the community lacked an airstrip, I circled the Hudson's Bay Company's low white buildings and noticed rows of airplane ski tracks. A steady stream of air traffic from nearby Thompson kept the village supplied with the necessities of life.

We landed in a splash of slush.

I turned around using full movements of the rudder pedals and bursts of engine power for a high-speed taxi to a solid patch of ice on which to park. Moments later, a Thompson-based Lamb Airways Cessna 180 alighted nearby with the same-sized load of people and freight. He taxied close to CF-SLH and blasted his tail around to park beside my wing tip. A small crowd of Indians, a few whites, dogs and snow machines rushed from houses to gather around us.

Airplanes no longer caused excitement at remote locations such as Nelson House, but two rarely arrived together. Satisfied when they saw who we carried, people soon slipped back to their cosy little shacks. I came to know the other pilot Bill very well in the weeks ahead. We chatted amicably about the joys of winter flying in Manitoba and the day we would be trusted with our first de Havilland Beaver.

Few aboriginal people during the late 1960s used dogs for transportation since the snow machine's arrival in the north. A few huskies and mongrel dogs living on scraps were generally considered village nuisances. Some became pets and traces of others could be seen as hood fur in newly sewn parkas. A few scrawny animals cavorted not far from the airplanes as we talked.

A beige pup ambled toward us. I reached under the Cessna 180's sliding seat and retrieved the soggy remains of a lunch brought from a restaurant in The Pas. He wolfed it down, waggled his tail and then, realizing I could offer no more, the young animal flounced off to play with his canine friends. When Bill started his engine, the same little dog returned.

The Cessna 180 roared at full power as Bill jockeyed the throttle to break himself free of the slush. Throttled back, he began taxiing downwind into position for a clear takeoff run. The pup followed, gleeful and frisky for having something new to do in Nelson House. He nipped playfully at the rope trailing from the tail wheel and then ran between the steel legs of the landing gear.

Suddenly, in an attempt to worry the blur of the propeller, he leaped, teeth flashing, into the whirling, razor-sharp blades.

A horrifying crunch of metal into bone resounded across the lake above the engine noise. Thrown backwards, the pitiful, stricken creature emitted a piercing, human-like scream. He scrambled to his feet and began running in a desperate attempt to shake away the shock and pain. Blood sprayed everywhere, leaving steaming pools of bright red splotches in the snow.

Bill shut down the engine and stepped outside. Neither of us could do anything except watch. The dying pup slowly strangled in his own blood and sagged gradually to its knees, crying as life drained from its shattered face into the frozen surface. Both eyes were glazed and he rolled over on his side. All movement stopped, except for one final tremor. Aghast at having killed the harmless little beast, Bill picked up the warm body and looked toward the village. No one came out of the shacks or seemed to care. Nothing moved, save for a flock of black, hunchbacked ravens—vultures of the north—perched on poles.

Enroute back to The Pas, the shrieks of the mutilated pup stayed with me until the air base radioed me to stop at Cormorant Lake, a former 1930s flying boat base. An MTS or Manitoba

Telephone Service repairman dropped earlier that needed transportation home. Water covered the ice, someone said over the HF radio, but the Cessna would be safe. When I reached the place, the lake looked more like open water than solid ice but landing, other than a tremendous splash, caused no problems.

I parked near a collection of decrepit buildings beside the railway line to Churchill. Many, dirty-faced, rag-clothed children emerged from a squalid cabin and rushed over to have a look at the latest "wump-teh-go-shay" or white man. They told me the telephone man needed more time. With little else to do, I followed them to see what help he needed to carry equipment to the airplane.

Outside the tar paper cabin, a large pile of empty Johnny Walker whisky bottles and muskrat bones blocked the only entrance. Five tiny pups rooting in garbage quarreled and snapped over a hairy scrap of moose hide. Inside, the repairman applied the finishing touches to a telephone on the wall as a very dark-skinned girl watched intently.

Melba was munching on a yellow object when she caught sight of me. Smiling, she extended a fat grimy hand, offering what I could only surmise might be toast. Several morsels of it dropped with a slop to the earthen floor. Not wanting to offend her, for there couldn't be much food in that household, I politely declined. One puppy shuffled in and was promptly kicked outside by Melba's rubber boot.

She turned back to me, still smiling, still offering. The repairman noticed my predicament and started a conversation with Melba who, I presumed, encountered few visitors in Cormorant Lake. He talked as he worked and Melba continued nibbling but now and again, she pressed me to accept her gracious hospitality. Picking up a tool box and a coil of wire, I politely beat it back to the airplane.

On the leg home to Grace Lake, the MTS man informed me just how fortunate I had been. To my surprise, Melba not only exceeded the age of nineteen and owned several kids, but she also usually offered far more than just toast.

After a quiet evening in the hotel bar, someone passed the word that Lamb Airways needed a Cessna 180 pilot to complete a Canadian Wildlife Service contract in the Arctic. The "feds" leased a small airplane to supplement a de Havilland Beaver already working in the barrenlands, west of Rankin Inlet on Hudson Bay's west coast. Eager to check out of the Attic and desperate to see new lands, I volunteered. Soon I stepped from a Transair Douglas DC-4 in one of the most desolate, unappealing airports northern Canada could offer: Churchill.

Considering my lack of experience in the art of tundra navigation, the base manager hoped to ride along for several days. Until then, my closest brush with the Arctic occurred when I discovered a pile of aeronautical charts someone left under the seat of a de Havilland Otter. I spent hours daydreaming over those charts.

A checkout and familiarization flight would have been greatly welcomed; but the base was shorthanded, and extra work drew the base manager away from Churchill. The company expected the new man to fend for himself.

When accepting the assignment in The Pas, head office warned me the wildlife biologist who requested the airplane had already proved difficult to work with. We would be together day and night, and stories of his impatience with pilots already filtered south. This hardly seemed a pleasant way to begin, but Jack Lamb claimed if the worst happened, I would not be the only pilot who refused to fly with him. Anxious to go, but apprehensive about the territory and the infamous biologist, my only chance to survive and look like a true company man would be to get along, no matter what anyone said or did.

The wildlife biologist, a dark-haired, arrogant man, knew the north intimately after having completed several seasons on caribou surveys. Without a "Hello" or "How are you?" he made it clear that he disliked flying with someone who had never flown in the Northwest Territories. Derogatory remarks concerning my age, the airplane's condition and Lamb Airways continued hour after hour. Considered timid but never patient, I surprised myself by listening without reply to every word and epithet he threw. To my credit, in spite of his obnoxious nature, we never came to blows.

After I had been assigned a Cessna 180, registered CF-SLJ,

we departed Churchill on the first day of June and paralleled the west coast of Hudson Bay. Bright white ice extended out into deep seas, but dozens of sharp-edged, black leads pointed toward open pools of turquoise meltwater. We watched sea birds of many colors, shapes and sizes whirl around the exposed areas. Some darted into the sea and others walked patiently along the ice flow edges.

For an hour, Arctic flying seemed ridiculously easy in the bright blue sky with an unbelievably accurate aeronautical chart folded on my knee. Several times, we slipped low to watch rows of dark, cucumber-shaped seals diving into holes to escape the airplane's 230-horsepower noise. A southbound single Otter radioed the location of a pod of beluga whales a few miles offshore. We borrowed a few minutes to wing eastward and marveled at the splendor of the white 1,200-pound sea mammals splashing in the spring sunlight.

Past Eskimo Point, 141 miles north of Churchill, the clear skies and unlimited visibility still held; the northwestern horizon showed traces of darkening cloud and fog sneaking inland from the open sea. Before long, the sky turned overcast and blowing snow began obscuring the land. With no other option, we turned around for Eskimo Point.

Circling the village, I sighted scores of brightly colored cubicles along the rocky shoreline. Several huge fishing boats called "Peterheads" were locked in ice not far from an immense pile of square stern canoes. The overcast conditions hindered any chances of selecting previously used airplane tracks. Everywhere, we saw hundreds of black dots, some in clusters and others sprinkled haphazardly.

Carefully selecting a clear area, we turned on final approach and landed. Mild weather meltwater splashed up and over the windshield, but we came to a stop quickly without striking anything. A few feet away, I studied a mound of the little dark spots we had observed while circling. Unable to guess their purpose, I skidded across the ice and kicked one.

They were honey bags.

Each one held fifty pounds of human excrement. The settlement homes didn't have plumbing and consequently, most residents used a five-gallon pail lined with plastic. Periodically, someone collected the oozing sacs and dumped them on the Hudson Bay ice. When spring arrived, the floes drifted to deep water and melted, thus solving Eskimo Point's sewage-disposal problem. In later years, a liquid sewage lagoon southeast of the village served the same purpose.

Honey bags surrounded our Cessna 180, so we decided to leave it on the spot. The wildlife biologist didn't seem pleased with the prospect of spending a night; however, as the weather worsened, he knew we couldn't continue. Walking toward the land, we plunged into damp snow up to our waists. The day's thaw didn't make walking any easier. Before we made it very far, a snow machine whirled from around the corner of a building and sped toward us.

The driver, we learned, represented Eskimo Point's Anglican Church. He wasn't friendly and asked who we were and what kind of business brought us to the coast of Hudson Bay. Satisfied, he adjusted the round white collar on his neck and started the machine. Exhausted from pulling my long legs through the deep snow, I assumed he would offer us a ride and nearly sat on the seat behind him. Instead, he gunned the engine and roared away so fast, I nearly fell backwards onto the biologist.

The wind picked up and our wet clothes began chilling our bodies. We staggered several more steps when another snow machine driver saw our plight. He, too, pulled alongside us. Until now, I had never seen an Eskimo. Dressed in a plastic, yellow parka and white rubber boots, this man didn't match the stereotyped image described in southern Ontario's schools. With a smile so wide I thought his face would split, he gestured toward his machine.

Exhausted, I flopped onto the back and held my sleeping bag against my chest. He bumped across ruts and through slush holes before depositing me in front of a single-storey plywood building. He drove away to pick up the biologist. Alone now, I walked up the seven wooden steps of a small veranda leading into some kind of office.

I knocked, and stepped inside. Immediately, a host of unfamiliar odors, colors and sounds assailed me. Along the walls, a dozen Eskimo people sat side by side on wooden benches. The women wore bright white amautuks, or wide-sleeved throw-over parkas, with oversized hoods in which they carried their children. One mother silently breast fed her child and another stood up to make room for me. The men used brown army surplus overcoats and many wore brown-gray sealskin boots. Most had removed their heavier clothing and piled it in a corner.

In a few moments, a squat *Kabluna* came into the room. He recognized me as a stranger needing somewhere to spend the night and gruffly informed me that bunk beds could be found in the adjacent building.

That evening, we received an invitation to visit another settlement official's home. On the way, we realized that all non-native residences in Eskimo Point were two-storey, elaborate affairs. The Eskimo people survived in plywood boxes with thin walls and warped floors.

After dinner with the official and his wife, several taps at the door announced the arrival of two school teachers carrying guitars. One looked barely old enough to leave her southern home. Her room mate, a striking, long-haired blonde in her late twenties, specialized in folk singing. She told us she spent several winters teaching in settlements across the north. Soon, another knock announced a pair of nurses and they too matched the others in personality and good looks.

The evening turned out to be the most enjoyable during my time above the tree line. Even the biologist mellowed and joined in a sing-along.

In the morning, a half-inch of solid, clear ice covered everything in the village after the weather system dissipated and passed on to the other side of Hudson Bay. Several sharp raps with my fists quickly cleared the Cessna 180 and we piled aboard. Ahead of the nose, more honey bags littered the sea ice. Evidently, we were leaving on collection day.

Nevertheless, we had no choice but to hope their contents froze solid during the night. On takeoff the Cessna 180 smashed across several before the wheel/skis smacked into a drift and booted us into the air. Not all the bags were solid, I noticed, peering at the wing struts.

We continued up the flat, rocky coast toward Rankin Inlet, where a tall wooden mine shaft on the seaward edge of the village acted as a visual beacon. The North Rankin Nickel Mine had provided the locals with a source of revenue from 1955 to 1962, but now stood abandoned. The village prospered and eventually became the capital of the District of Keewatin. On the gravel airstrip, a Lamb Airways de Havilland Beaver taxied toward a trio of metal-sided shacks. It formed the other half of the two-airplane caribou survey team.

Bill, the same person who flew into Nelson House weeks before, was the pilot. He felt as anxious as I to move inland, where weather would be easier on the nerves. As I hand-pumped the wing tanks full of red 80/87 aviation gasoline from ten-gallon drums, we discussed our impressions of the Arctic. We worked side by side for several weeks, shared the same tent and became good friends.

Neither of us cared for the manner in which the Canadian Wildlife Service planned to carry out its caribou survey. Since 1948, the Wildlife Service concentrated studies on a group of animals they called the Manitoba-Keewatin herd. The Cessna 180 served as an aerial reconnaissance platform for finding the hapless creatures as they migrated from northern Manitoba wintering ranges to calving grounds near Baker Lake, Rankin Inlet and Chesterfield Inlet. The biologists and their assistants intended to obtain information on herd structure, reproduction and nutritional status from examinations of specimens.

For the project, they needed to "collect" Barren Ground Caribou by indiscriminately massacring large numbers of the helpless animals. The Beaver's role, besides supplying campsites with food and moving men from Rankin Inlet to the main camp, involved flying in killing crews with large-bore rifles. Their arsenal included some semiautomatic military models.

My task entailed flying search patterns a few hundred feet above the ground. The biologists expected to use paint marks on the wing struts as guides in aerial counting. Our reports pinpointed the caribou locations, and soon Bill would carry hunters from camp to kill site. The slaughter commenced soon after he landed close to the unsuspecting herds. Caribou rarely ran; they became so curious they sometimes walked up to the idling Beaver.

The biologists selected a base camp eighty-eight miles northwest of Rankin Inlet. Maps showed white, featureless areas with nothing more than blue coloring to denote lakes and rivers. My first trip away from the easy navigation of Hudson Bay's coastline had to be "right on the money." If we missed MacQuoid Lake, the next settlement might be Yellowknife, about 600 miles west. On this trip, and all subsequent flights in this strange, starkly beautiful land, I left with as much fuel as the Cessna 180 could carry.

On the initial ride to MacQuoid Lake, my passenger left no doubts about how strongly he resented having to fly with the "kid from the south." Back in Eskimo Point, I began to think he might be part human after all; alas, he remained a steadfast asshole all the time I knew him. Rough and arrogant, he shamed two Eskimo skinners, who had never been aloft, into the airplane and crammed their gear around them. He spoke rudely to anyone who crossed his path or questioned his methods.

Surprisingly, my first venture from the gravel runway of Rankin Inlet went well. The lake ice contrasted sharply with the somber, rocky ground and made map reading quite easy. Every frozen body along the way contained a glimmering meltwater surface layer. I knew such conditions almost doubled takeoff runs, so we selected only the longest places for landing in the weeks ahead.

No one expected a Holiday Inn in the Barrens, yet I was surprised to find that the pilots' tent lacked a sewn-in floor. As Bill and I selected sleeping sides under the mildewed canvas, spring sunlight penetrated the roof and warmed the inside. Stretching out with thoughts of how fortunate we were to have a paid camping trip, I had little else to do until the following day. Our clients didn't appear organized and it quickly became obvious we'd need plenty of patience in the days to come.

Suddenly, out of the corner of my eye, I spotted a darting movement on a lichen-covered rock. Nothing reappeared so, with the Cessna 180 refueled to the gas caps and logbook updated, I drifted off to sleep. Paid camping trip, for sure.

Later, waking slowly, my eyes took a few moments to focus on the ceiling of the tent. Large, black blotches covered the canvas everywhere. One moved, then another and instantly, I snapped into full awareness, threw my sleeping bag aside and bolted outside like a shot from a high-powered target rifle.

Dozens of quarter-sized hairy spiders covered our sleeping bags, socks, clothes, and shaving kits. Unseasonal warmth had enticed these loathsome, bristling creatures to emerge from beneath every rock and crevasse under the floor area covered by the tent. Overcoming my *arachnophobia*, we killed enough of the nasty things to make the place habitable. Each night I slept in that canvas home, I carefully checked my sleeping bag.

After the third day at MacQuoid Lake, the biologists still couldn't make up their minds about which direction they wanted us to fly. By midafternoon, the sky turned overcast and soon, gently falling snowflakes changed into a heavy, nonstop snowfall. No one moved from their Coleman stoves for two days. When the storm ended, what appeared before our eyes reminded me of the stereotyped concepts many people carry of the Arctic.

Sparkling, fingernail-size snowflakes obliterated every landmark from horizon to horizon. Never before had I seen such seemingly limitless expanses apparently devoid of human touch, with nothing for the eyes to cling to except our tents. Around the camp, water bodies and shorelines no longer existed as landmarks. Now, low-level navigation in the achromatic barrenlands became an almost insurmountable task. For someone with only a few days experience "north of 60," flying would be extremely challenging.

As I gazed with wonder from the pilot's seat of the Cessna 180 at this panorama of land without bottom or edge, my biologist seat mate read my mind.

"If you can't handle it, I'll get somebody who bloody well will," he snapped.

With no excuse available, I had to go flying. Even the spiders retreated to their tiny rock caves and huddled together.

Our search for caribou went well at first, as plots coincided properly with the complex latitude and longitude grids on the aeronautical charts. Considering my conspicuous lack of expertise in the breathtaking central Canadian Arctic, the airplane stayed nicely on track as we cruised past boulder after boulder.

From MacQuoid, we paralleled the long, jagged shoreline of Kaminuriak Lake. To keep on the survey lines, I measured recognizable shorelines with a protractor, aligned the airplane with the surface features and reset the directional gyro every fifteen minutes.

After thirty minutes, we arrived at the southernmost part of the plot and turned northbound. As time passed and the biologist placed little dots on his map to show caribou, the concentration became tiring. Each time the Cessna 180 drifted off course, keeping a running fix became more difficult. At last, just as the biologist expected, it happened.

I last recalled seeing a small piece of speckled ice marked on the map as Derby Lake. Moments after it passed out of sight beyond the tail, we became totally lost. Frantically flying from lake to lake and ridge to ridge, in hopes of picking up identifiable landmarks in the encompassing whiteness, proved a waste of time.

Then he started.

"You fool! You stupid, god-damn fool!" he began, and pounded his fists hard against the instrument panel. "Why in hell they sent a kid like you in the first place I'll never understand. J-e-e-ezus Christ!"

He ranted on and on, never offering to help find our way back to MacQuoid Lake. Realizing the seriousness of our situation, I carefully calculated that unburned fuel left us with less than three hours in which to locate the tented campsite. An easterly heading would eventually take us to Hudson Bay, but how far it might be, I had no idea. Our only alternative, other than running out of gasoline and landing in a meltwater lake to wait for spring, meant holding the original northerly heading. Because the directional gyro couldn't be trusted and needed resetting every fifteen minutes, heading north seemed to offer us the best chance.

The Cessna 180's magnetic compass never showed any indication of reading accurately from the moment I saw the airplane in Churchill. During my first walkaround inspection, I had brought the problem to the attention of the company's base mechanic. He had looked up from his copy of the *Tundra Times* to sneer, "....don't need it. You got maps, don't you?"

Somewhere ahead lay Chesterfield Inlet, with its east-west length totaling 187 miles. Back in The Pas weeks before, one of the Lamb brothers had offered some last-minute advice before my departure. Never, never, he said, fly aimlessly around looking for something recognizable. Instead, Dennis Lamb added, find one prominent landmark and circle it. While going around and around, calm down, review and carefully but calmly plan.

After wasting an hour's fuel, a mental coin flip determined an approximate northerly course with a slight tilt to the northeast, in case the gyro proved to be too inaccurate. Despite another hour of holding a reasonably straight heading as closely as possible, nothing resembling the hundreds of lakes, rivers and eskers matched the features on the map.

Barely discernible in the flat terrain ahead of the nose, some bluish-white blocks of jumbled ice appeared. It must be Chesterfield, I thought, and tried to compare a lengthy bay with the one on the chart. By now, the biologist, having exhausted his store of epithets, resigned himself to fate as he sulked in the seat beside me.

Lost in the Arctic for more than two hours, we stumbled across Chesterfield Inlet near a landmark called Cross Bay. A few quick calculations and measurements with a ruler and I calculated MacQuoid Lake and supper over a Coleman stove waited only sixty miles away. After resetting the directional gyro, I noticed the biologist roused himself from his sulk. Other than a disgruntled look my way, he never said another word.

During our hectic wandering, the slaughtering crew successfully destroyed a pocket of the main caribou herd not twenty minutes from our tents. Postponing supper, we overflew camp and soon located the red Beaver down on a lake. From our 1,500-foot altitude, caribou carcasses dotted the snow, their match-stick legs splayed in all directions. When we landed, the skinners barely looked at us and continued their grisly chores.

Each man used an *ulu,* or crescent-shaped iron Eskimo knife. Even under the overcast sky, their silver blades reflected eerily in the light as they flashed up and down slicing legs, shoulders and intestines. Axes, too, were used and pieces of skin and bone chips flew everywhere. Tiny white fragments stuck to parkas and looked much like Christmas sugar candies.

Never having seen *Tuktu* up close, I wandered from corpse to corpse, quite surprised at the small size of the adults. Some literally lost their heads, and others had exploded chests. All were very, very dead. Hair, blood and organs lay everywhere.

The Eskimo men, bare hands darkened now with blood, showed their expertise. One named Peryouar could skin a caribou in seconds. The ripping sound he made when separating hide from flesh made me turn away. Another man noticed a parasitic group of writhing yellow warble fly larvae embedded in the back of an adult caribou. As they flopped about, torn from their once-living host, he poked them out from beneath the skin with his thumb and, grinning, popped these aqueous delicacies into his mouth.

When I stepped across a heap of bodies, I came upon a small, fawn-coloured caribou calf, somehow untouched in the terrible carnage. It ambled over to a dead female caribou and nuzzled the soft brown belly. Everyone stopped and stared at the tiny creature.

Probably only a few days old, the young animal raised its head and looked around at the stillness of its own kind laying lifeless all around. Confused, it wandered from corpse to corpse and once, stumbled across a pile of legs tossed onto the snow for later examination.

The wildlife biologists had no other choice. Even now, we suspected wolves waited quietly out of sight behind the ridges. One of the senior men picked up his large-bore cannon and injected a round into the chamber. The wide, soft eyes of the calf showed no trace of fear as it faced the giant standing before him.

With a backward glance at its bleeding mother, the sad little creature raised its head to stare innocently into the gun barrel. The powerful, ear-shattering blast shook all of us.

Bill, disgusted, left the scene and secluded himself in his airplane. Moments later, I joined him. We sat, angry and mortified at the Canadian Wildlife Service which carried out this bloodbath under the banner of research. To pass the time and distract our minds, Bill showed me how to work the fuel primer and start the Beaver's 450-horsepower radial engine. The Eskimos outside and the eager biologists continued hacking and bagging caribou parts.

When everyone finished their work, Bill and I loaded his Beaver for the short hop to MacQuoid. He planned to drop the men off and continue onwards with the sample bags to Rankin Inlet. Inside, rifles and other gear nearly reached the Beaver's quilted ceiling. Piled high, still-warm quarters of bloody meat stained everything they touched. Little room remained, so two Eskimos rode in the Cessna 180 with me.

As Bill applied throttle to swing into wind for takeoff, his heavy airplane refused to move because its weight generated enough heat to freeze the skis to the ice. Several of us pushed and rocked the wing struts, while he alternately blasted the engine back and forth. At last, with a few sharp kicks to the back of each ski, they released their grip and CF-EYZ slid away.

Moments later, I attempted to follow but my airplane was also solidly frozen in. Passengers disembarked and, despite the cold propeller slipstream, they strained with all their strength to break us free. Suddenly, the Cessna 180 lurched ahead but I dared not stop too soon. Instead, I taxied through meltwater pools and across snow humps. With full left rudder, control wheel forward and plenty of engine power to swing the tail, I came around to pick up the passengers.

Without stopping, I managed another noisy turn and, as slowly as possible, yelled above the idling propeller for them to run beside the airplane and jump in. One slipped and went down full length into the icy water. He raised himself and then caught up to the Cessna 180. Another hopped on the ski, held the door open while his companion slithered inside and then he too writhed and wormed his way toward the back seat.

Badly overloaded, we slammed across the lake trying to reach takeoff speed. Several times, we nearly became airborne, but soggy drifts slowed us down. The shoreline began narrowing into a small, arrow-shaped bay. I had no other choice except to yank us into the air, hoping the wings wouldn't lose their lift and plunge us into the rocky shore.

By carefully bleeding off flap a notch at a time, we attained a safe climbing speed and joined the Beaver. Bill had circled overhead knowing I might have problems. We flew in formation back to MacQuoid Lake, where I watched him land and leave a foaming trail of bubbles in the meltwater.

As the days warmed, takeoffs became longer and longer when the lake ice began crystallizing and surface melt became too deep for taxiing. In one long, drawn-out run away from camp, the crews lost sight of the Cessna 180 as I struggled for miles to lift cleanly from the surface. Treating airplanes so roughly didn't appeal to either Bill or me. The next day, the survey ended and we moved the camp back to Rankin Inlet.

The wildlife biologists left the Keewatin on a scheduled southbound Douglas DC-3 and the Eskimos returned to their families. While checking the journey logbooks, I noticed that CF-SLJ's routine inspection was overdue. Relaying details down to head office in The Pas, I settled myself into a bunkhouse to wait for a mechanic from Churchill. Soon, someone handed me a radiogram. It read, "Send logbook."

Three days later, the logbook came back on a Transair freighter. On one of its snow-stained pages, a signature and stamp certified a completed inspection. By the time a qualified person examined the Cessna 180's engine and airframe, over a hundred hours had gone by.

After several days of constant coastal fog and freezing rain, Bill and I flew down the Hudson Bay coast to our secondary base in Churchill. High winds held us both in port, but Bill left during the first available good weather. In The Pas, newly opened water created a desperate need for seaplanes, and Bill's Beaver required a changeover from wheel-skis to floats. I never saw him again. He left the airline for somewhere in western Canada and was killed in a flight training accident. As for me, a last-minute call came in for a ski plane on a contract close to the same area I'd left a few days before.

To everyone's surprise, the lake country northwest of Churchill underwent another freeze. Meltwater disappeared and so did the snow. Navigating became much easier and a mineral exploration company asked for a Cessna 180 to fly a geologist from

Toronto. Red-headed Tom Skimming of Inco arrived in Churchill. Just an hour or so after he stepped from the airliner, we were cruising above the Hudson Bay shoreline.

The contract required that the airplane fly for several weeks at Cullaton Lake, 217 miles northwest and 120 miles west of Eskimo Point. The company planned to move in a large group of diamond-drilling men and expected Skimming to prepare the camp when he wasn't prospecting. The Cessna 180 on skis could easily handle the local ice conditions. We also planned to land with wheels on a patch of ground Inco scraped from the tundra and called an airstrip.

Skimming knew the Arctic well, having spent years working in every corner of the Northwest Territories. He brought no prejudice about climbing into a single-engine airplane with a scrawny newcomer from southern Ontario. Not once did he ever question my judgment or demand an overload.

Inco had kept a crew working throughout the previous winter. When they could no longer maneuver the company's heavy exploration equipment in late spring, they pulled everyone out for a month. Only one man stayed behind as a caretaker. All he had to do was start the engines of the drilling equipment from time to time to keep them lubricated. Skimming predicted this fellow would be pleased to see us, especially since we had almost nothing but food packed to the ceiling.

Our flight from Churchill to Cullaton Lake took place in clear skies at 8,000 feet. Cullaton was only a few miles west of a huge landmark called South Henik Lake. At first, I saw nothing resembling any sort of landing site. When our estimated time of arrival came due, Skimming tapped me on the shoulder and pointed out the tan-colored airstrip near a piece of rising ground known as White Mountain. In later years, Cullaton Lake became a gold-mining community with hundreds of men and women stationed there. Large aerial freighters from Churchill and Thompson kept them supplied with scheduled flights nearly every day.

Not quite out of the tree line, small stunted conifers dotted the area. Sometimes, we saw pockets of caribou struggling to catch up with the main body of the Manitoba-Keewatin herd, which had been attacked by the biologists a week before. A tiny brown building beside some yellow construction equipment marked the home I would share with Skimming and the caretaker for the next few weeks. As we made a low pass to examine the airstrip surface, I saw someone walking along a rutted path. By the time we touched down, a figure sat waiting on an empty fuel drum.

As we stepped out, a short heavy man waddled toward us. Judging by his slow pace, he'd need some time to reach us, so Skimming and I began unloading the freight and sleeping bags. From an unsealed manilla envelope spilled a collection of letters, paychecks and grocery manifests into a puddle of slush.

Sensing someone behind me, I turned and very nearly dropped an armload of bread. Before us, stood the most foul, filthy old man I'd ever seen. What at first I took to be a sun-burned Eskimo's copper-tone skin turned out to be dirt caked so thickly, that small, glossy pebbles of it bordered the edges of his T-shirt. White patches on the man's arms and neck were places where cakes of grime had fallen away in tile-size chunks. Nuggets of yellowish ear wax matched the rheum caking the orbits of both eyes.

Skimming never said a word as the aged caretaker smiled through a blackened mouth. We both knew that isolation here at Cullaton Lake probably accounted for most of the missing mental cylinders. The man existed in a sorrowful, baffled state many northerners described as "bushed." Nothing less than a rubdown with steel wool would render our mangy new friend presentable.

The work from Cullaton Lake proved interesting. No snow existed now—only hard, runway-like ice surfaces on which to land. Open water developing along the shorelines forced us to carry a small inflatable life raft so he could complete his exploratory tasks. When the weather warmed, I passed the spare time between flights by waxing my beloved Cessna 180's metal surfaces.

Often left alone when Skimming disappeared on his gold quests, tundra-watching became my new obsession. In this part of the barrenlands, small trees weren't the only plant life. On the sweeping slopes that rose above the chocolate bogs, dwarf scrubs formed little patches of glossy green. On the hard ancient rocks under my rubber boots, lichens of many kinds became my private studies.

To most people who trudged about the Arctic, lichens represented nothing more than lowly organisms but I found the varieties fascinating. Yellow, black, crusty ones resembled patterns on my navigational maps and reindeer moss grew everywhere in gray-white clumps or singly in tiny, tree-like shapes. Knowing that explorer Sir John Franklin nearly starved not far from our campsite on Cullaton, I tasted rock tripe. After chewing several shreds, I knew right away that I'd have perished, had my name been on the list of men who accompanied him.

Once, an opportunity came my way to follow a lone caribou at close range. A medium-size, clumsy-looking creature, with huge brown antlers, bulbous knees and wide curious eyes, he walked casually toward the Cessna 180 as I watched from beneath the wing. His fur looked as if he'd lost a battle with a student barber. When he noticed me, his whole body flexed, ready to run. As he clopped away, his head and antlers stayed almost perfectly motionless while the lower parts of his body elongated in a series of fluid, snakelike motions.

In the coming summer, Skimming said, a Canso tanker airplane would deliver loads of diesel fuel into the airstrip. We spent the rest of our day blasting boulders and moving them to smooth the surface for the incoming airplane. Working with dynamite didn't count for a minute in my pilot's logbook, but it proved to be a valuable addition to my "experience repertoire."

By now, the lakes softened too much for landings, even with the light Cessna 180. Gray spots on the ice turned to black, signaling the end of the Selco contract. We planned on leaving for Churchill when Skimming returned from one last two-day walk to a campsite near Cullaton Lake.

On our final night, I stayed outside longer than usual. I stared at a breathtaking sky of haunting orange and black, caused by forest fires hundreds of miles southwest of us. Later, inside my sleeping bag, I remained awake, enjoying the silence until the old man came back from repairing a bulldozer. With my bag spread between some grocery boxes, I felt comfortable and drifted off to sleep, watching the afterglow of twilight cast a pink hue on to the plywood floor.

It seemed as if I hadn't been long asleep, dreaming of rivers and waterfalls hurrying along in springtime, as ice pans and crystals separated from shorelines. I opened my eyes and, strangely, still heard water tinkling somewhere close by. Odd, I thought, no bubbly brooks or streams existed for many miles and those that did couldn't move, encased in solid ice as they were. I listened carefully, shaking myself fully awake. The sound persisted.

Suddenly, I leaped out of my sleeping bag. In the dim light across the room, I saw someone silhouetted near the window. The old man was sleep walking. Lost deeply in his dreams, he thought himself in a lavatory during his youthful days, urinating full force into a shiny porcelain bowl.

My sharp angry yell awoke him. Instead of a shiny toilet bowl, he discovered he was was discharging great cataracts of steaming yellow fluid into baskets containing our food. Dazed and groggy with the sudden return to reality, he looked at me, fumbled with his dirty fingers and then carried on with his business. The next hint—a can of Libby's beans—aroused his full attention and he stopped. Still foggy, the old man stomped back to his sleeping bag and returned to sleep. In the morning, he remembered nothing and denied making the gigantic amber stains and rivulets drying upon our bacon, bread and eggs.

Two days later, we made our last takeoff from Cullaton Lake's airstrip. The caretaker stayed behind to wait for the Canso flying fuel tanker. Several hours later we located the flat boulder shorelines of Hudson Bay, followed the rocks south as cloud forced us down to fifty feet. When Churchill's grain elevators appeared, we could barely see their tops as we landed on the gravel runway.

Skimming quickly found a seat on a commercial flight for Winnipeg and disappeared into the cosy depths of Transair's Douglas DC-4. Sorry to see him leave, I learned later he requested my services for a summer's contract in the Chantry-Bathurst Inlet area. Much to my regret, Skimming and I never crossed paths again.

After several days, I heard The Pas head office telephone the base manager. He acknowledged instructions to send the CF-SLJ south for changeover to floats. At the time, my seaplane experience amounted to little more than a five-hour endorsement on a Piper J-3 Cub.

After returning to The Pas work settled into a routine. Lamb Airways' de Havilland Otters, Beavers, and Cessna 180s came and went, while I attempted to master float flying. Unofficial policy seemed to decree that no experienced old timers showed the new pilots how to keep themselves out of trouble. We learned on our own.

Flights took me in all directions to places that, only a few months before, meant nothing more to me than names in an atlas. Sometimes, my enthusiasm led to predicaments when I could barely make it back to base before running out of fuel. Other times, weather dropped below safe legal limits. In one case, I found myself following railway tracks at low level to Lynn Lake. Sloppy snow flakes nearly the size of tractor tires began flashing past the windshield. Unwisely, I pushed on into the murk.

Soon the wings carried so much slush it seemed impossible to stay in the air. Too low above the tracks, I dared not change direction, nor could I find somewhere to land so we kept flogging toward Lynn Lake. My passenger assured me once we found the town, a right turn would put us over the airport.

A gray water tower appeared in the gloom; simultaneously, several roof tops nearly clipped the tail wheel. I made a quick hard right turn but couldn't find a runway. Desperate, I brought the throttle back, cranked the flap down and prepared to land on a dark ribbon of road at the south end of town. Excitedly, the passenger yelled, "There! Off to our left, we saw a long, wet black strip of asphalt."

That night I stayed in Lynn Lake.

I returned two days later to The Pas and began float flying. On the water, high-speed step turns brought me back to the dock quickly and made me look like a high-time pro. Getting in and out of short lakes above legal gross weights became a practiced art. Someone reminded me never to forget to pull up the water rudders before takeoff. These small, fin-like devices at the rear end of the floats provided steering on the lake surface. After turning into wind, a pilot raised them *via* a cable in the cockpit. If forgotten, landing forces could slam them up hard enough against the floats to crack metal.

On bad weather days, I drank coffee with the Lamb Airways' veterans. In the evenings, trip after trip to the local bars persuaded me that I belonged in the ranks of hardened, high-time pilots. Awe-struck and eager, I listened to the stories of others. In one tale, a competitor landed a Noorduyn Norseman at Cumberland House on the Saskatchewan River, sixty miles from The Pas. As the pilot taxied through the silty water and floating driftwood toward the cream-colored mud banks, he noticed a party in progress among the local Indians. It began to break up as he approached.

Desperate for a flight to civilization, the party goers begged the pilot for a seat. In this case, money counted. The experienced "driver" knew that lean times could happen any day in the aviation business. The Indians paid dearly until not an inch to sit or stand remained inside the Norseman. More customers begged to go, but the pilot could barely squeeze the bulging doors shut against a press of sweating bodies.

He pushed away, scrambled up the ladder into the cockpit and fired up the radial engine. Moments later, he began a roaring takeoff along the winding waterway and staggered into the air for Prince Albert, 150 miles southwest along the Saskatchewan River. Behind him, passengers without seat belts held tightly to each other as the deafening engine noise sobered them all. The pilot felt comfortable with the window slightly open, a pleasant breeze cooling his face.

With plenty of rudder trim and extra foot pressure on the pedal, the Norseman flew a little sloppier than usual. Cruise speed stayed several knots below the Norseman standard. A hot day, he thought. The airplane's getting old and the old girl's endured many a load sliding along its wooden floor. Soon, he parked at his seaplane base.

Stepping down onto the dock, he realized he had carried a stowaway. Clutching the outside ladder between the airplane's belly and the float, a haggard-looking Cree unclenched his fingers, rubbed his eyes and staggered along the wharf. Apparently, the not-quite-sober character had jumped on as the airplane taxied away at Cumberland House and rode the route clinging to the oil-slicked ladder rungs.

Unimpressed, the pilot charged him full fare.

V During an early-morning trip to Norway House, my only passenger introduced himself as a British doctor. After takeoff, he remained pensive as we cruised above the flat, swampy land north of mighty Lake Winnipeg. As we reached Playgreen Lake, he unexpectedly burst into a long spell of laughter. He giggled and tittered nonstop for the rest of the flight. Before we docked at Norway House, he regained his composure and explained the reason for his mirth.

The previous day, a man target practicing with an illegal handgun at The Pas's gravel pit, panicked when he caught sight of a Royal Canadian Mounted Police vehicle patrolling nearby. The weapon required a permit he didn't have. Frightened, he jammed the loaded pistol into his pocket, overlooking the fact that his finger remained on the trigger. The gun discharged. My passenger had spent several hours rebuilding what remained of the man's reproductive member.

As weather warmed, the company decided to send me to Thompson for an indefinite period. For thirty consecutive days, charter flights from Thompson kept me on the move. In that period, I slept in transient houses, bunkhouses and camp sites in twenty-two different locations throughout Manitoba and Saskatchewan. One trip called for a week-long flight with one passenger to colorful communities such as Pukatawagan, Brochet, Snow Lake, Sherridon and many others. His task of arranging accommodations for a government-sponsored musical troupe to entertain the Indian people in Canada's centennial year, took several hours at each stop.

These blissful educational times came to an unanticipated conclusion shortly after we returned to Thompson. During my first day back in "Nickel Town," a de Havilland Otter landed on the Burntwood River and parked behind my Cessna 180.

The right rear door opened and out bounded a half-dozen attractive women. Most wore short skirts, and brought with them a mountain-sized pile of luggage. The base manager informed the watching crowd of pilots and mechanics that these pretty ladies were all school teachers. With contracts ended, Lamb Airways accepted a charter to move them from Indian reserves in June and back again during the fall.

The dispatcher beckoned me to the office. Someone needed a trip from Kelsey Dam to Thompson. In spite of my suggestion that he consider another pilot—since watching the stunning school teachers demanded my full attention—he prodded me toward the Cessna 180.

While the white-armed maidens watched, I carefully pre-flighted the airplane. Playing the dashing "Joe Bush Pilot" role, I untied the ropes and decided not to wait for help in getting away from the dock.

Keeping my mind on the teachers, I slipped into the cockpit and pushed the starter button. As the propeller blades turned over, the river current eased the floats back toward the dock. Thinking I'd have sufficient clearance from anything ahead, I tramped right rudder pedal and increased throttle the instant the engine caught.

My favorite Cessna 180 went straight ahead and crashed into the next airplane.

As long as I live, I will forever remember the sound and shudders of that propeller chewing deeply into the wing tip of the other Cessna 180. A semi-oval, fibreglass wingtip cover broke loose, flew up and landed near the astonished teachers.

I had forgotten to lower the water rudders.

The two airplanes remained locked, nose to wing. The only way to separate them meant climbing onto the wing, and applying creative bashes with a wooden paddle—all under the gaze of tittering strangers.

One of the airline owners stepped outside the office to determine the cause of excitement as the Cessnas separated. When he reached the dock, the current drifted CF-SLH and me toward the river center.

Not exactly appreciative of the sight of his money makers out of action, the airline owner volunteered some tart remarks about my parentage. After an order to return to the dock, the tone of our conversation escalated and I suggested he perform an impossible biological function upon himself. Paddling in the strong current felt like I was using a popsicle stick to berth the Queen Elizabeth II. Eventually, inch by inch, I crept closer to the dock until someone threw a rope.

As the dock hands assessed the damage, several taxi cabs arrived to take the teachers to the airport. By the time they left, I heard nonstop giggling about the unscheduled Burntwood River demonstration. I still live in fear of someday hearing someone say, "Oh, I remember you. You're the guy who...... "

Surprisingly, the damage to my Cessna 180 seemed slight. The propeller lacked a mark and looked fit for flight, although its opponent would not see service until a new wing tip could be installed in The Pas.

The base manager snappily ordered me to complete the trip. Relieved that he didn't fire me, I left immediately and soon landed across the high-tension lines at Kelsey Dam. Three men stood waiting with tool boxes, suitcases and metal poles. After they crowded inside the airplane, I sailed as closely as possible to the downwind side of the lake. Black and silver high-tension power lines linked by enormous steel towers surrounded us.

Throttle to the wall, the Cessna 180 dragged itself onto the step and we were airborne. Too slow, I held the nose level to increase airspeed and then eased into a steep climb over the metal lines. Minutes later, clear of danger, I followed the Apussigamasi River and passed Moak Lake on the right before spotting the distant smelter smoke in Thompson.

On final approach for landing, I applied several notches of flap as the voice of another pilot rattled through the overhead radio speaker. In a Lamb Airways' Otter, he planned to land behind me. With luck, I could get down and park well out of his way on the dock. As the floats touched, I eased in enough throttle to stay on the step, but the engine shook several times and vibrated in its mounts. Settling into the water, I had no idea what caused it and knew the mechanics had pronounced CF-SLH safe to fly. Humbled by the base manager's lecture, I thought perhaps my lack of float experience might be responsible.

"Keep it moving. Keep it moving," shouted the Otter pilot.

Unfortunately for him, he needed to slow down and follow behind since he couldn't pass on the narrow river.

My passengers left the seaplane base quickly — a yellow truck waited for them. Knowing that my propeller-crunching episode had placed me on thin ice with the company, I kept away from the office. Another Lamb brother who arrived from Churchill appeared on the scene. He saw me hiding behind the tail of an Otter as the dock boy refueled the wing tanks and the Cessna 180's oil.

"So what the hell happened to you?" he demanded, extracting a filter cigarette from a crumpled paper package. His lower lip suddenly seemed to take on a life of its own as it quivered in anticipation of my answer. Along one edge, I saw a tiny yellow trough that marked him as a heavy smoker.

As I prepared an excuse, the dock boy suddenly gasped, "My God, look at this!"

We turned.

He had opened a small trap door on top of the cowling ahead of the windshield to pour in a quart of engine oil. Since Cessna designers never predicted that their products might operate away from ladders and service trucks in the Canadian bush, our man had to climb as high as he could by wedging one foot on a step and gripping the propeller.

"Look, for God's sake. Look at this," he repeated. "I don't believe this. Look."

With one hand, he moved the top propeller blade back and forth several inches in its hub while the other remained firmly fixed in place. A fibre block inside the pitch-change mechanism had broken during the collision with the other airplane. Why the blade didn't shake loose, especially during the long, maximum-power climb over the wires back at Kelsey Dam, I couldn't understand. My three passengers and I had been only heartbeats away from merging with eternity. In the boss's words, "You nearly got bumped off."

The Lamb brother did not move. With feet planted in the sand, he swivelled his head and looked at me. Seconds later came those words that would stay with me for the rest of my life:

"Better take a walk on down the road, boy."

For a few seconds, the magnitude of his meaning didn't sink in. Slowly, very slowly, the import of what he said began to penetrate. My world suddenly went blurry and I staggered backwards several steps. Luckily, the company's half-ton truck prevented me from falling over backwards. Like comic strip or cartoon characters, the shock had nearly made me collapse.

The situation didn't seem funny, although a mechanic standing within listening distance snickered loudly. Fired from a job I enjoyed more than anything else in my career. I couldn't believe it had happened. No longer invincible in a Cessna 180 above northern Manitoba, I understood that overconfidence and an inability to recognize limitations finally caught up to me.

Nothing remained for me to do except leave the seaplane base. All trains and buses had departed and the scheduled Transair DC-4 was sold out. The company booted me out of the staff house and not one room remained in any hotel in town. I walked to a shopping plaza and discovered a mass of telephones. For an hour, I called every commercial bush airline I could think of and usually received the same answer.

"You're in Thompson? Hey, why don't you give Lamb Airways a call?" they said. After letting them know how the famous family fired me, a long silence followed. "Well, if we need somebody, we'll call you." No one ever asked for a telephone number or address.

Stranded with little money, I had nowhere to go and eventually arrived in Winnipeg and began calling for a job. Finally a far away voice in Parry Sound, Ontario, sounded slightly interested, although perceptively cool.

"As it happens, we might need somebody right away," the chief pilot said. "How much flying time have you got?"

I told him about the last few months' activities. A long silence followed and then the usual, "Might call you back." Before he hung up, I rattled off the number of the hotel.

One more number on my list remained but it too proved a waste of time. My aviation career was over. Abruptly, the telephone rang.

"You there?" a voice asked. It was the Georgian Bay Airways' operations manager in Parry Sound. "If you can make it here right away, we'd like to talk to you."

The next day I entered the office of Georgian Bay Airways. By now, the deep depression of the past few days had dispersed and I felt hopeful, determined to watch my step.

4 Moon River Mail Run

The operations manager demanded to see my logbook, which I meekly handed over. For twenty minutes, he leafed through page after page, stopped at the end of my entries and then flipped through the paper again. He dragged an adding machine across his desk and punched numbers into it.

"Forty? Wait a minute. What the hell do you mean, forty? You told me you had 400."

"No, sir. I did not."

"My God. Forty hours on floats. That's no good."

Suddenly, I realized no one had guaranteed me a job. Without warning, he smashed my logbook down upon his glass-topped desk. A small jar fell over and paper clips scattered across the floor.

"Stay here!" he barked as he stormed out of the room.

Seconds later, I heard the door of the general manager's office slam shut. Game over, I thought. Not a hope. All of this was for nothing.

I peeked toward the next room where the general manager glared back at me. He mouthed a few short words to his associate, shrugged his shoulders and threw his hands in the air.

The stomp of heavy boots heralded the operations manager's return. He dropped his huge frame into his chair and whipped off his eyeglasses. Lost in what appeared to be morbid contemplation, the man who held my future in his hands remained silent.

"Well, we need somebody right now and you're here....You get the shot kid," he snapped.

Georgian Bay Airways began operating from the Parry Sound waterfront in 1946 when its principal owner, Frank D. Powell, accepted a discharge from the Royal Canadian Air Force. Over the years, the company's pilots flew from bases in Ontario, and northern Quebec. The company pioneered northern Ontario commuter airlines and, in later years, entered the aerial fire fighting business with Consolidated Canso water bombers.

During the summer of 1967, my employment with the company became a nonstop catalogue of enjoyable flying hours over the magnificent Georgian Bay coastline. Decades later, I realized that fate had treated me kindly. If I had not been dismissed from Lamb Airways, my overconfidence would probably have brought me to a tragic end against a rock at Chantrey Inlet.

At Parry Sound, Georgian Bay Airways kept a powder-blue de Havilland Beaver with paint so old that flakes fell into the water when the engine started. Sharing the dock were two other airplanes: a red and white Super Cub with ringworm circles under its door and a banana yellow rarity called a Found Brothers FBA-2C. Occasionally, itinerant Lake and Republic Seabee amphibians crumpled their noses on the dock, and sometimes Sudbury-based Noorduyn Norsemen of Austin Airways taxied in for fuel.

Having been fired from my last job, I knew it would take time before anyone trusted me completely with an airplane. At first, my duties consisted of pumping floats and handling luggage but before long, the "Airways," as locals called the airline, began paying me two cents per mile on the Super Cub and slightly more on the others.

Each morning, dock boys checked the oil and placed a standard load of fuel in each wing or belly tank. As a pilot, I held the ultimate responsibility for the customers' safety as well as my own. Every trip, I either placed my hand on the fuel caps or visually made sure they were in place.

The Airways' territory on the east side of Lake Huron contained more than 80,000 islands, from Waubaushene on the south end to Wikwemikang on the north. Inland, hundreds of lakes with private camps and commercial tourist lodges kept pilots busy. Most customers drove to Parry Sound from Michigan, Illinois and New York. Rarely did an Airways' airplane carry Canadians, except the year-round residents who lived on the islands.

Sightseeing drew many passersby. On one trip, a piano player from the nearby Kipling Hotel brought his performing monkey along. The animal had never been on an airplane and no one at Georgian Bay Airways could recall ever having had a monkey onboard. Seconds after takeoff the monkey went berserk. By the time its greasy-headed owner subdued the crazed creature, its feces and vomit coated the cockpit.

Another trip involved an aristocratic British family visiting Canada for the first time. After they crossed the Atlantic via a BOAC Boeing 707 jetliner, they rode from Toronto's international airport to Orillia in a chauffeur-driven limousine. At Orillia, I waited in the rain with the Beaver.

As luck would have it, my earlier charter involved hauling fishermen from their camp sites into Parry Sound. The odor of bass entrails and the sight of fish scales plastered against the floor and walls didn't evince what I would have called "a sniffle of exceeding pleasure" from the chubby British matriarch.

Nevertheless, having journeyed this far, she adopted a stiff British upper lip and forced her two squally children aboard. Moments later, we left Lake Couchiching behind. As we flew northwestwards, it began raining so hard that I began searching for a sheltered place to wait for better weather. Luckily, a shallow groove in the trees to my left indicated the Moon River, which led to her destination on Georgian Bay. Dropping lower we continued on with barely enough forward visibility to see.

At our altitude, no outstanding features appeared and the matriarch wondered aloud how we Canadian bush pilots could possibly know where we were. Unknown to her, I'd flown innumerable trips in the area and knew every rock, hydro line and waterfall along the way.

We arrived as planned, circled an island and landed in the rain. Overwhelmed that I had located a specific piece of acreage in the middle of what she considered virgin wilderness, the stocky woman planted a slobbery kiss upon my cheek. Slipping a five-dollar tip into my hand, she stepped back and pronounced me, "Aw-fully clevah." Slightly spellbound by the compliment, I returned to Parry Sound a few minutes after official sunset.

The next morning, a dock boy parked a four-legged animal near the Piper Super Cub. At first glance, it resembled a tall, Mexican iguana but moments later I deduced the pathetic creature must have been some species of dog.

Instead of fur, a hard shell-like substance covered every inch of its skin. Deep, moist depressions with grotesque, threadlike outgrowths marked spots that once held hair follicles. Large, vague lumps with dark, central pits must have been ears, judging by their location. The sad, sightless eyes were opaque and nearly surrounded by flaps of dry skin. "Bubbles" needed a ride to Wildgoose Island.

Before long, the dock boy chained the dog to the Piper Super Cub's rear seat and I left for Wildgoose. Navigation with fine-scale topographical charts didn't come easily in the islands, but soon Spider Point slid under the plane's nose and our destination was in sight.

As I banked into a gentle left turn, I saw the cottage below, or at least what people called a cottage in this part of holiday country. It was a two-story, gabled place topped by a red-tiled roof and costly latticework along its length. With half flap, the airplane touched the water gently and taxied toward the island.

A woman waiting on the dock looked to be in her midtwenties. Exquisitely shaped like a Bolshoi ballerina, she stood by a high-back chair not far from the house. The unmistakable tan of the very rich colored her arms and shoulders. Long, beautiful, blonde hair covered her ears, flowed below her shoulders and ended out of sight behind her back. Teeth as white as the flowers that edged a shoreline near our air base, complemented a pair of striking green eyes. A fashion model, I thought, as the propeller stopped and the right wing tip gently touched a flagpole.

A young man grabbed the strut. The dog was quiet as I untied his chain and gently lifted him out of the airplane. Slowly, and shakily, he ambled away.

The woman stood, smiled and called the dog but, like a delicately handcrafted Czechoslovakian chandelier swinging in a summer breeze, she swayed unsteadily. As the sun streamed through the broken cloud above, the hound shuffled his ravaged body to her side. Her hand reached down toward the dog. Heedless of the animal's repulsive condition, she picked him up, drew him into her arms, and caressed him gently.

At that instant, I realized that she too was blind. The dog and the woman continued greeting each other as I eased the Super Cub toward deeper water. Paddling quietly in Georgian Bay, no one seemed to notice my departure.

I never saw that delicate Dresden figurine again. Before the summer ended, the young man told me his sister had died of a disease, the name of which I couldn't pronounce. In the fall, the family closed their cottage and never returned to Wildgoose Island.

As my flying hours increased at Georgian Bay Airways, the other employees and chief pilot Stanley King, accepted the fact that in my not-so-distant past, I had erred. Now they knew that I no longer saw myself as know-it-all, "Joe Bush Pilot." By asking questions, refusing heavy loads, and not rushing thoughtlessly into assigned tasks, it seemed I might remain in the world I enjoyed. With reestablished credibility, I was trusted with every airplane in Georgian Bay's fleet.

Customers frequently needed the Found FBA-2C to carry family members and a reasonable load of groceries. Canadian-built, the box-shaped wonder registered CF-SDB turned out to be a well-designed, short-haul airplane. Heavy on the controls, it took all my strength to release the overhead flap handle slowly after takeoff. The Found was powerful and could outperform any Cessna on the market. Robust, it lacked wing struts. More than one distracted pilot reached for a support that wasn't there and fell into a lake. I shared most of my work with Stanley King, a man whose mind was a lake of experience as large as Nippissing. He frequently offered advice to inexperienced pilots but never pushed himself on anyone unwilling to listen. When a trip looked as if it might exceed my limitations, he volunteered to fly for me. Later, Bert Archer, considered legendary in Canada's aviation circles, dropped by to help at busy times, especially during brief fall hunting seasons.

As the summer went on, the company dispatched me on monotonous forest-fire patrols. Detection observers from the Ontario Department of Lands and Forests accompanied me and either fell asleep or decorated the Super Cub's floorboards with their breakfasts. Other routine trips included taking supply teachers to Sugar Bay's elementary school and taking rubber-booted commercial fishermen to Sans Souci. Sometimes, world-famous sculptor Robert Murray booked a ride to his private retreat on Lookout Island.

One afternoon, a fully outfitted scuba diver flip-flopped from his station wagon into the base and requested a trip over Lake Huron's swells. He described a sunken barge not far from the Western Islands as a collection of shoals inhabited by nothing but seagulls. We warned him that high waves might make a landing impossible, but he insisted on going.

For the first time in weeks, Lake Huron's usually rolling surface remained almost calm, with only a six-inch chop. We circled until we spotted a dark, square shape far out in deep water. After pinpointing the barge site as closely as possible, we landed. The diver stepped off the Super Cub's float and disappeared in a frothy swirl of bubbles. An hour later, he surfaced.

"No luck. Couldn't find anything," he gasped. "Let's get out of here and come back again after I get more air."

Exhausted, he climbed onto the float after I took his cumbersome air tank and stored it behind the back seat. On the horizon, low cloud had turned dark black with white swirls at the bottom; a rain squall would soon hit the area. We returned to Parry Sound as the dock boy threw extra ropes on the other airplanes. Peeved at not being able to return to the Westerns, our customer left and never returned. His barge still lies submerged somewhere on the bottom of Lake Huron, loaded with whatever induced him to track it down. Several times, I swung out over the open water but couldn't locate the vessel again.

Several times a week, someone flew the Moon River Mail Run. Its romantic name referred to a small home that served as a post office southeast of Parry Sound. Tourists, encouraged by

Georgian Bay Airways' colorful brochures, tended to think of the short but usually turbulent hop as a glamorous journey.

Most people, able to successfully extricate themselves from the Super Cub's cramped rear seat, considered the surrounding hardwood forests and natural white waters as a world far different from the cluttered one they knew back home. Others threw up. Some dropped their expensive Canons, Hasselblads, or Nikons when they stepped on the gargantuan, well-fed bull snakes inhabiting rock piles along the shoreline.

According to one pilot, Moon River's exceptional muskellunge fishing couldn't be beaten. One rumor concerned a woman whose tiny dog was supposedly swallowed by one of these sharklike creatures.

Slightly north of Moon River, a well-known Canadian department store family established a small farm to provide fresh vegetables and raise horses. Hay, grain and livestock feed formed part of our regular inbound loads to Boundary Lake. Late one afternoon, our booking sheet listed Parry Sound's veterinarian. A horse with a throat infection couldn't swallow and would probably die a lingering death by starvation.

"I'll need help. Can you stay?" asked the vet as I tied the Super Cub securely to the boathouse dock.

City-raised, I knew nothing about horses except that their mouths had powerful, bone-crunching jaws. I also knew that they had four legs ending in blunt instruments that could maim inattentive Super Cub pilots. With little effort, any horse could sense someone with phobias toward biting, kicking animals. Anxious to overcome the stigma of my Thompson fiasco, I decided to stay and become a veterinarian's helper.

What awaited us in the barn hardly matched my idea of a graceful steed. The creature stood in yellowish brown ooze that sloshed over the tops of my desert boots and down between my toes. Rotted, peg-like stumps ran unevenly along its scabrous lips and foam dribbled from the lower jaw down its chest.

I felt sorry for the animal, realizing he could be facing his last days. The veterinarian opened his black leather bag from which he extracted something resembling a grotesque, orange snake. It turned out to be ribbed, rubber tubing. On the floor nearby,

Boundary Lake's caretaker placed several pails of porridge-like material.

"Gotta get some food into him," mumbled the vet. "Now, hold his head."

He took the closest end of the tubing and inserted it into the beast's left nostril. The horse's ears flattened and all four legs splayed apart. Seized in spasmodic, whooping convulsions, the tank-size horse tried to rear but couldn't because of my weight. A hoof slammed down upon my instep. Somehow, I maintained my grip around the beast's sweaty neck.

The horse's olive brown eyes bulged outward. For an instant they seemed ready to explode into a thousand tiny fragments of ligaments, humors and retinas. Its nostril flared so wide that I expected it to split and extend along the animal's cheek. As the unruffled vet slid the tube deeper, I looked around to see if it would emerge from beneath the tail.

Face-to-face, those angry eyes looked directly into mine and its great mouth opened. As I contemplated life without a face or shoulder, I caught a glimpse of its long, pink throat sluggering into the darkness of its stomach. A gigantic tongue writhed and flapped between its jaws. All of a sudden, a stream of loathsome, brown fluid shot outward from the throat. Horrified, I watched it the band of slime rocket across the stable, except the portion interrupted by my face. The mess filtered through my hair and slid slowly down my shoulders.

"Whoa, easy, Boy," said the vet, trying to calm the horse. He inserted a funnel into the free end of the hose and began pouring in pails of pablum. An hour later, the vet reeled the hose out like a giant, scummy earthworm. Disgusted, I slithered back to the dock. The next day on the Moon River Mail Run, I passed over Boundary Lake and saw the animal tethered outside.

My trips began ranging farther away from the base. A water-survey contract took me into Ontario's beautiful Algonquin Park. Another charter called for a flight to Lake Erie's sandy beach with a load of racing fans. Luckily, Lake Erie's swells failed to swamp the sturdy Found.

Southbound flights to ferry-choked harbors became exciting on windy days. Once, I used the Piper Super Cub to pick up a

British businessman and take him to metropolitan Toronto for a conference. As luck would have it, winds increased to twenty-five knots. When we arrived over the harbor's gray, crashing water, gusts of wind slammed into the crests and kicked up clouds of spray. With not enough fuel to return to Parry Sound and an anxious customer in the back seat, it seemed wise to aim for a sheltered area. Logs, boats and debris hindered my intended touchdown spot but a huge ferry passed by, I landed in the calm left by its wake.

Taxiing to a dock proved to be more difficult and hazardous. Titanic swells threatened to overturn us and each time the airplane's nose slammed down, water-soaked spark plugs nearly stopped the engine. A flat-bottomed service boat made its way toward us. Despite the unbelievable pitching, its crew managed to come alongside and match our movements. Two men held the wing struts to guide us to a buoy.

One man said they expected the Cub to go under and thought they would be rescuing us from drowning.

We tied up in a sheltered area and went to the dock by boat. Wet, exhausted and with no hope of carrying out a safe takeoff, I realized I had to stay in Toronto overnight, but I didn't have a cent in my wallet. My passenger reached into his pocket, then remembered he hadn't exchanged his British pound notes for Canadian dollars. Searching further, he discovered a twenty-five-cent coin in his jacket, which happened to be the exact price of a ferryboat ticket to the mainland.

I suggested he carry on to his conference; I would call a friend to rescue me. Two hours later, a flying buddy arrived and we left the airport to rock the night away in big city Toronto. In the morning, the Super Cub was still afloat.

Boundary Lake became a more frequent run as fall approached. In this isolated pothole, the caretaker and his wife lived year round. Whenever I saw them, they were bickering loudly, their quarrels frequently spilling over to whatever pilot drew the dreaded duty of flying into Boundary.

After an exciting day of moving cottagers, I returned to hear the base manager's dictum to leave for Boundary Lake. The caretakers demanded a ride to town for a medical appointment. I stood by as the dock boy pumped gasoline into the Found and then left as quickly as possible. By the time the floats touched Boundary Lake, the sun had nearly set. Taxiing closer, I noticed something disquieting in the way the couple stood on the dock.

The instant the two-blade propeller stopped, they began ranting. "Where the hell have you been?" Bella shrieked. "We wanted a god-damn airplane hours ago."

Bella was a large woman. Her arms ended in fingers so short, I thought at first they lacked knuckles. Grit-filled hair hung over her forehead and a slanted white scar angled down from her eyebrow. Her thin-framed husband lacked a hair upon his head. He also lacked teeth, which caused his lips to sink so far back into his mouth, I thought they had been amputated.

"I said, where the beegeezus have you been?" Bella shouted again. "When we tell you we want out of here, we mean right now!"

Attempts to persuade her that pilots only did what dispatchers told them proved fruitless. Small flecks of foam began appearing at the edges of her mouth. For all I knew, her medical appointment could be a rabies check with Parry Sound's veterinarian. When I voiced my thoughts, her anger became so consuming that even her husband backed away.

Snarling and snapping, they boarded the Found. Its Lycoming engine started instantly and we taxied toward the lake's west end. Boundary Lake lacked enough length to make pilots feel at ease and there were few places to land in case of an emergency. Granite hills with sharp-tipped pine and rock-hard poplar trees waited to claim overloaded airplanes. Also, the lake's "L" shape increased the takeoff distance, as an airplane had to roar around the corner.

Distracted by the haggling of my passengers, I slowly eased in the throttle. As usual, the magnificent Found quickly left the lake's surface. Only after clearing the hills did I dare reduce engine power and raise flaps for a better climb. We landed in Parry Sound minutes later. Shortly before going home, the manager called me into his office.

"How much fuel did you have for Boundary?" he asked.

"I don't know. The usual, I guess." With dozens of short hops every week, trips blended together and became routine.

"Go have a look," he suggested.

I looked inside the Found's cockpit and saw that both wing root gauges indicated zero fuel, which was not enough to float the corks inside the tanks. This was impossible, I thought, as we always landed with something showing on the needle. I slipped outside to check the fuel caps. Both were missing.

Evidently, the dock boy didn't replace them and, in my haste, I failed to check each one. My preoccupation with two quarreling eccentrics also caused me to neglect the cockpit gauges as I taxied from the dock in Boundary Lake. Every drop of gasoline had been siphoned out by the airflow.

No one could explain what kept the engine running on takeoff over those stony hills. If fate, luck, or whatever it was, hadn't played a part, the caretakers would never have been heard again. Worse, my rashness could have transformed a classic airplane into a twisted mass of useless metal sitting on a craggy hillside.

Near the end of the period at which I planned to leave Georgian Bay Airways for university, a humiliating incident took place. In later years, an overwhelming fear that someone would learn about it remained with me everywhere I traveled.

"Tomorrow, you've got an early trip from Iron City Fishing Club," said the dispatcher. "Take one passenger to Penetanguishene and then come back for a load to Boundary Lake."

The next morning, I was in a rush after sleeping through my alarm. I postponed two important pre-departure duties. However, at Iron City, an exclusive club for steel executives from Pittsburg, Pennsylvania, the floats could be pumped and I could probably find a bathroom to take care of the other duty.

After circling the lake, I landed and step-taxied to the Iron City dock. For the first time in the history of Canadian aviation, a passenger was ready to go. A United States marine, in full dress uniform with a dangling silver sword, had hired the Piper Super Cub to rush to Penetanguishene. There, a limousine stood by to take him to a Lear jet at Toronto's international airport. Fortunately, the Super Cub carried tight floats which could be pumped later. As for its frazzled pilot, I would also have to wait.

After leveling a few hundred feet above the islands, I looked longingly back at Iron City. Somewhere in that cluster of neat white cottages, dining rooms and tennis courts, I knew a bathroom existed. Nevertheless, in what an American tourist once described as the "Great Canadian Bush Pilot Tradition," it seemed within the bounds of propriety to contain myself and carry on. Every jolt of turbulence reminded my body that a bathroom stop would soon be necessary. Luckily, the sleeping community of Penetanguishene appeared below the Edo 2000 floats, and we landed.

"This isn't Midland. I want Midland," my passenger snapped.

Damn! The dispatcher had clearly said Penetanguishene. I quickly applied takeoff flap and slammed the throttle forward. Moments later, we were across town and touching down in the proper bay. A long, black limousine waited and the driver quickly took my customer's bags. As for my over-strained body, no washroom was in sight. Restaurants and service stations didn't open until regular business hours. If my concentration held, I could safely reach Parry Sound in less than thirty minutes.

Enroute home, cottages dotted every island. As Honey Harbor passed slowly off the right wing tip, I felt pressure below my bloated stomach. Near Beausoleil Island, the pressure peaked in uncountable sharp twinges and then mercifully subsided.

Being an airplane pilot really was a good life, I thought, as the Super Cub crawled on. I rocked the wings at a sailboat anchored in a pretty, tree-lined cove, and a sailor waved back at me. At that instant, a bolt of pain struck my midsection and I vowed to propitiate whatever gods looked after Super Cub pilots as white-hot lightning daggered through my limbs.

So help me God, never again would haste spoil my day, even if it meant keeping the entire United States Marine Corps waiting at the Iron City dock. My idealistic view of flying for a living changed as the Super Cub chugged on. The wind shifted and slowed my forward speed. This time, the excruciating spasms increased until I released the control column and pushed inward on my abdomen. I dove toward a cottage-lined inlet on the mainland.

Boats beside every dock forced me to a boulder-covered shoreline. Cottagers, interrupted by the sudden appearance of an airplane, flattened their noses against windowpanes. One spectator sat in a lawn chair yards away from my parking spot with a coffee cup angled properly to his lips.

As the right float bumped a rock, I reached frantically for a rope. The privacy of a clump of juniper waited close by but there was no rope to be found.

After completing inspections, Georgian Bay Airways' mechanics didn't return the airplane's tie-down ropes to the baggage compartment. A quick search netted me nothing more than a short piece of string that barely fit around a huge, mossy boulder. Oblivious to the strangers' stares, I jogged toward the trees.

Damn! The string slipped and wind blew the airplane toward deeper water. I ran back, threw myself into the bay, and dragged the Super Cub to shore. As I tweaked the knot again, I leaned against an overriding world of pain. I turned and began a final, desperate sprint toward the juniper.

Six steps later........

Discomfited, I slithered shamefully back into the airplane. The crowd of cottagers giggled as my reddened thumb pressed the silver starter button. Enroute to Parry Sound, I no longer sat comfortably in Mr. Piper's product. Shaking, shivering and chattering, I felt more like a disembodied foot squelching in a swamp-soaked rubber boot.

In Parry Sound, an overpowering essence inside the fecund cockpit overwhelmed my equilibrium. Carefully, checking to ensure no souvenirs trickled down my pants, I staggered in the direction of a bathtub. Many years later, at a friend's graduation ceremony, the story of my encounter above Georgian Bay escaped my lips. The audience—all elementary schoolteachers with wine glasses primly perched between fingers—beseeched me never to tell the tale again.

Labor Day weekend marked the season's end and since my wise parents inculcated the concept that education was more important than flogging airplanes across Canada's wild country I returned to university. By January 1968, I began mailing out applications for summer employment. Jobs were not plentiful but

an answer arrived from a company in Victoria on Vancouver
Island.

5 Legend

Flying Fireman Ltd. flew enormous, powerful airplanes called Cansos, or Catalina water bombers as Americans called them. With a wing span of 104 feet and a pair of 1,200-horse-power engines, each weighed almost seventeen tons. The addition of long doors on their bellies enabled them to scoop 8,000 pounds of liquid from a lake and drop it into the flames of a forest fire.

In April, I opened the small door of a hangar at Victoria's international airport and saw several Cansos, some on jacks with landing gear barely touching the cement floor and others with cowlings removed from their radial engines. One lacked a windshield, but several white-coveralled mechanics worked precariously from ladders to replace the plexiglass panels.

I found the chief pilot beside an oak desk in a small cubicle nearby. We knew each other from my Fort Nelson days on the Piper Super Cubs. He frowned when I walked in.

"So what are you doing here?" he asked. "You didn't get my message?"

Apparently, a letter telling me that the promised copilot job wouldn't be available did not reach my residence. Only one of two airplanes purchased from Mexico for water-bombing conversion arrived in Canada. With one Canso for the fire season, the company needed fewer pilots.

Air fare to Victoria had cost me my last dollar. I slumped disconsolately into a chair and pondered my next move. Luckily, a woman in the next office had overheard the conversation. The widow of the late owner and founder, she managed the Flying Fireman.

"Don't worry about it. We'll find something for you," she said and left with the chief pilot. In a few moments, he returned and beckoned me into the hangar.

"Keep yourself busy," he snapped, obviously not pleased with having his decision overruled.

Several hours later, as I studied the Cansos closely, the chief pilot approached me to say a copilot opening existed after all. Someone had taken a job with a major airline and wouldn't be back for the season. Salary, he explained, would be no more than $500 per month and $15 per flying hour. This was a fortune in 1968, considering my lack of heavy-piston engine experience and no instrument rating.

Flying Fireman Ltd. had been in business for three years when I was hired. Despite the loss of its founder, in a flying accident, the organization expanded rapidly and a career with them looked promising. My summers would be spent in Canada on forest fires in British Columbia and Alberta. If their bids were successful, travel to Australia looked like a definite possibility.

In 1968, Canso copilots didn't require flight training or ground-school classes. During my first day, a mechanic demonstrated landing-gear emergency procedures to qualify me for the job. My long, lanky build was the main attribute for accompanying older, senior pilots on refresher flights at the season's start. Lowering the main wheels, in case of a malfunction, meant removing the water-tank lid and climbing inside through a narrow opening. It was a dirty task because of the slimy, soup-like material used to gel the water dropped on fires.

Like all airplanes in the Fireman's fleet, my assigned Canso looked immaculate after a complete rebuild. While waiting for my chance to ride in the right seat, two pilots flew it to a nearby practice area. During a water pickup, they struck a log and jammed the nose wheel in the up position. Wrinkled metal prevented a lake landing to make repairs, so they returned to the airport and declared an emergency approach.

Dismayed, I knew that if they did any damage, the company would either keep me grounded until after the repairs were done or let me go. I watched the pilot turn for a strip of fire-retardant foam applied to the runway by airport fire trucks. The copilot, a fat British refugee who considered himself a Greek god, was ordered to scramble to the rear the instant the main wheels touched. The captain planned a tail-down landing and hoped to hold the nose up as long as possible. His copilot's bulk would help keep the tail down after the airplane contacted the surface. I watched helplessly.

The huge airplane ran along the runway for a moment, then the front end slammed down hard on the pavement. Sparks cascaded from the nose as it slid into the foam. There were no crew injuries, but repairs wouldn't be completed until late in the season. This left me with the choice of leaving the company or waiting while working on the hangar floor. Flying Fireman seemed to have a future, so staying with them, I thought, would be the wiser choice.

During my Lamb Airways epoch, the airline had forced pilots to do whatever chores were handy when they were not flying. This meant sweeping hangar floors, piling lumber or "bucking" rivets inside seaplane float compartments. At Flying Fireman, I simply walked out and joined the mechanics. Most were surprised. They hadn't encountered a pilot who knew how to rivet.

Weeks had passed when a request came from the Alberta Forestry Service for water bombers to the northern part of the province. After a freezing voyage across the Rocky Mountains and an overnight stop in Kamloops, the pilots and I arrived at Lac La Biche. On all sides of the horizon, forest fires raged out of control. Fire-fighting airplanes of every kind worked closely together from a 4,300-foot, grass-covered runway.

Despite plenty of air traffic at Lac La Biche's uncontrolled airport, there were no near-misses or collisions. Not yet a Canso copilot, I helped mechanics prepare the company's airplanes for flight. When the forest fires were under control, word came from Victoria for me to go to Prince George as a copilot. Coincidentally, a Cessna 205 needed a ferry flight to the same airport. Another pilot and I soon pointed the tiny airplane west.

After a long haul through British Columbia's crooked valleys where rain showers forced us to fly low, we spotted several tall columns of smoke. Thinking we might have turned around somehow and flown back into Alberta, we rechecked our maps. No, it was Prince George. What we saw turned out to be discharges from five pulp mills surrounding the city.

Within a few days of our arrival, Flying Fireman promoted a experienced copilot to captain. After several seasons, Tom Swanson deserved the advancement. In the previous year, management had scheduled Swanson to fly with the founder of the company, but at the last minute he was replaced by another copilot. He climbed out of the Canso and watched it leave. A short time later, word came that the airplane had crashed and burned twenty-two miles northwest of Victoria.

Now assigned a left seat, Swanson had yet to make his first flight as pilot-in-command. An affable type, he requested me as copilot and we flew together on his inaugural trip as captain. That evening, head office ordered him south to bomb fires on Vancouver Island. Much to my chagrin, the chief pilot forced me to stay in Prince George because Swanson needed a more experienced crewman, he said. A few days later, Swanson and copilot Tom Worley died after clipping trees with their wing tip. Ironically, the accident took place within a few miles of Swanson's close call the previous year.

Their deaths shocked everyone. For me, these two men became the first people I'd known to lose their lives to aviation. The accident made it painfully clear that fighting fires from the air was high-risk business. I no longer felt as safe as I had in the Piper Super Cubs or in the other tiny training airplanes in my logbook. The huge Cansos couldn't be thrown around easily. I was determined to handle them carefully and seek advice from more experienced pilots. Manipulating heavy water bombers above the flames was not a place to learn alone.

Management indicated they might team me up with a famous pilot I had met in Fort Nelson during my fire patrol work. Well known in flying circles, he had pioneered airmail routes into the

Yukon and Northwest Territories during the 1930s. In World War II he used his experience to switch over to four engine transports and delivered them throughout North America. As for Cansos, his flying time in "Pigboats" was more than triple my total logged hours. The man had become a legend, and I, young and impressionable, couldn't believe my luck. The seasoned expert and the eager novice would fly together.

My first days with the living legend were different from what I had expected. After finishing the preflight inspection, I climbed the metal ladder beneath the blister, closed the hatch, and made my way toward the copilot seat. Settling in, I looked toward the captain.

"Now get this straight, you little bastard. You sit there and keep your god-damned hands off this airplane. Don't touch a thing until I say so," he barked. "You're only there because the law says you have to be there, so keep your mouth shut."

As he snapped at me to start the auxilliary power unit, I could see a very long summer ahead. This became my main duty as the airplane's designers had placed all APU switches on the copilot's side, out of the captain's reach. During the period I spent on the Canso, my hero never expressed a kind word, nor did he try teaching the art of aerial fire fighting. Not once did he permit me to land, take off or carry out a water pickup.

The spectacular scenery in this region of British Columbia proved to be the season's highlight. One fire-fighting mission took us above the immense, newly constructed Peace River Dam. North of Prince George and toward one of our few forest fires of the season, a tremendous flood water lake spread far ahead of the airplane's nose. Countless stumps, branches and logs dotted the sides of Williston Lake, making it a dangerous water pickup area. No airplane dared land for fear of puncturing a hull.

Once, the British Columbia Forest Service called out a pair of Cansos to investigate smokes spotted near the Prince George airport. In the dense, green conifers, we picked out what, at first, looked like deliberately set bonfires. However, no one lived in the area and the thickness of the spruce prevented trappers or hunters from traveling through. Lightning, we knew, walked across the country occasionally and started scattered spot fires.

There was no wind that day, so the smokes drifted straight up in bright white plumes.

A smoke at the base of a cliff topped by a level plateau seemed impossible to reach with a load of water. Dropping from directly above would be ineffective, and a parallel approach along a rock ledge left little maneuvering room. Although most people despised my captain's attitude toward copilots, he deserved his reputation as one of Canada's top fire-fighting pilots.

With a full load scooped from a nearby river, he brought the ponderous airplane to treetop level and aimed directly at the base of the cliff. With no escape route on either side, he couldn't climb above the plateau or make normal left or right turns without hitting the hill.

Undaunted, he continued toward a small feather of bright, white smoke. Concerned, I said nothing and watched his finger slide over and press the bomb button. As the load released, my eyes went to the instrument panel and my fingers eased throttles to climb power as the captain wanted.

Blue sky filled the windshield as the airplane struggled upward in a vertical climb. Just as the wings felt ready to lose their lift, the scenery changed from blue to green as we pivoted around on a wing tip. My loosened safety belt barely held me in my seat and we now faced straight down. He yanked the throttles closed as the airframe shuddered and in seconds, my cheeks sagged, dragging my body into the seat as he eased out of the dive.

The captain's maneuver—called a stall turn—worked. We hit the target dead-on and snuffed out the flames, but thirty minutes later, my hands still trembled. The airport joke that day concerned "the look on Grant's face."

Lightning, I learned, didn't cause all of British Columbia's fires. We journeyed south of Prince George to Williams Lake, to drop water on what locals described as "rodeo fires." Well known for its western flavor, the community held a gala rodeo event every year to attract cowboys from across Canada. Although most participants came to demonstrate their riding and roping talents, certain unscrupulous breeds of people also attended to earn extra cash setting fires.

Undetected, these seedy types slipped into the pine and

spruce near Williams Lake to start small fires. Their actions sometimes developed from tiny nests of flames into awesome conflagrations that consumed hundreds of acres. The British Columbia Forest Service called upon every able-bodied person who could handle a shovel and fire hose. Wages and overtime brought in extra cash for those who struck the silent match.

While parked at Williams Lake with two Canso water bombers, we received a call to drop on flames twelve miles from the airport. The captain selected a long, narrow pickup lake and after the usual run of sixteen to twenty-two seconds, the tanks were full. We watched for streamers of white foam bursting from the overflow vents on the Canso's sides, and then flicked a switch to raise the pickup probes.

I looked up from the instrument panel in time to see a gigantic bird, its wings spread wide, fly directly at the nose of the airplane. Coming closer, I could see features on its white neck and tail. I realized we were on a collision path with an adult bald eagle. At the last possible second, the eagle turned and flashed by my window, close enough for me to see a pair of black and yellow eyes.

The huge creature would hit the propeller, I thought. I waited to hear a thud and the noise of an engine out of balance from broken propeller blades. Miraculously, he made it and sailed behind the airplane without hurting himself or us.

We returned to Williams Lake where the mechanics carefully looked the engine over. Only a few inches of space separated the propeller tips from the fuselage behind my seat. The eagle had either flown through the gap or had unaccountably missed the three-blade propeller turning at over 2,000 revolutions per minute. Undamaged, we loaded the mechanics and returned to Prince George to wait for more fire calls.

Through the generosity of the British Columbia Forest Service, someone arranged a public fire-fighting demonstration. Several buses and hundreds of spectators gathered at the Prince George airport to watch the show. Forestry workers placed clusters of hydrogen-filled targets near the middle of the runways. The plan was to dispatch both Cansos to show how Flying Fireman Ltd. fought fires.

Our water bombers had parked close together the previous evening with the bird dog tucked underneath our wings. At pre-arranged times, all three airplanes started engines simultaneously. On signal, the tiny Cessna 337 taxied toward the takeoff runway. The first Canso followed seconds later.

On my left, my captain gently advanced the overhead throttles to join the parade. The heavy water bomber didn't move so he applied more power. Still, we didn't budge. With both powerful engines almost at maximum settings, the Canso stayed in place while the other two airplanes waited patiently. My captain brought the throttles back to idle. We both knew why the big airplane stayed in one spot. I had forgotten to remove the parking chocks from beneath the wheels.

Expecting a tremendous verbal barrage, I was surprised when the captain said nothing. His look of disgust quickly added to my haste as I unfastened my safety belt, crawled to the rear and opened the exit hatch. The ladder fell to the ground as I tried to hook it into its slots. Before hundreds of witnesses, I pushed, kicked and twisted the chocks from underneath the big rubber tires. It really seemed that copilots—at least one of them—were absolutely useless in the water bombing business.

After that, the demonstration went well. There was no doubt that the sights and sounds of the massive Consolidated Canso water bombers impressed the spectators. Both airplanes hit their targets dead center and burst the balloons.

That afternoon, another captain related his part in a similar event the previous year. Often, pilots were asked if water bombers scooped fish from lakes during a pickup run. We answered that only water could fit through the narrow openings of the pickup probes; but we knew a few people didn't believe us. As a practical joke, the captain drove to a Prince George seafood store to buy a few pounds of whole fish. After he and his copilot picked up their water load, he crawled back to the tank, unscrewed the lid, and threw the fish inside. To this day, he said, some people who witnessed the prank are convinced that water-bomber pilots have fish dinners after they're called to a forest fire.

Few other trips materialized during the season. That summer of 1968, it rained more than anyone in the British Columbia's

Forest Service could remember. Day after day, until the end of the contract, rain continued soaking the streets of Prince George, as well as every pine needle and poplar leaf from the Pacific's west coast to the Alberta border. In the previous year, Flying Fireman's pilots logged almost 300 hours of flying time. During my stint, I managed to acquire fifty meager hours but held high hopes of earning a fortune. As luck would have it, those who returned the next year enjoyed over 275 hours in the air.

Since the season turned out poorly and my hopes of learning from the aviation legend were shattered, I looked forward to seeing Ontario again. My eagerness to return home had little to do with continuing my studies. It was because I looked forward to an important event on October 12—my wedding.

On the last day of work, a Beechcraft 18 owner offered me a ride to Victoria. For several hours, without a cloud from Prince George to Vancouver Island, I enjoyed a parade of mountains in many shapes and sizes. At Victoria's head office, after a few good-byes consisting of "too bad the summer didn't work out for you," I boarded an airliner for a hop to Toronto—the end of a disappointing fire season.

6   Rock-Rimmed and Wide Waxed

After wedding Linda Ina Sinclair, whom I had met at a Belleville, Ontario high school in 1961, we settled into the business of completing my education. Linda supported us while I attended another year in Waterloo. To earn extra cash, I became a part-time flight instructor at the Waterloo-Wellington Flying Club.

Studies went poorly during my last university year, mainly because my thoughts stayed in the clouds back in British Columbia. As exam week approached, the annual search for aviation employment began. This time I intended to find year-round work; but, few flying positions turned up. A surplus of more qualified pilots made the situation appear almost hopeless.

Anxious to relocate in the north, Linda and I waited for an offer from a bush airline. When I contacted former employer Georgian Bay Airways in Parrry Sound, they welcomed me, having decided to re-open flight training in Piper Super Cubs. At least I knew the people and felt confident Linda would enjoy the area as much as I did.

Full-time in Parry Sound, I expected to earn more than I did as a summer pilot. Despite high expectations, my salary was nearly the same as my previous stint with the Airways. Mileage rates on the Piper Super Cub stood at two cents.

During my two-year absence, the engineering staff painted

the de Havilland Beaver and Found FBA-2C a striking yellow and red. Both looked as if they had recently rolled through factory doors. The Piper Super Cub carried a similar scheme. The airplanes flew well and it felt like their tubing, fabric, and plexiglass welcomed me back.

My instructor rating proved to be the asset Georgian Bay Airway's management appreciated most. I was determined to operate a successful school and fly charters when not teaching students. I soon discovered many potential license candidates in the Parry Sound area. As word about the flight school spread, people began calling.

Some had enrolled years before but the instructor had quit, they waited patiently for a replacement. Others arrived with doubts about boarding a "rag and tube" Super Cub on floats; they needed a little persuasion before undertaking a sample flying lesson.

Warm days generally meant afternoon turbulence. Anyone who became airsick hesitated to sign on the dotted line. Before long, I discovered that flying westward over Georgian Bay usually resulted in a calm and stable flight. After potential customers gazed down at the rock-ringed islands between Midland and Byng Inlet, they started flying training.

Students at Parry Sound differed from those I taught in larger centers. Nearly all spent their lives around boats or machinery; consequently, it didn't take long to teach them to maneuver a double-ruddered Super Cub on the water. Wise in the ways of boating, few damaged a float while docking. Everyone who ventured into the office became memorable.

One man measured six feet, six inches in height and looked far more like a walking rail fence than a human being. Watching him fold up like an accordion into the front seat of an airplane usually drew the mechanics from our hangar. In contrast, another man barely reached five feet and weighed over 250 pounds. In spite of his massive bulk, he proved to be a quick learner and an excellent pilot. So did a young woman named Lucia who taught elementary school. Her appearance on the dock also guaranteed the mechanics wouldn't return to work until she disappeared over the horizon in the Super Cub.

Teaching the basics of flight during weekdays and ground school classes left me with little time for charter work. In open-water season, trips took place in the Beaver or the Found, just as they had when I worked for Georgian Bay Airways two years before. In winter, we utilized a Cessna 180 on skis. Not often did I leave the docks or classroom without putting in sixteen-hour duty days. My understanding wife rarely saw me.

I renewed my friendship with the Found FBA-2C. As my hours in the aircraft increased, it again became evident the Canadian-built wonder outclassed any Cessna 180 or 185. Challenging to handle, it felt heavy on the controls as many of detractors claimed. Once, I made the unforgivable mistake of relaxing too soon after landing at Boundary Lake. Front-end heavy, it pitched forward on the noses of the floats at such an angle, water covered the windshield and splashed inside through the fresh air vents.

On a holiday weekend, a short wiry man arrived at the office with a dozen kegs of marine gasoline, some sleeping bags and his ten-year-old daughter. A regular customer at the Airways, he requested a flight into a lake northeast of Parry Sound. After studying the chart, I concluded that his destination lacked adequate length to land.

"I been goin' in there for ten years with a big yellow airplane," he insisted. "Ain't never had no trouble."

Thinking for a moment, I remembered that Georgian Bay Airways once operated yellow Noorduyn Norsemen.

"You must mean a Norseman," I replied. "If something that big can get in there, surely to God there must be room for a little Found. Let's go."

With extra fuel in the wings left over from the day before, we came off the water quickly and tracked northeast across Mill Lake. In twenty minutes, his destination came in sight. The water body edging outwards from a high-tree shoreline certainly didn't seem large enough for a Found-sized airplane, much less a Norseman. Nevertheless, convinced that the larger freighter had once handled this spot, I decided not to disappoint a paying customer.

With power reduced, we approached as slowly as possible, nose high above the hardwood trees. The instant the last deciduous leaf passed beneath the floats, I wrenched the throttle back to idle and we dropped out of the sky toward the ripples. A reflexive blast of engine power stopped the aircraft from smashing into the lake hard enough to drive the float struts upward. Still, the jolt shook all three of us.

Surprised at the abrupt touchdown and distracted by maps falling from the top of the instrument panel into my lap, I neglected to return the throttle back to idle. Instead of decelerating, the Found picked up speed, roaring toward the lake side.

"Jee-ee-sus Kee-ee-rist," I gasped. Beside me, her father gaped at the tree trunks rushing toward him.

I yanked the throttle with one hand and slammed the control wheel full forward with the other. White foam and water sprayed up and over the top of the roof and onto the tail, vibrating the controls in my hands. The airplane dropped its nose and stood nearly vertical for a moment. Another millisecond and we would have gone completely over on our back.

When the shaken Found dropped back level, the maps sailed from my lap and struck the windshield. Still moving forward, the airplane had enough momentum to damage the floats if we bumped the rocks. I turned the switches off quickly. The propeller stopped and the rubber nose protectors of each float slid over a submerged log as we came to a halt.

"We're at the wrong end of the lake," barked my passenger. "What'd you park here for?"

I walked forward along the float and stepped to shore. Pushing on the nose with all my strength, I missed the first attempt and nearly fell into the water. After a few more back-straining shoves, the airplane floated free and backwards to deeper depths. No dents appeared on the floats. We were lucky. As we taxied slowly to the cabin, I hinted that this tiny patch couldn't have held a Noorduyn Norseman. The little girl leaned forward and thrust her teddy bear into her father's lap. Their cottage, well back in a stand of poplar and birch, lacked a dock so I parked beside a pile of boards held horizontal by some boulders.

As we unloaded, the father suddenly remarked, "Well, y'know, it only had two seats."

The airplane he claimed to be a Norseman was not the famous pug-nosed, 600-horsepower freighter after all, but a Piper Super Cub. I should have known better than to take the word of a non-pilot customer when it came to airplane sizes and performances.

Leaving the lake didn't turn out to be an easy matter either. Performing what may have been the first and last takeoff of a Found FBA-2C from this tiny opening in the forest, required every inch of available space. At the far end of the lake, I shut the engine off and paddled backwards until the tail contacted some overhanging willow branches.

The Lycoming started quickly. With zero flap, I snapped the throttle to the wall and desperately kept as straight a run as possible. After a few seconds, I reached for the flap lever above my right shoulder and applied half. The Found left the water at sixty miles per hour, nose up, barely clearing the trees. For an instant, it sagged and mushed downwards. A gust of wind provided an extra second of lift and we climbed away at 500 feet per minute.

Back at base, a quick check of the booking sheet revealed that our customer and his daughter reserved the Found for their return flight two days later. I crossed out "Found" and wrote in "Super Cub—two trips."

Frequently, fog floated in from Lake Huron and shut our business down for days. Customers lined the docks, anxious to fly to their weekend retreats as quickly as we could haul them. When weather cleared, we flew all day long. Every airplane kept busy, including the single-passenger Super Cub. Sometimes, a Cessna 180 would be pressed into service as well, but none of us cared for the "Wichita Wonder," for it couldn't match the Found or Beaver in practicality and load capacity.

Most Georgian Bay Airways customers rarely winced at the prices to fly them to their islands or marble-floored lakeshore retreats. Thunderbirds, Cadillacs and chauffeur-driven Lincolns filled the company parking lot. In spite of the wealth, few passengers were snobbish. Once they stepped upon our dock, most were relaxed and pleased to be away from business-oriented worlds.

One family frequently chartered to an island near Shawanaga Inlet, a few miles northwest of Parry Sound. Always friendly toward the pilots, they seemed a close family. The patriarch, a man well into his sixties, clearly loved and respected his daughter, who happened to be about my own age. She, in turn, worshiped the man and rarely came to Canada without him. The mother, we noticed, seemed quite high-strung and temperamental, especially when weather held us up.

One midweek day in August, the dispatcher received a frantic radio telephone call. This was normally a quiet time, since the bulk of the company's flying took place Friday nights and Monday mornings.

"Right now! Come right now!" a woman shouted. "He's sick! He's had a heart attack! Come right now!"

In panic, the caller slammed the radio telephone down without telling anyone who or where she was. We waited anxiously for another call while the dock boy scrambled to top the Found's fuel tanks. We didn't know if the trip would be short or long, but we often flew medevac emergencies to Toronto Island Airport.

We waited. Only a few daylight hours remained and seaplanes couldn't legally fly at night in Canada. No one touched the telephone. Some people called for bookings but after a hurried explanation they hung up immediately. At last, the lady who made the urgent plea telephoned again. It was our Shawanaga Inlet family. Within minutes, I ripped the Found from the water and turned northwest.

On the horizon over Lake Huron, low clouds came down to skim the surface. Rain would begin soon. Having dropped the family off several times, I knew the area well and didn't need to circle. Below, two figures waved white towels, as I taxied toward their dock I could see that their faces showed deep concern.

The daughter had managed to drag and carry her father to a plastic lawn chair on the dock, where he sprawled unconscious. Shallow breathing indicated serious trouble. With surprising strength, the woman lifted the end of the lawn chair and beckoned me to grab the other. Together, we moved him to the Found and slid his limp body into the back. The mother crowded in beside him and the daughter came up front, reaching over the seat to hold her father's hand. Tears welled from her eyes and her mother began wailing the instant I left the dock.

"Can you get us to Toronto?" the woman asked. I learned later she had recently completed her second year of medical school.

A quick radio call back to the office for a weather forecast revealed conditions would be barely within limits. Clouds no longer waited far out on Lake Huron; instead, they rolled inland across the islands and turned to rain. As we flew along the coastline and over Midland, I glanced at the passenger beside me. Fear of losing her father gave way to a look of defiance, then pity. Just as quickly her expression melted into helpless submission as she pondered the thought that he might not live. She released his hand only to wipe away her tears and then grasped him again. The mother said little, deep in her own grief. She leaned her head against her husband and held him closely.

Toronto's ceilings stayed low. Thanks to the area's air traffic control, we arrived safely at Toronto Island Airport. A harbor commission boat stood by to transfer the man to an idling ambulance. As the family stepped away, the younger woman stopped and waved good-bye.

Later that year, I saw them together again. The quick flight south and subsequent cardiac treatment saved the man's life.

Although I respected the Found and enjoyed the Piper Super Cub, nothing was more pleasurable than a trip in the de Havilland Beaver. Gentle to fly, easy to land, the tremendous, low-lift wing allowed it to handle very short lakes.

The Beaver had far more cabin room and seats than anything else at the dock. Unloading usually meant heavy work, as it carried awkward objects such as propane bottles, wood stoves and refrigerators. With the Airways, I carried my first external load, a long canvas canoe knitted to the floats with several ropes.

By Labor Day, much of the work had diminished. Fortunately, Georgian Bay Airways successfully bid on a short-term contract with Ontario Hydro to haul a painting crew from Parry Sound to lakes paralleling hydro lines north of town. Once on site, the men spent their day painting towers. At day's end, they would be picked up for a return flight to Parry Sound.

The contract called for a Beaver; however, a demand for an extra airplane at our South Porcupine base south of Timmins took the airplane away. To replace it, we found another Cessna 180 that had spent time at Moosonee on James Bay. Not exactly pristine, it failed to match the Parry Sound airplanes in appearance.

Some say the life story of a bushplane can be read by looking at its ceiling. A gouged, tobacco-stained headliner and hundreds of fish scales plastered to the walls and floor attested to a colorful career. Ontario Hydro wanted its contracted Beaver but could do nothing except settle for the dilapidated Cessna 180.

The paint crew didn't seem impressed and a wildcat strike nearly erupted in the office. Finally, the foreman persuaded his men to board. Once inside, I reached for the starter button, expecting the mighty 230-horsepower engine to leap to life. Only the mortifying sound of stillness greeted our ears.

The dock boy swung the airplane back and tied it up as the mechanic came out of the hangar. In his hand, he held a huge wrench, so large it obviously couldn't fit any bolt on the Cessna 180. He sometimes ran into starting troubles with other types and knew it to be a solenoid again. The engine usually started after a few sharp blows with a heavy object. I opened the cowling, and the mechanic reached in and delivered two quick raps with a wrench. He refastened the cowling securely and suggested I try again.

The two-blade propeller turned over several times, the engine coughed and then caught fire. After a shot with a fire extinguisher to squelch the flames, the mechanic looked inside again. All okay, he said. We tried again. My passengers shifted restlessly in their seats.

The engine started well this time and we left Parry Sound's harbor to follow the hydro line north. The trip lasted thirty minutes and required landing as closely as possible to the first unpainted tower beside a railway track. Circling, I saw that the only suitable spot happened to be an extremely slim stretch of water. To stop safely before a narrows, we'd have to touch down at a wide area closer to the electrical lines. Once unloaded, taxiing through the constricted spot would place the airplane in a favorable takeoff position.

No matter how familiar a pilot becomes with the way his

airplane flies or how often he completes perfect approaches, he never knows exactly how the landings will turn out. Anyone with a pilot's license understands the bizarre sinking feeling the instant he realizes he has "blown it," knowing the landing will be hard.

My passengers seemed familiar with airplanes. As I eased the throttle back for landing, one muttered to his seat companion, "Is he crazy?"

Spoiled by many hours of flying over long lakes and low shorelines, I rounded out above the water nearly thirty feet too high. A terrible, helpless sensation told me we were about to smash into the lake, maybe hard enough to break the floats.

Sure enough, the left float struck first, throwing us back into the air. We went down again on the opposite side. In the excitement of keeping the wings level, I lost my grip on the control wheel. The Cessna 180 pitched forward almost onto its nose before quickly settling back right-side-up. "Some arrival," mumbled the man on my right.

Leaving the confined area with the empty airplane didn't present a problem. Returning before dark, I surmised that the exhausted painters didn't look forward to the trip home. Naturally, we were lighter on fuel than the early-moring flight.

Nevertheless, tail to shore, we began the takeoff run as the passengers gripped their seats. At the narrows, a gust of wind boosted us into the air; however, as we accelerated into the wider section, the wind died and lift decreased to a point where the floats hit the water again. After several skips and one full, engine-roaring leap, the overworked Cessna 180 crept airborne. As the aircraft nudged slowly to a proper climb, we passed underneath some wires suspended between a pair of hydro towers.

With four of us, plus paint cans, brushes and lunch pails aboard, we couldn't clear the trees at the lake's far end. There wasn't enough room to yank the throttle back and stop to try again. Running onto the shoreline could result in serious damage. As I raised the nose, the Cessna 180's airspeed dropped dangerously.

I could continue straight ahead, or turn left or right. The panorama filling the windshield changed from a solid gray mass into individual trees with sharp needles and broad branches. An abrupt turn to my side put us in the clear. Once I leveled the wings, we flew on for another ten minutes before we dared to move. Anyone witnessing the takeoff would have seen nothing but the yellow tip of the rudder cutting through the bush. The next day, the Beaver returned to Parry Sound, but the painting crew requested another pilot.

The Parry Sound area had a well-deserved reputation for its successful two-week annual deer and moose hunt. Camp and lodge owners booked airplanes two years ahead to guarantee their flights. Often, they found themselves disappointed to miss the season's opening day when fog obliterated the far end of our docks. When that happened, beagle hounds, coon hounds and fox hounds howled as their owners stamped impatiently in the hangar. One hunter who couldn't wait to attack something delved into a stack of beer cases and consumed dozens before his buddies stopped him. Shambling toward the Beaver, he climbed up to look into the cockpit at the switches, instruments, buttons and levers.

"Them pilots don't want to fly," he announced. "This airplane's full of gadgets."

Trying to convince him that the pilots were paid mileage rates and were therefore not pleased to sit around drinking coffee would be a waste of time. Few non-pilots understood the limitations poor weather imposed on us.

Hunting safari packages advertised in outdoor magazines usually showed pretty white tents or log cabins on cleared sites with neatly stacked firewood. When the happy hordes of hunters arrived at Parry Sound, we found ourselves hauling the implements that would ensure such scenes greeted their eyes. Leaky chain saws, moldy tents, broken bottles and dribbly eggs became part of our hauls from the first day of hunting season to the last. Canoes on the sides of airplanes often froze ropes so tightly we needed screwdrivers or sometimes an axe to free them.

Every hunter who drove down the hill toward our office seemed huge and overweight. All wore bush boots stained from tramping through bush country the previous year. We sometimes found rifles and shotguns fully loaded with safeties off. Although

I never saw an accidental discharge at Georgian Bay Airways, every pilot checked each weapon before loading it aboard his airplane.

In late fall, darkness came early, as did sub-zero temperatures, when ice crept outwards from shorelines to reduce takeoff space. More than once, we smashed our way with paddles to make the last few yards to shore, slipping and sliding on ice-covered airplanes. We often crawled toward the rear of a float to free frozen water rudders. Worse, with bare hands we pried float plugs out of the ice with screw drivers. More than one pilot missed a step and fell into a semi-frozen lake.

Our tourist-oriented airplanes, spotless during most of the year, doubled as flying meat wagons soon after opening day. Interiors became gory and slimy with slow-gelling animal fluids and sticky with foul-smelling hair that penetrated even the brown paper bags we brought along for lunch. At pickup time, we loaded lifeless deer, moose and bear carcasses. By dusk, our hair was matted with dried blood; our hands and face were greasy with animal fats; and our fingers were gouged or lacerated as we helped our customers unload their meat into trucks. "Flying the Hunt," as we called it, entailed some of the dirtiest, coldest work in aviation—truly different from the traditional tasks of airline pilots.

We usually came to know our hunters well. Unlike the summer tourist trade in which more than 90 percent of the clientele drove in from the United States, the hunters lived mainly in southern Ontario. Some camps remained empty all year, except for the two-week season. One lake-side lodge had been in the same family for generations.

Every year, we serviced a camp in an exceptionally short lake, ten minutes flying time northeast of Parry Sound. Only Super Cubs and lightly loaded Beavers could get in safely. Usually, the family that owned it arrived at our base a day or two before opening with enough freight to last the hunt. Nephews, cousins, uncles and every male in the clan helped carry their goods to dock side.

On the first run, we arranged seating for at least two passengers. The rest drove along a bush road to within a few miles of camp and walked in with the rifles. They finished the trip by boats left hidden in the bush.

Everyone at the Airways enjoyed their camaraderie and willingness to help load our airplanes. None complained about our costs, nor did they dispute the fact that we could only haul light freight in something as large as the Beaver. In the aviation business, we found it surprising when customers took the word of a pilot.

During a return to Parry Sound after a pickup at Wabwashkesh Lake, I flew the Found directly over the camp. Our company pilots habitually flew out of their way over the camp to ensure no emergencies existed. In this case, a small boat lay on the shore at the opposite side of the camp. This was strange, I thought, since the size of the clan customarily demanded two boats. I couldn't see the other one anywhere.

Suddenly, a flash of yellow caught my eye. Curious, I banked the airplane right and looked down to see three frantically waving figures in rain coats. They seemed desperate to attract my attention as I circled several times. With a load of propane bottles and wooden boxes of dead batteries packed to the ceiling, I concluded that a landing was out of the question in the Found. However, I knew pilot Robert Petkau would be passing by shortly with an empty airplane.

Petkau agreed to investigate, so I continued to Parry Sound. Before long, we learned that a terrible tragedy had taken place. When the family arrived on foot at the edge of the lake, they discovered someone had blasted holes in their boats. One sustained severe damage, but they decided that the other was in good enough condition to move the group.

Without life jackets and at night, they crowded into the boat and set off for camp. The tiny, overloaded vessel went down and four men perished—two sons, their father and grandfather. The survivors swam to shore and walked to the cabin, where they spent a long night waiting for the first airplane to pass by.

A Department of Lands and Forests de Havilland Turbo-beaver, flown by veteran pilot Douglas Calver, brought police scuba divers to locate the bodies. After a short, cold dive, the divers quickly located them and placed each in a dark plastic body bag.

Calver took on the unpleasant task of ferrying the victims from the short lake to a waiting hearse in Parry Sound.

Not everyone who preferred the solitude of cabins on isolated lakes spent time prowling the forests for moose or deer. We frequently flew an eccentric, forty-year-old man into Island Lake, thirty minutes north of town. Always alone, he stayed for several days. A cigar connoisseur, he always kept an unlit one between his teeth and mashed it inch by inch into a yellow, glutinous mess beneath his lips. Even with the lake only a few feet from his cabin door, he never washed.

On schedule, I dropped into his lake on a Friday evening. After swinging the tail of the Piper Super Cub around, I stepped over a rusty fuel drum and some crushed tin cans and knocked on his door. He appeared, sleepy but ready to go, and threw a crumpled, dirty packsack into the airplane. Enroute, he began to laugh long and hard. When he tapped me on the shoulder, I eased the throttle back to reduce the noise.

"I left my false teeth on the table," he cackled, his cigar bobbing up and down with every syllable. "Can you imagine how that'll scare anybody who breaks in?"

"I guess so," I shrugged, and continued cruising southward, soon landing at Parry Sound. He followed me to the office to settle his account where the sight of our young receptionist stopped him in his tracks. An attractive woman with reddish-brown hair, she seemed embarrassed at his attention. As she wrote out a receipt and took his money, the client began putting "the make" on her, ignoring the shiny new wedding band on her finger. She was polite but kept glancing my way.

"Look, we really should get to know each other," he said. "What do you think?"

She didn't answer. Her pretty face turned crimson.

"Why don't we go for a drink, just you and I?" he said, leaning so close the odor of his chewed cigar drifted across the counter top. She drew back several steps.

"Why don't you ask my husband?" she said with a polite smile. "He's standing right beside you."

Dumbfounded, our client went silent. Before I had a chance to say anything to the guy who had just tried to pick up my wife, he slunk outside, slipped into his car and drove on toward Toronto.

When hunting season ended, activity at Georgian Bay Airways slowed considerably. Trips to Sugar Bay School to drop inspectors or occasional jaunts to San Souci's general store relieved the monotony of many no-fly days. Our Moon River Mail Run was reduced to one flight per week. Our regulars—the cottagers—returned to the city until spring.

Flying over island-country in winter resulted in little more than glimpses of snow machines flitting between lakes. Ice fishermen traveled in their peculiar little "scoots" or flat-bottomed boats driven by rear-mounted airplane motors. Sometimes, we discovered snowshoe tracks left by trappers along the shorelines. Wherever we went, we saw boarded-up windows of winterized cottages. Dramas of life and death took place among the upturned boats, frozen docks and covered eaves. Wolf, deer, squirrels and many other animals left their marks. Black ravens hovering above the quiet forest often signaled the end of some creature overtaken by a predator.

Teaching the basics of winter flying brought many interesting situations. One of the first to sign on parked his Volkswagen beside the office door and questioned the rental rates of Piper Super Cubs. He carried a dignified air and told me he needed to fly for health reasons. A perceptive doctor suggested he find a therapeutic way to spend his time, for Father Patrick J. Byrne took his spiritual vocation seriously. I agreed with the doctor's choice—flying airplanes was a relaxing way to spend a day.

At first, Pat gave us the impression he might lack the mechanical aptitude to handle airplanes well enough to complete our thirty-five-hour flying program. Unlike many Georgian Bay Airways students, he had spent most of his life dedicated to academics. Nevertheless, after being told of possible extra hours, he carried on. Sometimes we repeated exercises several times. At one point I lost my temper and told Pat he had as much chance of getting through the course as hearing the Pope pass air.

Pat proved me wrong, and soloed a Piper Super Cub on floats. From that day on, his skills improved tremendously. His joy of discovering the delights of flight above the elegance of bush country became a pleasure to watch. Not long after freeze-up, however, when mechanics, Ross McEwen and Leo Sipala changed the airplane from floats to skis, Pat gave me a horrendous fright.

A private pilot licence on skis or floats required cross-country navigation exercises of at least 200 miles. At the Airways, students plotted a course to North Bay then south to Orillia and home to Parry Sound. On the initial trip, they rode with an instructor and on the second, went alone, reversing the route. Careful preflight planning had to be demonstrated before leaving the harbor.

Each season after the harbor ice became solid enough, senior pilot Stan King marked a short runway with conifers cut from the nearby bush. An experienced pilot, he required little room to takeoff and land even when dreaded "white-out" conditions made flying difficult. Students, I knew, needed more space, so I spent an afternoon tripling the length of our makeshift runway.

"White-out" referred to situations in which unbroken snow, combined with overcast skies, blotted out all ground references. High-time pilots compared it to flying in a milk bottle. Estimating the correct height from which to change a glide into a landing involved using our cut conifers as a guide. Away from base, we approached as closely as possible to shorelines or searched for dark objects like wind-bared rocks or well-worn snow-machine trails.

Pat progressed extremely well toward his license and the time arrived for his cross-country solo. As taught, he checked the weather conditions and preflighted a Piper PA-18 registered CF-LAI shortly after sunrise. Within a few hours, we completed the dual trip successfully with barely an error in navigation. Now, he would carry out a solo run and then a flight test would mark the completion of the private pilot course.

Dressed for warmth, he resembled a penguin in his bulky parka and warm winter boots. However, if the unthinkable happened and he went down somewhere in the slush, Pat would never freeze. As he left the snow-packed runway, I saw thin trails of exhaust silhouetted against the tree line—indicative of a cold, clear day. He turned toward Orillia expecting to return by mid-afternoon.

As the only pilot on duty this day, I had completed a Cessna 180 trip to Sugar Bay. Several teachers needed a ride to the school, and I had to wait for them before returning to Parry Sound. Soon, I noticed a dark bank of clouds with light bottoms over Georgian Bay. Before long, quarter-size snowflakes streaked past the windshield. Ten minutes later, we returned to town.

As expected, Pat telephoned the air base after each landing. Concerned that he would encounter the approaching snowstorm, I rushed to call him back at North Bay, but he had departed fifteen minutes before. Hopefully, Pat would see the cloud and lowering visibility en route, and return to safer weather some-where else. I was not aware that the advancing storm stalled a few miles east of Parry Sound. Beyond its white-curtained edges, clear skies prevailed.

Private pilot candidates didn't have experience in instrument flying to handle out-of-sight-of-ground conditions. Although Pat excelled in glassy water and white-out landings, nearly all of his training took place under simulated conditions. Whether clear thinking would prevail in real-life circumstances, I could only hope, as snow began accumulating on our runway.

No other pilots dropped by as the weather went below safe limits. Most of the staff went home, but no further word on Pat's progress came in. Without a doubt, he would assume his safety was assured until almost within sight of Mill Lake.

Pacing the floor, I listened carefully for the Super Cub in the gloom. Unable to bear the office heat, I stepped outside and noticed the freshly fallen snow now reached my ankles. Only an hour before, it lacked enough depth to create a footprint. Perhaps my overdue student had landed somewhere to spend the night or turned around to head for North Bay. If not, even an experienced pilot would barely be able to land in an all-encompassing white-out.

Sheltering myself under the tied-down wing of the Cessna 180, I tried to ignore the cold. A freight train rumbled in from the east side of town and thundered across the steel railway bridge behind our office. Cursing it for obliterating all other sounds, I waited for the click-clack of steel wheels on steel rails to fade away.

I could hear an occasional automobile drive past and sometimes snow machines plunged through snow drifts at the south end of the bay. One muffled sound somewhere near the air base caught my attention. I hoped it would be the Super Cub. It had to be, I realized, but snow came down so heavily, the top of a hill across the river disappeared from view.

Suddenly, a burst of engine power broke the silence—it was Father Patrick Byrne.

He barely cleared the nearby bridge and at the last moment, a pair of aluminum skis passed overhead, the white bottoms of the airplane's wings barely visible. I saw the profile of a determined pilot in the cockpit, intent on lining up with our runway markers.

Pat quickly faded from sight. I heard him increase his engine power and then reduce it so the airplane could descend slowly. Pat had been taught how to "feel his way" by manipulating the throttle carefully. For several moments, the only sound I heard was the plop of snowflakes on the Cessna 180 wing.

At last, I heard the faint purr of an idling engine and saw the Piper Super Cub taxiing toward the air base, carefully following the row of conifers. Its wings rocked right and left as it went from drift to drift. Pat swung the airplane around and shut off the engine.

He exited slowly, his face the color of snow. Unable to turn around for fear of losing control, Pat explained, he had no other choice but to fly straight ahead to the base, instead of turning back to North Bay. Around his neck, a rosary swung from side to side.

"Bet you tore that thing all to hell," I said pointing to the rosary and tying the airplane securely into the ice. We went to the office where I signed his logbook. A few weeks later, Father Byrne received his private pilot license. Not long after, he moved from Parry Sound to Ottawa, but continued his pleasure flying. We kept in touch over the years and his letters always mentioned his favorite Super Cub, CF-LAI.

After working almost seven days a week nonstop and encouraging more Parry Sound residents to learn to fly, I decided to ask for time off to enjoy the company of our receptionist. Total holidays coming to me amounted to over twenty days. I placed my request before the manager for two consecutive weeks. He considered my time off for at least five seconds.

"I can't have you pilots screwing the company like this," he said. "We'll give you a week and that's it."

By the time we parted that day, he agreed to my original request; however, his response made me examine the facts of my working life. Perhaps full-time flying wasn't the way after all, especially for a married man with the prospect of children in the future.

At the time, major airlines held no fascination for me, nor did the idea of carrying corporate luggage. Linda and I decided that an application to North Bay Teachers College might be a path to a normal life. My fanaticism for airplanes, however, remained undaunted and I hoped that flying during summers would suffice.

7   Stormin' Norman

I graduated in May 1971 as an elementary school teacher. The West Parry Sound Board of Education offered a job at Foley Public School, east of the town. Since the school term began in September, I planned to fly somewhere new in Canada for the summer. With more experience now, I was thrilled to see several offers come my way.

"NOW HAVE PILOT POSITION AVAILABLE IN NORMAN WELLS ARE YOU INTERESTED," read a May 5, 1971 telegram from Northward Aviation Ltd., a company that had acquired the Pacific Western Airlines bush division years before. "PLEASE REPLY COLLECT."

I looked forward to a season in the western Northwest Territories. Linda found a secretarial position in Toronto; during my absence she would stay with her parents.

First, Northward wanted me to stop in Edmonton. As part of the hope-you-like-it-here introduction, my new employer presented me with a crest bearing the company logo, a winged Pegasus with the words: "The Flying Packhorse People" in blue lettering. Later, customers informed me they had facetiously nicknamed the organization, "The Flying Jackass People."

Someone thrust an airline ticket in my hand and told me Yellowknife would be home until breakup at Norman Wells. My arrival in the capital of the Northwest Territories coincided with a Sunday; no one worked on weekends in early spring. A red and white de Havilland Otter with Northward's logo on its tail bobbed gently at a long gravel dock. Behind me, a large, unpainted, two-storey building served as a base office. Finding the front door locked, I knocked but got no response and looked up to see a blonde-haired man staring from the second-floor window.

"What the hell do you want?" he asked.

Assuming he worked for Northward, I told him I planned to stay in Yellowknife before going to Norman Wells. He continued staring, said nothing and then disappeared. Minutes later, the door unlocked and I dragged my suitcases into the office. He stood there, watching every move I made.

"Jeezus-christ, you're a stupid looking son-of-a-bitch," he said.

Astounded, I stood open-mouthed, not knowing what to say. Seeing my stunned expression, he began laughing long and hard. Finally, he stopped and introduced himself as the owner of a one-man helicopter company called Aero Arctic. Over the next few days, I learned that practical jokes on unsuspecting newcomers were his forte.

He wasn't finished yet. Standing in the middle of the hardwood floor, I looked for some place to store my suitcases. My new acquaintance pointed to a door opposite a stairwell.

"That's the pilot's room," he said. "Put your stuff in there."

After dragging my battered luggage across the room, I opened the door to find a closet packed with brooms, mops and wash pails.

The next day, Northwards's Yellowknife staff reported for work. The base manager didn't show until shortly before lunch. While waiting, I fell asleep in a chair until the abrupt slam of a door woke me.

"A school teacher? Nobody told me they were sending a god-damn school teacher," he said, when someone made an introduction. "Jeez, we got three pilots sitting around here now with nothing to fly so what the hell do I do with you?"

To pass the time, the base manager suggested I unload airplanes at the seaplane base and airport. In one case, a Twin Otter on floats taxied in after a changeover from wheels. Another day, the head mechanic needed someone to change over a well-worn single Otter registered CF-CZO. I recognized it from magazine advertisements as one of a pair sold to Canadian Pacific Airlines in the early 1950s.

When nearly finished on CF-CZ0, a dusty pickup truck drove up to the airplane and someone yelled, "You!" from the cab.

"Hey, you," one of the senior pilots repeated. "Want to get checked out on the Otter?"

Underneath the airplane tightening bolts, I snapped my head up so quickly, I bashed it against the sharp metal step. Although blood ran out of a deep cut along the left side of my face, I held a rag against the gouge and jumped into the truck. An Otter checkout had been hinted at by the operations manager in Edmonton. Now the opportunity to fly one of the de Havilland Beaver's big brothers had finally arrived.

Ron Warnick flew the Otter CF-VVY for almost an hour demonstrating, takeoffs and landings on Great Slave Lake. Most pilots new to the ten-passenger airplane had a tendency to leave the water and climb away with the nose placed excessively high. The "Stoneboat," a nickname I learned in later years, handled the opposite way. Once airborne, the pilot had to push the nose down before climbing.

Plenty of pilots destroyed propellers when taking off from runways after forgetting the Otter's peculiarities. One pilot, I was told, broke a blade during his first takeoff to deliver a newly overhauled Otter to Whitehorse, Yukon, from Oshawa, Ontario. He quickly borrowed a hacksaw, cut the other blade tips to match and never told his employer.

Our flight went well and after thirty minutes with me in the pilot's seat, Warnick suggested we taxi back to the dock. For over an hour, I practiced alone wherever I could find open water.

Around the edge of Yellowknife, I saw abandoned buildings everywhere and guessed they were once active during the gold rush days that created the town. Drab rocks interspersed with tiny spruce trees looked only slightly like tundra. They seemed more like Sudbury's sulfur-killed hills more than the barrenlands on the Hudson Bay coast.

Later that afternoon, I went to the office to find out if word had arrived from Edmonton concerning my move to Northward's base at Norman Wells. On the telex machine, Ron Warnick had typed "....happy with Grant's checkout." The chief pilot answered by saying he expected to travel to Yellowknife to do my flight proficiency test. The message also implied that soon, someone would be going to "the Wells."

Breakup came slowly near Yellowknife. Although the many bays around Great Slave Lake were free of ice weeks before, few of the company's regular customers north of town saw open water yet. Yellowknife was a lively place to spend my leisure time, especially after a winter at North Bay Teachers College.

Yellowknife was born after a gold discovery in 1896 by miners en route to the Yukon. More exploration and development took place in 1934 and two years later, the place grew into a boom town. Bushplanes parked at every empty space on the lake shore and flew hundreds of trips with every imaginable type of freight. Some ranged north to pitchblende deposits on Great Bear Lake and helped to support the sites which produced most of the world's uranium and radium. During my stay in 1971, silver and gold mining as well as tourism made up Northward Aviation's main sources of revenue.

The people who flew in the Northwest Territories weren't fascinated with ping pong scores, pizza quality or other trivia that occupied conversations in the "cultivated" south. Airplanes and only airplanes interested them. Some northerners tried to leave aviation but they always returned to flying. In my case, I'd already committed myself as a school teacher and intended to enjoy the job, whatever the price.

"I mean it," I said one evening in the Hoist Room bar. "Discussion closed."

"Bullshit. You'll last two years as a school teacher and you'll be back flying airplanes," said Duncan Matheson, one of the most respected pilots in the Canadian Arctic. His words turned out to be prophetic.

A telephone call the next day suggested I accompany another pilot to Norman Wells. Before we could leave Yellowknife, however, the weather fogged in and held us at the seaplace base.

When it lifted, we learned that ice had blown back into the seaplane docks on Dot Lake beside the MacKenzie River at Norman Wells. No one parked a floatplane on the swift MacKenzie, especially in spring time, when fast water carried away anything tied to the shoreline.

To get navigating experience, I volunteered as Ron Warnick's helper for a flight to a silver mine near Great Bear Lake. We landed at Terra close to Port Radium with tool boxes and as many groceries as we could legally carry. For the return, an equal number of passengers occupied the seats along one wall. We also carried nine, 100-pound bags of silver concentrate valued at $600 each. The map reading proved easy in the clear weather as we enjoyed vistas of countless lakes of distinctive shapes and sizes everywhere.

Next day, I repacked my bags and waited for the Otter assigned to Norman Wells. Word had it that life at this MacKenzie River Northward base might not be easy. With three pilots and two airplanes, flying time wouldn't be plentiful. Worse, somebody said, accommodation for me entailed staying with the senior pilot and his wife.

The 400-mile flight would be the longest in my life without a landing. From Yellowknife, we crossed the sparse, black, spruce-and-willow country near Fort Rae, a village populated by Dogrib Dene and Satudene tribes. We then carried on to gigantic Lac la Martre. Everywhere we looked, lakes shimmered toward rising land in the northwest. Some were flat, olive green and sparkling, while others were a dark, indigo blue.

With nothing more than a few wisps of high, scattered cloud and barely a breath of wind on the water below, we picked out the light blue of Great Bear Lake and its high purple shorelines. Not far from Norman Wells, our maps began showing many small lakes. With hills and rivers as guideposts, navigation was a picnic.

As we approached the petroleum-oriented community of the Wells, burning red flares of excess gas from oil rigs caught our attention. On the left, the MacKenzie River looked appallingly dirty, with tree stumps, logs and chocolate water flowing toward the Arctic Ocean. On our right, a stretch of hills called the

102

Norman Range protected the adjacent lowlands from mountain winds.

To my surprise, my fellow Northward pilot exercised his seniority to fly the last few miles. We switched seats in the air so he could buzz a woman friend in the village and claim the honor of landing the season's first floatplane on Dot Lake. Before long, we settled into the water and tied up at a long, skimpily built dock flanked by dozens of red fuel drums. The ice had disappeared completely.

Since this would be my last year as a full-time, year-round commercial pilot, I intended to enjoy every minute. During the ride to the village, I learned that other accommodations, besides the base pilot's home, had been arranged. A good sign, I thought. The mechanics at Norman Wells waxed ecstatic about the work ahead. We were told we'd have "so much flying, you'll never be able to stand it." Anxious to log as many hours in Beavers and Otters as possible, I looked forward to what promised to be a feverish pace.

Northward operated a red, white and blue Beaver on gigantic balloon tires, along with an Otter and a Cessna 206 on tricycle landing gear from the airport. On my first day, the Cessna 206 hung suspended from a tripod near the office. For some reason, the fragile little airplane disappeared and never flew a minute with Northward. Another Beaver on floats at Dot Lake handled the seaplane work. The Otter that we delivered from Yellowknife would see many trips along the MacKenzie. Evidently, however, the base pilot preferred leaving the wheel work to junior pilots.

"They had no use for you in the big city, I see," remarked acting base manager Steve, who left soon afterward for Wardair in Yellowknife. "I suppose as long as you're here, we'll have to do something with you."

As sometimes happens with short-term, seasonal jobs, not many managers in Canadian bush airlines waste much thought on pilot accommodations. They forget that airplane drivers must sleep, which is not easy in twenty-four-hour daylight. My room in the mostly male town turned out to be a corner in the room of a decrepit, clapboard building beside a liquor store.

The pea-soup color of the blistered paint on the outside walls reminded me of crushed grasshoppers on prairie highways during droughts. Aptly named the Greenhouse, the hovel's dank, gloomy interior suggested that the previous occupants perhaps really didn't care for Norman Wells or Northward Aviation. If they did, the place may have been left in cleaner shape before they fled south to sanity.

Caked tracks of gumbo mud, drink-stained walls and cigarette-burned furniture littered each room. As I dropped my suitcase on a ripped, urine-dotted mattress, choking clouds of cigarette ashes flew up and through the unscreened bedroom window. Under the bed hid dust bunnies the size of cotton-tail rabbits.

Before leaving Yellowknife, I bought a sack of potatoes and a case of canned beans. Sheer hunger forced me to venture warily into the kitchen. In the porcelain sink, a galvanized dish pan overflowed with a chartreuse-colored furry mold. A layer of dead blowflies and tiny white worms lined the window sills and rodent-sized insects scurried in herds when anyone approached the cupboard doors.

Many places I'd stayed in Canada lacked heat and hot water. Not the Greenhouse. Scalding hot was the only temperature in the plumbing system and that included the greenish yellow liquid in the toilet bowl. Anyone flushing the toilet while still sitting on it wound up with painful blisters in an embarrassing location.

At the airport, I took a close look at the Otter on balloon tires. If this de Havilland marvel seemed huge before in Yellowknife, the large blobs of low-pressure rubber pioneered by Weldy Phipps in 1958 made it tower even further above my head. Never having flown one on wheels, I decided to ask for a check ride. The first takeoff frightened me: the tail rose so quickly, it nearly clipped the propeller on the runway. Years before, I'd seen a Royal Canadian Air Force Otter do the same thing at Buttonville Airport, north of Toronto.

On landing, the airplane had to be plunked squarely on its main wheels with tail wheel held off the ground as long as possible. No three-point landings were allowed in these airplanes, the check pilot warned. Even with a light wind blowing across Norman Wells' runway, the Otter demanded plenty of attention to keep straight. More severe crosswinds would come later, I knew.

After a short break, I did several solo circuits and returned to try the tundra-tired Beaver. It, too, showed a few peculiar landing quirks. When the wide, low-pressure wheels grabbed the surface, the airplane slowed abruptly with a pronounced nose-down tilt. As part of the checklist, I made sure my heels touched the floor, clear of the brakes.

A typical northern airplane, Beaver CF-HEP looked like it had seen its share of hard work. Oil and exhaust stains seeped from behind the cowlings. Dents or scrapes from previous years blended into the paint. White spittle stains marked the floor; I guessed correctly that previous passengers didn't enjoy their bouts of turbulent air. No matter how slipshod the airplane looked, the Beaver proved itself a dependable workhorse and had never failed a Norman Wells pilot.

While airplanes operating from Norman Wells appeared to be typical bushplanes, most of the work they did differed from charter flying in other parts of Canada. Some trips were easy—the MacKenzie River acted as an excellent aerial highway north and south of our base. Since few settlements existed in this corner of the country, long legs meant good mileage. Westward, shaded foothills warned of mountains and beyond them waited solid cliffs and unpredictable winds. Beyond the cliffs, I saw endless miles of gray-blue pebbles skirting the black, interglacial hills.

For several days, no one seemed to know what to do with me. Senior pilots did the flying when weather permitted. Springtime rain squalls inundated the area and created mud everywhere. When the cloud cover dissipated, a glance across the river at the MacKenzie Mountains showed snow still hovering on the tops and creeping down into valleys. Someone warned me that water runoff raised the river's level by as much as six feet. This usually brought more floating stumps and logs. One touch on a seaplane float could sink an expensive airplane.

At last, Edmonton head office telexed a senior pilot to leave Norman Wells and report to Yellowknife. This meant my flying would probably begin the next day. Sure enough, my first trip was to a muddy airstrip beside the MacKenzie River, south of Fort Norman. An Ontario mineral exploration company called Heath and Sherwood managed a drill site several miles inland from the Dahadinni River. A large operation, they needed regular food and fuel runs.

As I touched at Dahadinni, a Bell 47 helicopter hovered above the airstrip's west side and landed as the Beaver's propeller stopped. The pilot began slinging groceries to a collection of orange boxes used as bunkhouses and workshops. Northward wanted several more hops back and forth the same day to the Dahadinni airstrip, an hour each way until sunset. By the time I returned to Norman Wells, another request for the Beaver waited on the telex.

A Northern Canada Power Company technician needed a ride to Dene Indian village of Fort Norman. On the northern bank of the MacKenzie River at its junction with the Great Bear River, the place carried the native name of Tulita, meaning, "where the two rivers meet." Originally a trading post in 1810, Fort Norman's strategic location made it a transportation center for Arctic explorers like Sir John Franklin. In modern times, hunting, fishing and general tourism provided revenue for the Dene and Metis residents.

The technician wanted to inspect a power line at low level, so navigation to Fort Norman was effortless—I just followed a cut trail in the trees. While we took a break in the village, he told me one of his work mates once hired an Alouette helicopter to help repair a wind-damaged pole.

Dangling beneath the helicopter, the repairman suddenly found himself falling after the pilot panicked and punched the emergency release button. Thanks to the cushioning spruce needles and low height of the trees, he wound up with little more than a few painful gouges.

A highlight of my stay in Norman Wells took place shortly after a flight from Heath and Sherwood's Dahadinni camp. Steve England loaded the Otter and, knowing no other trips were on the books, asked if I'd care to go along. Sixty minutes later, we landed at Dahadinni to unload and took off again, this time southwest toward the mountains.

We climbed steadily and map-read toward the deeply canyoned Redstone River, where we followed a dark valley lined by an occasional patch of scrub spruce. At 8,000 feet, the highest peaks were only a few hundred feet beneath the wheels. Initially, the sky stayed clear but half way to Little Dall Lake, a high, thin overcast developed.

Not far from the south Redstone, we spotted a flat, white body of ice high up on a plateau. At one end, a drill rig and several canvas tents caught our attention. Steve couldn't be sure of the ice thickness, but a radio report from camp confirmed that enough was left to hold the Otter. Since customers in need of food, gasoline and mail often colored their estimates, Steve was hesitant. He circled the center of the lake to examine it closely for crevasses and soft spots.

Steve made a gentle touchdown, applied takeoff power and went around again. We felt no cracks; nor did the surface show any sign of dangerous areas. After the next approach, he landed and shut the engine off before we stopped rolling. After a close look at the pavement-like surface, we presumed the ice would last only until the first sunny day. A few hours of hot sunlight would be enough to "candle" the ice, or separate it into long, clear crystals.

With little else to do while the drill crew unloaded our airplane, I strolled away on my own. On all sides, mountains rose until they disappeared into cloud layers. As I looked up, a crack appeared in the gray sky above us. Streaming sunlight filtered through the haze to touch the wings of the Otter and the faces of the working men.

Beneath my feet, the once-drab ice suddenly was transformed into a turquoise blue. Nearby, I noticed a tiny pool of meltwater. Bending down, I put my lips into it and took the most delicious drink of pure, fresh liquid I'd ever tasted. Quiet enveloped us. Everyone stopped their work and gazed around at the cloud, rock and sky. The separated mists slowly melded together again and broke the spell. The men shook their heads and resumed the tasks.

On the return, Steve sat pensively in the pilot's seat. We both knew that few people had ever enjoyed splendor like that at Little

Dall Lake. I snapped a few photographs from 9,000 feet and put my camera away, glad to have made the trip.

In the early 1940s, wartime shortages dictated a need for a petroleum pipeline to transfer oil from Norman Wells to refineries in Whitehorse. The resulting Canol Road project became the largest construction job since the Panama Canal. Thousands of men and tons of equipment moved into what many considered wasteland. Decades later during my stay at Norman Wells, little remained to symbolize the sacrifices made, except faint trails marked by occasional derelict U.S. Army trucks.

Bridges no longer existed and supply airstrips along the Canol disappeared, as scrub vegetation slowly reclaimed the country. By the time I came to Wells, it was known as a rich man's nature trail, but those of us at Northward rarely saw it. Few lakes alongside the road were big enough to hold our airplanes and no settlements remained intact.

One day, a European French doctor and his male traveling companion stepped off a Pacific Western jet and into our base office. They wanted to charter an airplane for an adventure conceived, we guessed, in a chateau in France. Their concept of sport involved a dropoff on the Canol Road, 198 miles into the Yukon mountains then a hike back to Norman Wells. They needed logistical support for this wilderness expedition, and the doctor had developed a brilliant plan.

Instead of carrying food supplies, they wanted an air drop every 20 miles along their route. After the prepared containers were dropped from the airplane, the pilot would land on the last available body of water from which the doctor and his ectomorphic friend would begin trekking back to Norman Wells. This all sounded somewhat logical to everyone in the office until the oddball pair arrived at Dot Lake the next morning.

Our Northward staff assumed that if anyone dropped twenty-pound cardboard boxes from the belly of an airplane, parachutes of some sort would be in order. The Frenchman wanted the containers shoved through the Beaver's floor hatch with nothing more than several wrappings of fluorescent-pink tape to slow their descent and cushion the landing. Trying to persuade our eccentric clients that nothing could survive the impact of from a half-mile fall proved fruitless.

Between the Frenchman's broken English and our arm-waving, we settled on a series of hand signals before takeoff. As junior pilot, I was chosen to make the trip. We climbed into the mufflerless company truck and drove along the mud road beside the river to Dot Lake. After stacking the boxes near the Beaver's rear cargo hatch, we departed with as much fuel as the tanks could hold.

Twenty-eight miles away at Dodo Canyon, a Death Valley-like phenomenon west of the Wells, we planned the first drop. By peering straight down into the gorge, the outline of Canol Road could barely be seen. As I reached for the throttle to reduce engine power, the doctor misinterpreted my movement as the signal to expel a box. Out it went.

As we watched, the small brilliant square container became a pink dot as it plummeted rapidly to the valley floor. Striking the earth beside the trail, it exploded into hundreds of tiny pieces. A flash of sunlight indicated broken glass food jars.

The doctor, English quickly forgotten, leaned forward as I returned the throttle to cruise position. Pursing his lips, he shouted more instructions. When he leaned between the front seats and I turned to look at him, his fetid breath nearly knocked me senseless. Every time we dropped a box, he waved his sleeveless arms wildly and placed his sweat-covered face close to mine to make me understand it was out.

By the time a half-dozen boxes exited through the Beaver's belly hatch, I began feeling nauseated. I sneaked an airsickness bag from beneath the right-hand passenger seat and kept it handy.

On one drop, a small patch of mountain vegetation caught fire from whatever exploded in the box. Luckily, plants or trees were sparse and the blaze quickly sputtered out. As we continued dropping, I became so absorbed in handling the airplane as the mountains grew higher, I failed to notice that fewer and fewer lakes appeared. The point of no return passed behind the Beaver's tail.

A quick glance at the chart put us close to Fuller Lake, supposedly the landable-sized water along the route. Horrified, I realized the few potholes we saw now and then were still frozen solid. Even if ice covered Fuller Lake, a landing would still be compulsory. We carried three, ten-gallon kegs of gasoline for the belly tanks for the return to Norman Wells.

The tops of the nearest mountains disappeared in drizzle. A small pond a few miles from Fuller Lake looked like solid ice, no doubt frozen to its rocky bottom. Drawing closer, the edge of our landable lake appeared through the mist and God, thank God, it was open.

Lack of sunshine made judging water depth and spotting shoals difficult as we bored through the rain to land. On touching down, I heard none of the horrible, metal-crunching sounds every pilot experiences eventually in his career. Once parked against a cluster of black boulders, my passengers jumped to shore with shoulder packs. With nothing other than a few fragile fishing poles as their defense against grizzly bears, they vanished into the scrub, leaving me on my own to refuel.

While draining the gasoline kegs into the airplane, I saw no sign of life in the valley. I heard no birds, no insects—not even a squirrel or chipmunk broke the eerie silence. Studying the majesty of my high surroundings, I had the strange feeling I didn't belong. Watching over my shoulder, I slowly paddled the airplane to deeper water, fired up the Pratt & Whitney engine and pointed the airplane eastward.

The overcast, having descended further now, forced me into cloud. Ten long minutes later, I made it on top to brilliant sunshine. The peaks slowly disappeared until the great, fat MacKenzie River took shape through occasional cloud breaks. After landing at the Wells, the dock boy placed the floor cover back in place and no one ever again dropped a load along the Canol Road. Transferred from Norman Wells later, I never heard of the two Frenchmen again, so I assumed they survived their trek.

Northward Aviation served "the three Fs": Fort Norman, Fort Franklin and Fort Good Hope. Fort Norman could always be reached by wheel or float airplanes, good weather or bad. No matter how low ceilings dropped, arriving at "Norman" meant simply flying low above the MacKenzie and watching the color of the rapidly moving water.

Normally, the MacKenzie retained the same consistency and shade of runoff as a child's sandbox. Where the water changed from brown to black and then clear along the shoreline, a pilot could anticipate a sharp left turn where the silt-free Great Bear River joined its bigger brother. Seaplane pilots simply closed the throttle and landed. Wheel pilots went for the airstrip.

The runway on a plateau above river level was long enough for a balloon-tired Beaver, but crosswinds nearly always blew. If not, intense dust clouds sometimes caused fifteen-minute waits for visual conditions to return. The only method of keeping grit from the engine involved taxiing rapidly, braking hard to swing around and shutting down the engine before the sandstorm enveloped the airplane.

Moving tuberculosis victims from these primitive airstrips became a customary but unpleasant task undertaken by Northward's Norman Well pilots. Medical staff at village clinics never had to tell us our passengers carried the dreaded disease, but we learned to recognize the signs—a sealed, silver can of sputum and a large manila envelope containing x-rays. Usually, the patient's family gathered when a child, parent or relative left the settlements for treatment in the south. Sometimes, this meant a long sojourn in a TB sanatorium. One twenty-three-year-old Cree woman told me she lived in the "San" for eleven years.

I never forgot an Indian girl with sad, dark eyes. She was about fourteen or fifteen years old and rode with me from Fort Norman to Norman Wells. She carried a tiny, squally baby who was also seriously ill, judging by the green, slimy phlegm drooling from its mouth and nose. Besides the standard tin can and x-ray, this young mother carried a pickle jar half-filled with gummy, blood-speckled saliva. By the time we'd left the ruts of Fort Norman's runway and landed twenty minutes later at the Wells, she had expectorated enough fluid to fill the container.

After parking beside the Pacific Western Airlines Boeing 737, I helped her and the baby out and guided her toward the Edmonton-bound jet. As I watched a flight attendant take the child, the horrible thought struck me that my ex-passenger no longer carried that revolting pickle jar. Expecting the worst, I rushed back to my Beaver and cautiously climbed the steps, opened the right front door and peered inside. She had thoughtfully placed the jar upright on the floor between the seats.

Not relishing the idea of using bare hands to pick up the jar, I returned later with a pair of borrowed rubber gloves. Despite my caution, the vile, slippery thing slid from my grasp and tipped against the flap handle. The amoeba-like contents emerged and slithered along the bakelite floor.

It took several hours and three rolls of paper towels before I finished separating the stringy mass from floor boards, seat cushions and flap handle. Using disinfectant from the survival kit, I also washed every inch of wall space, especially near the pilot's seat. No one else, other than myself dared to fly that particular plane until I left Northward for Ontario.

Fort Franklin was a log cabin community of 333 Hareskin Dene Indians on the north side of Great Bear Lake's Keith Arm. Surrounded by thinly forested land close to the tree line, the community depended on wheeled airplanes during my stay. The ice on Great Bear was no longer solid enough to hold a skiplane. Although open patches of water appeared, seaplanes didn't yet have enough takeoff space.

Navigation to the village on clear days was simple: first climb over the Norman Range and aim for the "Big Water" with a compass heading. A senior pilot described an alternate but longer, bad-weather route.

"If it goes the shits, drive on up the (MacKenzie) river, make a quick left at the (Great) Bear and follow it 'til you see the white dome-shaped church," he said.

With two nurses from Inuvik and their medical gear packed into a wheeled Beaver, I followed the senior pilot's wise advice and arrived over Fort Franklin despite some marginal ceilings along the way. With little time on wheeled Beavers, I felt dismayed to see that the airstrip measured little more than the ten-foot, two-inch track of my airplane. Worse, winds roared ninety degrees across the gravelly surface at more than thirty knots.

After two frightening attempts to land and subsequent go-arounds when houses appeared in front of the windshield instead of the runway, we struck the ground with a terrific whack. We stayed solidly on and, surprisingly, pointed in the correct direction. Later, the base manager told me at least two Otters ran off the runway the previous week. Taxiing to a point where my passengers could be dropped took twice as long. With not enough room to turn on the airstrip, I had no choice but to taxi to the far end, wheel around and come back.

As the propeller wound down, I glanced at my passengers. Both were completely oblivious to my struggle with the airplane. Neither one cared about the great moment in Canadian aviation history—my safe arrival on a short runway in a vicious crosswind. These two were seasoned veterans of the north, I thought, as we unloaded medical gear and a portable x-ray machine.

The load for the return to Norman Wells included a half-dozen passengers eager to reach Fort Franklin. Although not a trace of snow could be seen for miles, I heard a snow machine flopping toward the airstrip. Dragging along behind the badly treated, overworked Moto-Ski snow machine, a crudely made komatik sleigh bounced from rock to rock. A small wire crate secured across its boards helped hold it down.

As the driver drew closer, several terrified Husky puppies tried to chew through the wooden slats. Young and frisky, they looked like pudgy balls of fur as they rolled around in the cage.

The pups were destined for Norman Wells and placed on the first available flight to Fort Good Hope, nearly ninety miles northwest. Most northern villages still had a few dogs here and there, but these unfortunate creatures lived a miserable existence. Since gasoline-powered snow machines entered the Arctic picture, many once-noble Huskies of the barrenlands lived permanently in the open at the end of stakes plunged into the permafrost. Short lengths of chain knotted around their collarless necks led to the end of their wretched worlds.

Plainly, most became forgotten creatures, judging by the famished animals I had encountered. At Cambridge Bay on Victoria Island, three forlorn former sled dogs were staked in a flooded run-off area. Doomed to spend the rest of their lives sleeping, lying and eventually succumbing in the cold water, they rarely had enough energy or interest to howl at strangers walking by.

As the Hareskin Indian lifted the crate from the komatik and slid it into the Beaver, I noticed one pup lying in a corner. Spreading the wooden slats apart, I eased him out and held him. Once a playful lump of fluff like his brothers and sisters in the cage, the tiny animal's hide, ripped and hanging on one side, was sticky with gore and feces.

He lacked the strength to raise his head but the tiny white tip at the end of his tail wagged feebly. The Indian took the pathetic beast from my hands, shrugged, and with one, quick unexpected motion, slammed the helpless near-dead puppy against a boulder. Satisfied as the quivering pup's blood stained the sand and it became still, the owner grinned at me. Without a word, he kicked the bloody, bleeding carcass into a windswept patch of grass.

Aghast and enraged, I climbed the two steps into the Beaver, fired up the engine and slammed the door. The wind still blew hard across the strip but I don't remember one second of that takeoff. At Norman Wells, a mechanic removed the cage and placed the surviving puppies in the Greenhouse. Several days later someone must have found space for them on the flight to Fort Good Hope. When I came in to feed them, they were gone.

Despite the airline's internal problems, I enjoyed the flying and learned to adjust their pace. It wasn't frantic, but rarely a day slid by that a trip didn't come up. All went well until mid-June when a pair of replacement airplane mechanics arrived on the base. Before I even laid eyes on them, I heard them complain as they tramped up the Greenhouse stairs.

Nothing pleased these two. First, they informed the pilots we were living in the wrong place—the Greenhouse belonged to them. Next, they made it clear that a pilot's wife who came to the Wells to visit her husband, had no place on company premises. Worse, their utter contempt for pilots was obvious. In contrast, I had always believed pilots and mechanics shared equal responsibility. One couldn't live without the other, so both deserved the courtesy of mutual respect.

Nevertheless, I had come to Norman Wells to fly Beavers and Otters and I intended to do so, though few Otter trips came my way. Finally, a senior pilot requested a day off just as an Otter booking came in.

My first revenue Otter trip consisted of a group of drill rig workers bound for a site northwest down the MacKenzie. All four arrived at Dot Lake several hours late and had obviously enjoyed their previous evening downing whatever booze they could find in the Wells.

Their destination, I knew, wasn't the most pleasant place to land. Water visibility was no more than a quarter of an inch in the muddy river. At a bend called the San Sault Rapids, the current ran much faster than most of our stops along the route. Loaded with all the freight, fuel and people the Otter could take without sinking at the dock, we struggled off Dot Lake, turned right and followed the MacKenzie River at low altitude.

Senior pilots suggested I try the middle of the river, where there might be fewer hidden sandbars. Because of constant current and shoreline erosion, hazards could form overnight or shift location within a few hours. We landed safely without hitting anything. My near-sober passengers waded to shore and, at my insistence, helped swing the tail around to drag the airplane as far backwards as possible onto the gravel.

After emptying the cargo compartment, I jumped in, fired up the 600-horsepower engine and took off empty back to base. Hardly spectacular, my first revenue flight in an Otter turned out to be the last one before Northward Aviation called me elsewhere. The balance of my time was spent at Norman Wells in Beavers.

Pacific Western Airlines or "Pray While Aloft," as we called it, landed in Norman Wells on regularly scheduled flights to Inuvik from Edmonton, Yellowknife and Hay River. We knew the jet's arrival signaled the chance of a charter flight. Some passengers planned to travel on to Fort Good Hope or Arctic Red River. An elderly Indian lady, freshly discharged from a hospital in Calgary, journeyed with her grandson. She was barely able to move without a pair of canes, as we eased her into the back of a Beaver at Dot Lake.

A group of three men who had partied long and hard while "outside" could have used more time to unwind. Another pair of riders waited—a trapper and a tall Indian girl with the longest mane of jet black hair I'd ever seen. The additional revenue of so many extra customers meant extra revenue for the company, since Northward already received payment for hauling the twice-weekly mail. The drunks, who looked to me like a trio of pot-bellied bats, wouldn't be a problem if we flew high enough. Anyone with alcohol in their systems usually fell asleep at altitude.

Off the lake, I settled back to enjoy the fifty-five-minute run to Fort Good Hope. Not far out from the Wells, a glance back told me that nearly everyone was relaxed and appreciated the scenery along one of Canada's largest waterways. Below, a barge churned the water into raging white cataracts as it fought to hold a heading in the current. Smooth air and easy navigation nearly lulled to me to sleep until I heard a gurgling noise.

"The bag, use the bag!" I shouted.

Not quick enough, a semi-inebriated welder missed the coffee-stained, white paper bag held between his knees. As de Havilland Beaver CF-JXP droned on above the muddy brown river, he shuffled his splashed boots and tried to joke about Northward's poor inflight service.

Mid-June became surprisingly warm for an Arctic spring.

The sunlight heated the hills around us and sent up afternoon turbulence. Even the beet-nosed trapper and his blonde girlfriend said nothing.

Behind a row of sandy bluffs a few miles ahead, Fort Good Hope and its Hareskin Dene population of 454 waited for the mail. The landing in front of the oldest fur trading post in the lower MacKenzie Valley proved uneventful, other than a standard zigzag roundout to avoid floating stumps and discarded oil drums. With a ragged yellow rope, I managed to tie the airplane to a broken-down wooden wharf littered with rusty gas cans and smashed aluminum boats.

Once finished securing the Beaver and dragging a plank to the left rear passenger door, the customers, except the old lady, stepped out. The trapper and his female friend would stay in Fort Good Hope, as would the young boy and his grandmother. After takeoff, I planned to go directly to the barge with the three drunks. Counting heads, I noticed the elderly woman still hadn't vacated the Beaver.

Her grandson peered inside. The old lady slept peacefully,

her head propped comfortably against my sleeping bag. He clasped her by the shoulders and began shaking her gently. He continued rocking back and forth, a little harder each time, jabbering loudly. Panicking now, the young man desperately hauled off and slapped his grandmother hard across the face. He got no response. He yelled directly into her ear. Nothing. The boy hit her again. Still, she remained motionless. "Holy God," I thought, "she's dead!"

I jumped inside the airplane and we both shook the woman so hard, it seemed as if her head would snap off at the top of her neck. Finally, she stirred and opened her bloodshot eyes from what had to be the deepest sleep I had ever seen. Fully awake now and certainly alive, she administerd the most vociferous tongue-lashing ever given in the Northwest Territories. The relieved grandson and I stood back and let her rave.

Once away from Fort Good Hope's dock, the construction workers became far more active. By the time we leveled at 3,000 feet to search for their barge, a packsack gave birth to a forty-ounce bottle of Canadian Club rye whisky. Despite my request to keep it capped, the pale, brown fluid quickly disappeared down their gullets. Before long, life for the barge workers became a party thousands of feet above a historic Arctic waterway. Not for me, however. I remembered that the welder had already used every airsick bag in the Beaver.

Their barge was chained to the side of the river and would be home for my new back-slapping buddies until freeze-up. Riverboat traffic supplying native settlements from Hay River north to the Beaufort Sea counted as one of the most important Arctic enterprises. Should a load of fuel oil and timber run aground enroute, only an expensive airlift could keep a community supplied.

A log boom behind the barge served as a dock and on it, workmen bolted several trailers to serve as living quarters, tool shed, cook shack and dining room. A crew of ten men generally stayed on the job until winter forced them home.

My load of spirit-filled believers, now almost completely incapacitated and fully incoherent, could barely climb from the Beaver as it rocked against the logs. Once outside, they lurched along a line of wooden planks. None could pull himself up and over the sharp-edged lip of the barge.

Several brawny workmates grabbed them one at a time. A man on each arm and leg heaved them onto the steel floor as easily as if they were tossing bags of potatoes. The drunks struck with terrific thuds and I expected them to have at least a few broken bones. Miraculously unhurt, they pulled themselves along on elbows and potbellies toward their sleeping quarters.

Flabbergasted that human beings could survive such unbelievable abuse, I started back to the Beaver, but the cook called out to ask me for lunch. His spotless kitchen trailer stood in great contrast to the cockroach-infested Greenhouse of Norman Wells. I enjoyed a fine dinner—haute cuisine in comparison to beans, potatoes, tomato juice and chocolate bars on which I'd subsisted since leaving Yellowknife.

Later, as I landed at Dot Lake, the Pacific Western Boeing 737 passed overhead for the airport. On the southbound leg, it usually landed at the Wells. Much to my surprise, the base manager asked me to take another passenger to Fort Good Hope.

Rushing to the airport, I preflighted the wheeled Beaver and went to the terminal to find my passenger. Only one person waited in the office. She was a pretty young woman in her midtwenties and, as she told me later, about to enter teachers' college in the fall.

Not dressed for the MacKenzie Valley sub-Arctic, the white-armed maiden with raven black hair wore a tight mini-skirt. A bare-shouldered blouse left plenty of territory favored by black flies or mosquitos. Not a blemish marred the face and her teeth radiated like snow whenever she smiled, which was often.

Michele had never seen a spruce tree or understood how deadly the biting insects north of 60 could be. She opened the rear door, threw her luggage inside and climbed into the passenger seat.

She told me her boyfriend at Fort Good Hope worked as a geologist. I knew the man. His crew had asked me to check on a meat order a day or two before. Michele planned on surprising him and didn't bother letting anyone know her arrival time. I looked forward to seeing the look on the boyfriend's face when she arrived at Fort Good Hope.

No doubt the exploration crew thought I'd recovered their missing groceries and expected a few paper-wrapped packages of bacon, liver or steak. As we landed and swung the tail around, a cloud of dust enveloped the Beaver. As the dust settled, Michele opened her door and began climbing out. The maneuver seemed difficult in the tight skirt and I wondered why no one helped her.

When I came around to the side of the airplane, I saw everyone standing still, their mouths unashamedly drooped open. Michele stepped into the sand and looked around. She didn't see her boyfriend until he came out from behind a cook tent.

His jaw dropped so far I thought it might strike his belt. He stuttered something I couldn't hear. Finally, he came to his senses and escorted pretty Michele from the goggling crowd.

As I taxied away, I saw that not one man had moved. I never saw Michele again but the pilot who later delivered her to Pacific Western reported that she'd left the camp wearing baggy work pants, bush boots and a checkered woollen shirt.

In Norman Wells, a telex from Yellowknife ordered a pilot to fly Beaver CF-HEP south right away. Mechanics would install tundra tires so that it could finish a season in the High Arctic islands beyond the North American mainland. A Resolute Bay-based twin engine STOL type called a Dornier 28 had flipped upside down on Ellef Ringnes Island close to the North Pole.

Shaken, the Dornier pilot went to Inuvik to wait for another airplane and now, no experienced high timers on Northward's roster wanted anything to do with flying in the "Islands." In other words, my chances of being North Pole-bound wouldn't be because of any talent or enthusiasm. Simply, management discovered my name at the bottom of the barrel and nobody else wanted the job. I quickly volunteered.

Almost any airplane in Resolute Bay on Cornwallis Island eventually wound up in some kind of mishap. Not many people lost their lives in the tundra-tire business, but plenty left the Islands with an accident in their logbooks. Nevertheless, I craved any opportunity to explore the High Arctic. Head office pounced upon my offer.

Before leaving Norman Wells, the Beaver held every possible drop of fuel. In the rear, I carried three, ten-gallon metal kegs. The distance from the Wells exceeded the airplane's range, so a quick stop at Bennett Field, fifty miles southeast, made up the difference. Luckily, the sky stayed clear to Yellowknife. A tail wind reduced the total trip to three hours and forty minutes over the route we'd flown in the Otter weeks before.

8   Tell Him It's Good

When I arrived in Yellowknife, no one could tell me when I would be leaving for Resolute Bay. I checked into the Gold Range Hotel and enjoyed a long, hot shower that removed the last trace of Norman Wells from my hide.

At the air base, the base manager dropped a pile of aeronautical charts into my lap. That evening, I spread them on the hotel room floor and carefully plotted every inch of the trip. Beaver CF-HEP's lack of a long range fuel tank would require extra stops along the way.

The mechanics installed an astrocompass mount in the airplane, but no one knew how to use it. As more information dribbled in from Edmonton, someone told me I wouldn't be venturing into the High Arctic alone. Northward had sent a Scotsman named Sandy MacKenzie to Yellowknife. While waiting for him, I gathered rags, tools and whatever we needed to keep us as self-sufficient as possible.

Stories about island flying cropped up every time I approached someone on Northward's staff for advice. One pilot explained how a tundra-tired Beaver could land on the barrenlands one day, and be over on its back the next because of a little rain. Tales of high winds seemed plausible since the maps showed hundreds of square miles of flat areas with almost nothing to slow the breeze. In the northeast corner, glaciers and long stretches of water formed gale-scoured valleys. Some said wind-storms lasted for weeks. Still, I wanted to go.

Sandy MacKenzie finally arrived to teach me some tricks of survival. A barrel-chested Scot, he understood the Arctic well, having worked out of Resolute with the first wave of long-range Piper Super Cubs in the late 1950s. Anyone acquainted with Sandy acknowledged him as one of the best on big wheels.

Landing on unprepared, soggy, and sometimes snow-covered beach terraces, slopes and plateaus didn't come naturally to any pilots, particularly to those with seaplane time. Magnetic compasses were useless for Arctic navigation. Magnetic variation on Cornwallis Island was eighty degrees west at one point; and less than twenty miles away, it shifted ten degrees. On overcast days, a navigator needed to be highly skilled in map reading, since astrocompass bearings from the sun weren't available.

After going over every possible detail, we checked out of our hotel and headed for the airport. The Beaver looked huge on its modified Douglas DC-3 tires. The airplane seemed in excellent condition after thorough inspections by Northward's conscientious, Yellowknife-based mechanics. With Sandy in the right seat, we filed a twenty-four-hour flight notification in lieu of a flight plan because we couldn't plot any accurate times of arrival.

The engine started easily. Once checks were completed, we taxied toward the runway. I picked up the microphone to call the tower, but received no reply.

"The radio's dead," I observed.

"What?"

"It's dead," I repeated.

"Bullshit," said Sandy. "Let me try."

Sandy flicked the microphone button several times, then pounded the panel with his fist, but nothing changed. My right foot on the brake pivoted the Beaver snappily around and we taxied back to Northward's designated patch of gravel. So much for our first attempt to depart the "Gold City" for Resolute Bay.

We telephoned Northward's electronics man. As expected, he asked the question all avionics people learn during their first day in radio school: "Did you turn it on?"

After unloading beside a huge, silver Wardair Bristol

Freighter, we returned to Yellowknife and remained in town for another night. Somebody pulled the radio out and took it away for repairs.

After a night in the Yellowknife Inn, where we dined beside a glass-encased polar-bear hide, we returned to the Beaver. After the radio man reinstalled our radios, we tracked north across the taiga country. Our first leg lasted almost three hours to Port Radium on Great Bear Lake's east side. We handpumped our belly tanks full from several forty-five-gallon drums.

Our track to Coppermine took us across stretches of land that had been reduced to nothing more than surface, horizon and sky. At one stage, we passed over Bloody Falls, the scene of a massacre in 1771 where explorer Samuel Hearne couldn't stop an Indian party from attacking a group of helpless Eskimos. I looked beneath the tires, envisioning the one-sided slaughter and Hearne's struggle to reach the headwaters of the mighty Coppermine River. At the settlement, we refueled again with the help of two swarthy Eskimo men.

After takeoff, we crossed northeast above the panorama of Coronation Gulf. As far as we could see, turquoise ice and meltwater extended on forever. We reached Lady Franklin Point on the tip of Victoria Island and map-read to Cambridge Bay. In polar bear and seal country now, we searched the surface for signs of life. We saw nothing except flocks of snow geese alighting on a few ice-free stretches along the shorelines.

After Cambridge Bay and the luxury of an electric fuel pump to fill our tanks, we crossed Victoria Strait and headed for Spence Bay. Soon, we saw the meltwater of King William Island, where explorer Sir John Franklin and more than 100 of his shipmates perished. In the harsh, compelling beauty of the islands below, I imagined their horrible death march. Nearly 200 years later, we cruised serenely above their graveyard in the comfort of a de Havilland Beaver. Not once did the Pratt & Whitney engine falter.

Over Spence Bay, our calculations showed us 765 air miles from Yellowknife. Steep cliffs on both sides of the hamlet sheltered an excellent harbor. With winds gusting across a narrow sand strip at thirty knots, Sandy barked an order to land on the ice close to the Hudson's Bay store. The idea of placing an expensive Beaver on uncertain sea ice didn't seem at all appealing. Long, jagged cracks crisscrossed the surface. Holes, black with sea water, spread along shorelines close to empty fuel drums and honey bags. We parked short of a crack paralleling a snow-machine track.

A young Eskimo who had been fishing from a hole dropped his *leister,* or spear and walked to the idling Beaver. After paying him and his friend five dollars each, they rolled some fuel drums to the airplane.

A Northward Twin Otter appeared over a hill and landed close to us with a load of whale bone. Pilot Bob Platt sometimes accepted charters in which he and a group of Eskimos searched the nearby coast lines for carving material. He laughed at the notion of anyone taking something as small as a Beaver into the Arctic Islands. After Platt departed for his base at Cambridge Bay, we decided to stay the night.

Not the most picturesque village in the Arctic, Spence Bay existed on a pile of glacial till. Sea ice crawled up the shorelines. In some places, the Hudson's Bay manager told us, it measured six feet thick, although tremendous cracks frequently spread underneath the snow cover. No pilot on the coast dared land at Spence Bay without a meticulous aerial inspection.

From Spence, we needed enough fuel to fly 350 miles along the Boothia Peninsula and across the Somerset Island before Resolute Bay. In good weather, we could do the trip on belly tanks. If not, we would lack enough reserve to return to Spence. Sandy anticipated a tundra landing near an abandoned survey camp where we planned to refuel from two forty-five-gallon drums we carried.

The Spence Bay manager told us that land toward Bellot Strait was nothing but monotonous black rock and dirty white ice, but I found the scenery breathtaking. For miles on both sides of our wings, rugged, rounded hills and acres of pebble beaches passed beneath our wheels. Occasionally, we paused to circle over rings of ancient, weathered stones placed by early Eskimos to hold down their tents in Arctic gales.

Skirting kelp-covered shorelines, we watched as white beluga whales plunged through ocean rollers and seals disappeared head first into ice cracks. Soon, we arrived at Stanwell-Fletcher Lake. At this isolated jewel, forty-five miles north of the last of North America's mainland, we saw that modern mankind had recently been here.

In a tiny patch of green, we saw a few shreds of faded orange fabric on a tumbled-down, wood-framed tent. Around it, speckles of white, gray, and black spread out like the effluent from a dropped glass jar of marmalade. As check pilot, Sandy insisted we switch seats for the landing—our first of the season on unproven tundra. I pulled the pin on the control wheel, slid it over to him and slipped into the rear. Reaching forward, I held the wheel as Sandy unfastened his seat belt and moved to the left. Now we would land.

Sandy spent twenty minutes circling above the tent frame. I remembered our discussion concerning Arctic off airport landings. A pilot needed patience.

"The plants look right," Sandy shouted and continued circling.

Grassroots pilots in southern Ontario generally appreciated soft, green carpets of grass on which to land but, similar conditions in the Islands often meant trouble. Lushness indicated moist ground. When poppies, saxifrage, bell heather and other colorful plants grew in clumps with bare dry areas between them, the surface usually was considered solid enough to support an airplane.

When possible, Sandy explained, use slightly sloping terrain. This way, a pilot can fly below his touchdown point to search for moisture. Sunny days made the procedure easier since bright light reflected from the water. Normally, active layers of shallow tundra soil thawed each year, although rarely far below the frozen permafrost. If not too deep, it could help prevent tundra tires from sinking to the axles.

Satisfied, Sandy established the Beaver on final approach with full flaps. The slowest possible airspeed took us between the tent frame and a humpbacked ridge. The landing turned out to be a hell of a whack, but such touchdowns weren't unusual in the High Arctic. For a moment, I wondered about Sandy's long absence from airplanes. He noted my concern and told me the bounce was intentional to test the surface for wheel penetration.

Once down, he increased the Beaver's engine power, ran the wheels over the ground and took off again. An Arctic reality: if the tracks filled with water, we would look elsewhere to replenish our gas tanks. After another touchdown, Sandy braked hard to keep the tail up and preserve the fragile tail wheel.

"Get stopped quick, shut 'er down on the spot and never taxi until you get out and walk around," he said. "Look for soft areas and mark them. You never know when you'll be back."

Our Beaver carried a cardboard box of toilet tissue, pink survey tape and wood slats. The tape and slats outlined the take-off run and the biodegradable toilet paper tossed out the window unrolled and floated down to the landing zone to snag on lumps of soil. Besides showing wind direction, it marked the aerially inspected patch of ground. Because tundra looks much the same, it wasn't uncommon to discover a safe touchdown spot, only to lose it during a turn.

We rolled the drums sideways out of the left rear side door, and let them thunk into the soft ground. After hand-pumping in 80/87 gasoline, we decided to look around the abandoned camp.

The previous occupants were members of a geological party, judging by mildewed sample bags they left behind. They had thrown gasoline and naphtha tins outside their tent flap. Corroding peanut butter pails and ripped lard cans filled crevasses between crumpled sheets of black plastic. Small twirls of grass told us at least lemmings considered this offal habitable.

Damp tufts of white hair clung to boards ripped from the tent frame. Curious, I poked around and discovered another example of how some northerners treat domesticated animals. Two dead dogs lay in a heap, surrounded by mounds of powdery, white manure. Yellow nylon ropes led from their necks to wooden stakes. Whether someone shot or starved them, I couldn't tell, but their milk-white teeth were bared and their lips were cracked. Bending closer, I saw that they served as homes for tiny, writhing forms of life.

"These were working animals, not pets," said Sandy. A few hours later, we crossed Barrow Strait's brilliant white pack ice and landed on Resolute Bay's gravel runway. The air time totaled just over thirteen hours from Yellowknife.

Although Resolute Bay had a fuel dealer with electric pumps, Northward obtained gasoline from a mountain of drums piled close to a barracks belonging to J. C. Sproule and Associates. The company hauled bulk fuel at cheaper rates.

A rubber-booted, wizened Eskimo man from a nearby village showed us where to sleep and wash. One chipped porcelain basin served for a dozen men in the barracks. Nasty odors emanated from the rarely emptied toilet in the grungy bathroom. The camp's bread supplies and other foodstuffs rested under woollen blankets just a few feet away. It was many years before I could eat another slice of bread without recalling that vile smell.

The cook, a refugee from Saskatoon, Saskatchewan, didn't look the part. Instead of a white chef suit, he wore blue jeans and frayed, checkerboard shirts. Despite his long-haired and heavily tattooed appearance, no one faulted him for his unorthodox dress. He took his trade seriously and kept the barracks kitchen stocked with rows of pies, cakes and tarts twenty-four hours a day.

After a decent sleep in a wooden shed with foil-covered windows, I peered outside, anxious to get on with High Arctic flying. Dense fog with droplets like suspended ballbearings enveloped Cornwallis Island and kept even the Twin Otters and DC-3s grounded. Not even Pacific Western or Nordair dared approach Cornwallis Island with their Boeing 737 jets.

A Resolute Bay-based Beaver meant plenty of waiting with little flying. New to this part of the Northwest Territories, time passed quickly. In days to come, I appreciated the peculiar camaraderie shared by those who fly in the High Arctic. Experienced senior pilots became generous with advice on how to survive. Most, like me, had started in Beavers and Super Cubs.

Before long, tiny "x's" showing suitable landing places appeared on the frayed charts of my map collection. No one held back on the location of expensively placed gasoline caches. The only stipulation was, "Use a barrel, replace a barrel." Soon, my notebook bulged with suggestions on fuel economy and bad weather escape routes.

Our assignments included setting up and supplying geological survey camps in the Arctic Archipelago. Normally, helicopters or light airplanes flew field men out of fly camps to search for minerals. Noteworthy rock formations, like sulfur deposits or oil-bearing limestone, spotted from the air called for landings. As geologists walked and sampled, I either slept, read or explored the fascinating landscape on my own.

Many trips meant long hauls—the shortest measured 170 miles to a gas cache on Devon Island's Grinnell Peninsula. Fueling the Beaver CF-HEP became a persistent problem; however, installing an auxiliary tank involved major and costly modifications, a procedure Northward didn't consider worthwhile.

One of the first trips combined a training and sightseeing flight. We departed Resolute Bay not long after a final wisp of fog drifted south across Barrow Strait. Our destination happened to be a site I saw illustrated on an insurance company calendar many years before.

The flight to Beechey Island took less than thirty minutes. From fifteen miles back, we saw the flat top of the island. As we drew closer, vertical cliffs dropping sharply into the sea made me shudder as I thought of the men who first laid eyes on the place over 100 years ago. Destined to winter there, explorers searching for the Northwest Passage probably didn't realize at first that the island's north side was a sheltered shallow bay and gently sloping hill.

Sandy occupied the pilot's seat, which gave me a chance to look over the terrain. On top of the hill, a large white cross stood starkly against the dark wind-blown plateau. On the lower part, three graves lay near the remains of some kind of tumbled-down wooden structure. In later years, researchers excavated several graves and found the occupants preserved as if they died days before instead of more than a century ago.

Beechey didn't look frightening from the Beaver's comfortable cockpit, but Sandy couldn't locate a suitable landing area because of a strong crosswind. We banked back towards Cornwallis but decided to carry out a training exercise before returning to Resolute Bay.

Below, dozens of seals refused to leave their comfortable perches on the ice. We selected a beach ledge and after several

In 1963, the author bought a Piper J-3 thanks to the generosity of a Belleville, Ontario finance company when banks would not consider the $1,400 loan. For nearly three years, he flew the 65-h.p. airplane. Despite some foolish mistakes, he managed to survive the "apprenticeship" years.

This Luscombe trainer at Anglemont, British Columbia, was easily repaired by inserting a bolt in the broken landing gear, but fuel had drained leaving barely enough to return to Kelowna. The brief trip was one of the author's first out-of-province flights in 1966.

The Muskwa River area, southwest of Fort Nelson, was a customary fire patrol route. On the warm days it was refreshing to fly with the Piper PA-18's doors open.

Piper PA-18 CF-ONN provided many pleasurable hours on fire patrol in northeastern British Columbia. Here, at an airstrip in 1966 near the legendary Headless Valley of the Yukon, the airplane has its switches on for a quick getaway.

On the barrenlands west of Rankin Inlet, Northwest Territories, snow had melted from the land but in June 1967, the author landed regularly on frozen lakes. Here, biologists weigh caribou before the party's Inuit skinners butcher it.

At Rankin Inlet, Northwest Territories on June 3, 1967, the author and Cessna 180 CF-SLJ rendezvoused with the caribou survey party. Bound for the barrenlands south of Baker Lake, he spent several anxious hours lost above the Arctic whiteness.

The author ran a seaplane flight school in the late 1960s. With students such as Linda Sinclair of Parry Sound, Ontario, he logged hundreds of hours of exciting ski and float time.

In 1968, the author found himself based at Prince George, British Columbia, as a copilot on a Canso water bomber. Unfortunately, it rained nearly every day and few hours went into the logbook.

Fort Simpson in subzero weather during early 1974 was not a pleasant place. Captain and copilot shared the bone-numbing work. Here, the captain checks the Douglas DC-3's oil at daybreak.

In the MacKenzie Mountains near the Yukon border, Little Dall Lake served as an oil exploration camp in 1971. In late spring with winter snows gone, the frozen lake acted as an excellent obstacle-free runway for Northward Aviation's de Havilland Otter CF-CZP.

En route to Resolute Bay, Northwest Territories, on June 24, 1971, the author encountered discouraging words from a Northward Aviation's de Havilland Twin Otter pilot at Spence Bay. Despite warnings of rough territory and unpredictable weather, the author and instructor Sandy MacKenzie carry on.

Having read about Arctic Bay years before, the author visited this settlement on Admiralty Inlet and was not disappointed. He found the Inuit residents shy but friendly and always anxious to see the Orange Bird.

About 1400 to 1500 A.D., Thule culture Inuit used this Grinell Peninsula site on the northwest corner of Devon Island, 112 miles north of Resolute Bay, as a winter village.

En route to Clyde River on Baffin Island from Pangnirtung, the author marveled at the tremendous power of glacier ice. Almost inaccessible, these areas are nearly untouched by modern humans.

The author, marooned without any personal effects for more than a week in August, 1971, on dreary Ellef Ringnes Island due to poor takeoff conditions. The camp into which he had flown in gasoline and mail had run out of food.

The author's closest brush with total destruction occurred in this strange, highly modified, British Britten-Norman Trislander. A so-called expert in the passenger seat had almost decided to pull the propeller pitch controls backwards during a critical takeoff from Wawa, Ontario.

In 1973 the author had finally achieved his dream of flying the "Grand Old Lady." Part of the work involved hauling hay and fuel drums in the Douglas DC-3 to a private ranch west of the Alaska Highway.

Whaling by "Kabloona," or white men, had almost disappeared in the Baffin Island area by the late 1960s. However, in 1974 these enormous rendering pots at Pangnirtung were still filled with rancid animal blubber.

Today the author has a unique collection of Inuit art from communities in the Canadian Arctic. At Cape Dorset, west of Iqalit (formerly Frobisher Bay), this woman worked for hours in the Arctic breezes of Hudson Strait.

Throughout his travels, the author encountered Canadian Native peoples in the northern fringe of most provinces. The community of Summer Beaver northeast of Pickle Lake, Ontario, was typical of communities served by seaplanes and skiplanes.

Povungnituk, on eastern Hudson Bay, was one of the first Inuit settlements visited by the author when he became copilot on the Orange Bird in April, 1974.

The seal hunt at Sach's Harbour on Banks Island usually drew what few visitors there were to this vast island in the Beaufort Sea. In 1971, pelts could be bought in dried condition for less than five dollars.

Selecting a High Arctic landing surface could be made easier by observing vegetation. Plants growing closely together in green carpets usually spelled soft ground and danger. Widely spaced vegetation on southern Ellesmere Island indicated solid land.

Discarded fuel drums have always been a problem in the Canadian Arctic. At Leaf Bay in 1974, on Ungava Bay's west coast, Natives and non-Natives alike scattered these empty reminders of civilization everywhere.

Labrador, during the author's time in 1972, was known for constant fog, wind, and high tides. However, after storms passed and weather improved, villages like Hopedale on the Atlantic coast had a peculiar whitewashed beauty.

Labrador summers are blessed with plenty of sunshine. At Forteau on the Strait of Belle Isle near the Quebec Border, the author's Beaver kept company with a Labrador Airways' Otter during an overnight stop in July, 1972.

Small sea planes such as this Piper PA-11 at Kenora, Ontario, were docile and easy to fly; whether cruising on fire patrol, teaching nervous student pilots, or sideslipping into tiny ponds for water surveys.

In October, 1975, at Quebec's major airport, the nose wheel of the author's Aero Commander 680F collapsed. Other than a scraping of the belly and wheel-well doors, little damage occurred and the airplane returned to Mattagami, Quebec, the next day.

In August, 1972, the author accepted a brief contract with Les Ailes du Nord from Sept Îles. On this occasion, he was called upon to fly out a badly burned man as the fog dissipated enough to allow a landing and takeoff.

inspection passes above the gravel decided it might be safe. A few scattered plants suggested dry land; but this time Sandy flew lower than usual so that he could look up at the ledge. This way, he said, frost heaves or ditches showed up more clearly. We landed, looked for artifacts and took off again, finding nothing but a gigantic pile of rusty barrel hoops.

Every trip, Sandy drilled me repeatedly on how to determine direction. One involved a large, white book entitled, *Finding the Sun's True Bearing.* Using it became a simple matter of understanding Greenwich Mean Time, or GMT, and combining it with a few calculations. Its disadvantages lay in having to turn directly into sun before setting the directional gyro. Most pilots readjusted their headings every fifteen minutes. It worked well on clear days, but overcast skies forced pilots to count on map reading to keep them safe.

Next morning, the whoosh of the Nordair jet settling onto Resolute's gravel runway coincided with our first revenue trip. We planned to fly west to the approximate location of the Magnetic North Pole to drop off a three-barrel cache of aviation gasoline. Navigation to Bathurst Island with astronavigation and aeronautical charts proved simple. As days went on, I marveled at the accuracy of Arctic maps, in comparison with many I'd used in other areas of Canada.

For the first time since we began flying together, Sandy said "Good!" when I selected a spot on Bathurst without his assistance. Although he fidgeted in the ninety-degree crosswind along a 450-foot ridge, I saw his shoulders relax after touchdown. His patient instruction paid off as he watched me keep the tail up by application of brakes until the last second. We expected the ridge would be dry because of its height above the ice of Graham Moore Bay.

"Don't forget your sticks," he suggested as I slipped outside and walked ahead of the airplane. There, I placed a tiny stake wrapped with fluorescent pink tape to flutter in the wind.

We left the North Magnetic Pole and returned to Resolute Bay. After landing, we received word another trip would take us to Ellef Ringnes Island. Because of continuous daylight, we weren't rushed and took time to carefully plan the flight.

While waiting in the barracks, several pilots came in and described conditions at Devon Island. Fog persisted almost every warm day, they said, adding that cold-weather ice crystals kept visibility well below safe limits for days. Worse, landings on Ellef Ringnes could be extremely hazardous.

"You know why you're here, don't you?" said a pilot who flew a Twin Otter for Sun Oil Company. "There's a Door Knob (Dornier 28) upside down. It's still there beside the camp so God knows where you'll land."

We left Resolute Bay with every drop of gasoline the Beaver could hold. Behind us, roped-down cardboard cartons of steaks, soft drinks and more cases of vanilla extract than I'd ever seen made up the load. After flying directly north for over an hour, we began searching Devon Island's edges for a fuel cache dropped by Atlas Aviation's de Havilland Twin Otter. We topped our tanks and took off downhill.

To reach Ellef Ringnes Island, we could either go directly across sea ice to Cape Nathorst or remain close to land via Cornwall and Amund Ringnes Islands. We selected the land route and aimed for Cornwall Island's dark cliffs, barely visible across a bed of fog. At Amund Ringnes' Slime Peninsula, we turned left and located the shores of Ellef Ringnes. Sandy described the island as the world's biggest mud pie.

Our destination camp lay inland amid a group of hills so low they didn't appear on the map. As we repeatedly crisscrossed portions of the island, we couldn't locate our hungry customers.

No lakes existed on Ellef Ringnes, but several slowly flowing rivers emptied into the south-central coast areas. Braided channels sifted along flat-bottomed valleys and disappeared further inward toward the center. We saw no bird or animal life, and no empty fuel drum to indicate man had trekked the land.

A puff of white off to our right caught Sandy's attention. We flew toward it and were relieved to find a cluster of small, sparkling white tents surrounding a much larger one. A few yards away, the rotor blades of a Hiller helicopter slowly rotated to a standstill. About 100 yards from a gravel ridge, we saw the Door Knob upside down exactly in the middle of the only reasonable landing site. We had no choice but to land a few feet from the tents.

"This looks close," said Sandy, as I circled the tents and looked down at the men who came out to see the airplane. "We better switch seats."

"The hell with you," I argued. "The only way I'll learn to do this right is to do it."

Sandy sat and sulked. The best choice seemed to be a dry patch between the cook tent and the smaller residential area. It would be the tightest and shortest spot I'd ever landed an airplane.

Because of the proximity of nearby ridges, a steep approach was necessary. Besides, I justified to Sandy, we needed the steep angle to keep the tents in sight. The Beaver, a phenomenal performer at slow speed, held nicely at fifty miles per hour with full flap and plenty of engine power to keep the nose positioned.

"When you pull that power back, you better not sit there," Sandy warned. "It'll drop like a rock."

After gently easing the throttle off, I could see that the airplane was still about twenty feet higher than it should have been. Down it came and struck the ground a terrific blow. We careened back into the air, hanging unsteadily and shaking from the impact.

"Power! Power!" yelled Sandy.

The Beaver hit again but this time the bounce took us only half as high. As we sailed between the tents, a couple of panicked spectators ran as hastily as they could from the whirling propeller.

"You told me to bounce," I snapped, slamming the throttle wide open.

"Not that hard for Christ sake," Sandy bellowed. "Jee-zus, what the hell are you trying to do? For God's sake!"

Several more solid whacks followed; then, finally we stayed down. Groceries, gas cans and survival kit lay together in a jumbled heap on the aircraft's floor. As the propeller slowed to a stop, a half-dozen men rushed to the airplane to see if we were intact. Sandy, speechless now, removed himself from the right seat, stepped outside and examined the landing gear for damage.

Finding no wrinkles on the belly or near the wheel struts, we went to the cook tent and, in silence, enjoyed a steak dinner. As we ate, someone from the exploration crew brought in a soggy cardboard carton and mumbled something about eating scrambled eggs for a week.

After photographing the crashed Dornier on the hill, Sandy ordered me to fly twenty miles west toward the Danish Strait on the south end of Ellef Ringnes. He wanted to give me another lesson in Arctic flying lore. Airplanes rarely made ice landings in this area, but Sandy wanted to point out the differences between old ice and new. Old ice, the permanent pack that formed part of Prince Gustaf Adolph Sea, looked like a dirty, yellowish brown. The freshly frozen material was blue and reflected the dull, overcast light. Satisfied, we turned toward our fuel cache on Grinnell Peninsula and then returned to Resolute Bay.

That evening in the Arctic Circle Club, Sandy and I discussed my landing at Ellef Ringnes. It couldn't be classified as a gentle one, but conditions weren't easy. Unbeknownst to me, my performance had shown Sandy that, in spite of a few rough spots in my basic airplane handling, I was on my way to being considered safe in the High Arctic Islands.

Before returning to Edmonton, Sandy wanted another trip to be sure I could survive without him. A new camp would be installed on Melville Island with two airplanes flying in tents, food and exploration gear from Resolute. Working with us, a yellow and black Helio Courier equipped with smaller tires than our Beaver, would precede us to the site.

By deeming the situation "tight," for neither Sandy nor the Courier pilot had ever landed there, he elected himself as pilot. We removed everything inside except the pilot's seat. Tents flecked with ugly blotches of green mold went on top of plywood sheets, which would be later used as flooring.

Canned goods and rubber ground pads followed and we stacked rough-cut lumber lengths from front to back. More plywood sheeting lined the walls and in every corner we jammed bread, sleeping bags, toilet tissue, and canned butter. The only vacant space—a narrow horizontal slot toward the rear—would be my place this trip. Determined not to miss new territory, I squeezed myself in, but could only see through an opening above the Beaver's right front windshield.

According to a line drawn on my chart, the camp would be somewhere east of Hecla and Griper Bay. Map coloring showed many lowland creeks with occasional contour lines showing 950 feet. Blued creek symbols suggested small valleys and possible soft ground. The flight would take nearly two hours one way.

After takeoff from Resolute Bay, the weather across McDougall Sound, Bathurst Island and Byam Channel remained clear and smooth. My view of the outside world through the windshield stayed crystal blue and never varied. Finally, Sandy retarded the throttle and pumped down several degrees of flap.

As we circled left, low-level turbulence began shaking the airplane. Sandy looked his landing area over carefully. My ride became unpleasant as sharp ceiling vents dug painfully into my head and back. When the flaps came fully down, I knew we would be landing.

Suddenly, my micro-world changed from bright azure to solid brown as Sandy made his descending turn to final. As he power-approached, I pried a plywood section from the side window and peered outside. The aircraft flew between sand-topped hills and ridges, dangerously close to the Beaver's fragile wing tips. Worried, I pulled myself forward, ignoring the wooden slivers that pierced my forearms.

Frantically searching for some indication of where we were, I suddenly realized that Sandy was making a terrible mistake. Almost under the nose, a fast-flowing river with milky gray water rushed through the center of a narrow gorge. In seconds, we would collide with its rocky shoreline. From my horizontal position near the ceiling, I could do nothing except wait and hope my injuries would be minor.

We touched down on the near shore, lurched to the right and skipped. For an instant, the ludicrous vision of the Beaver upside down, sliding and smashing through a wall of water flashed through my mind. Either I'd be flung outside like a Zulu spear and pulverized against a rock or worse, I'd suffocate as fuel drums and other freight crushed the dying breath from my pinioned body.

149

White spray flew up over the huge, black nose and blurred my forward view. We shot across the river and careened onto the other side to dry land, and stopped with a screech of metal brakes. Sandy cut the switches. Momentarily paralyzed, I lay on my stomach, quivering and shaking at our escape from what had really seemed like a last trip.

Another trick: braided gravel streams were usually shallow and solid enough for big-wheeled Beavers. Sandy, who neglected to tell me about this little tidbit of Arctic lore in our preflight briefing, acknowledged that this piece of Melville Island wasn't for me. Had I landed there with my lack of experience, he'd have recommended to our Edmonton office that I finish my summer back in God-forsaken Norman Wells.

After unloading, we stopped for a quick cup of coffee brewed over a kerosene stove. I noticed Sandy eyeing the strings of toilet paper thrown out by the Helio Courier pilot. Most of it landed clear of the water and separated into long lengths.

"Laddie, you'd better roll that up. We can use it again," said the Scotsman. As his apprentice, I dutifully obeyed.

We finished an uneventful, fogless return trip to Resolute Bay. Thankful to be intact, I generously volunteered to buy several rounds of beer that night, a practiced habit which in future years served me well as a civil servant.

My first evening at the celebrated Arctic Circle Club was Sandy's last before his return to Yellowknife. The experience proved a good example of how attitudes change. The longer anybody works away from civilization, the more their perceptions of the opposite gender alter.

Not many women lived in Resolute. The few who did, stayed only a short time as school teachers or social workers in the nearby Inuit village. Nurses and cooks for oil camps in the barrenlands passed through, or sometimes pilots and mechanics brought their wives or girlfriends north for a visit.

As we entered the dimly lit room, we saw six men with hundreds of empty beer cans at their table. In the center of this happy group sat a solitary white woman with a cigarette planted in her mouth. She finished her drink and crushed the can between her fingers.

"Nurse," whispered Sandy.

I looked again and saw a face so heavily jowled that the weight of her cheeks created soggy, red-veined pouches beneath her eyes. Dark brown furrows surrounded her nose and a mismatched pair of pursed, cracked lips. Short, oily hair supported a dirty gray cap.

Her suitors plied her with rounds of drinks. At midnight, she drew on a pair of shabby running shoes, raised herself from the chair and made the floor boards squeak as if she had stepped on a nest of helpless house mice.

She reached for the nearest male and as she did she revealed a mass of curly brown hair under an armpit. With one hand, she deftly turned the peak of his helicopter hat upwards. Seconds later, this northern belle trundled away arm-in-arm with a smiling, love-starved companion for the evening.

The next afternoon, a drama took place over the airwaves. An oil company cook fell at Vanier Point and became paralyzed from the waist down. His work mates didn't dare move him while a plaintive voice on HF begged for a doctor and a medevac. In Resolute, we heard another airline broadcast that an airplane would be dispatched right away. No doctors were stationed in Resolute Bay but they would contact the only available nurse.

Radio chatter across the north stopped and everyone on Cornwallis Island awaited the departure of a medevac de Havilland Twin Otter. Before long, the dispatcher returned and, in a bitter tone said, the nurse refused to go.

I thought of the woman at the Arctic Circle Club the previous evening as the Vanier Point voice pleaded for help. A fog bank north of his island held off all day but a slight change in wind direction could quickly lower visibility below flyable limits.

At the end of a long silence, a crisp, professional voice of an overflying corporate pilot advised Vanier Point he'd overheard and would divert for landing. The emergency ended for an injured cook, but not another word broke the quiet for thirty minutes. That night, "Blocks-the-Sun" sat alone in the Arctic Circle Club.

As Sandy entered the Boeing 737 the next morning, a manager from an exploration company that had contracted the Bea-

151

ver, came down the big jet's stairs. Surprised that no authorization had arrived to establish gas caches, he told me to go to work. My job now entailed placing as many drums as possible, where they could be used later.

While waiting for assignments, I kept busy with non-flying duties. De Havilland Beaver CF-HEP was mine for the balance of the season and revenue flying time would soon come rolling in. Besides keeping it fully fueled, I made certain it carried extra High-Arctic equipment. Stored in the belly above the removable camera hatch, an extensive survival kit contained enough food to last for weeks. A sixty-pound life raft barely fitted into the baggage compartment, and on both sides, rags, oil cans, and ropes prevented it from shifting.

I swept the Beaver's interior and kept the airplane spotless. Two ten-gallon drums called "JICs" (or "Just-In-Case") rested behind the pilot's seat every flight. As weeks went on and hours increased, these little kegs often brought CF-HEP home.

After several days of Utopian weather, Art the dispatcher called me into his office. An oil company wanted a trip to Ellesmere Island, he told me. A Door Knob had attempted the flight but its pilot couldn't land because of his airplane's small standard wheels and the moist, muddy morass below.

"Chickenshit," Art sneered, as he leaned back in his chair and turned down the volume of his tape deck. His vantage point 260 miles from an unknown piece of ground on Ellesmere made me wonder who he was to question an experienced pilot's decision.

Recently retired from the Canadian Armed Forces as a cafeteria cook, Art had been in Resolute only a short time. One evening, in one of his back-slapping intoxicated binges, he revealed some reasons for his deep-seated hatred of pilots. It seemed his chief Air Force responsibility had involved meal preparation for aircrew who often expected him to cook after regular working hours. Now endowed with authority for the first time in his life, he despised anyone associated with aircraft, particularly those who flew them.

Art openly disparaged the Dornier pilot with remarks about babysitting the "fly boy." His slurs often extended to other pilots who flew the limited Piper PA-18 Super Cubs or awkward de Havilland Otters. He couldn't admit these people were highly experienced masters of the art of Arctic flying who landed where no human beings had walked before.

Many died in the north. In fact, a single Otter collided with an island not far from Resolute during my assignment there. The pilot became nothing more than a scorch mark on the side of a cliff and his death became a reminder that the work we did every day came with its own distinctive hazards.

During my early days at Resolute Bay, high-time pilots warned me that Ellesmere Island, the most northerly in the Arctic Archipelago, was sometimes unapproachable due to vicious weather. Polar winds funneled through Peary Channel and Massey Sound, and smashed against upthrusting mountains and downsloping glaciers. Steep-sided fjords and cliffs captured gales and twisted them into severe, metal-bending turbulence. In summer, fog formed rapidly. In spring and winter, continual white-out conditions reigned. Pilots who knew the island avoided Ellesmere when they could, but exploration camps and research parties working there needed their support.

With grocery boxes crammed to the ceiling, I left the comfort of Resolute in clear weather. Unlimited skies and visibility lasted until Bear Bay, a small pocket of Devon Island where it angled to form the Grinnell Peninsula. The Beaver did well until 8,000 feet, when thin air caused it to run out of throttle.

As North Kent Island slid under my finger on the map, I did one last astrocompass calculation as the clouds above mighty Ellesmere began forming an undercast to the island's southern edges. Open water surrounding North Kent apparently remained year-round because of perpetual winds and constant, low-level turbulence. On this day, from my perch over a mile high, I saw only glassy water. In the distance, I spotted a gigantic ice cap with a high point shown on the chart as 7,700 feet. The geologists in Bauman Fjord radioed reports of high wind and good visibility underneath the cloud.

Descending to stay in sight of the surface for easier map reading, I cruised at 1,000 feet above Norwegian Bay. Little snow remained in the valley. Further on, winds created miniature dust storms. The terrain resembled a bizarre moonscape under the ominous gray cloud cover as Hoved Island passed behind the Beaver's tail. Farther inland, as I map read carefully toward Bauman Fjord, whirling snow squalls whitened the braided streams. Two frantically waving human figures stood on the crest of a hill.

Another pilot had dropped the geologists in separate camps of two men each. A pre-positioned gas cache on a level plain nearby lessened my worries about return fuel. Circling the men became hazardous in the turbulence and gusts prevented anything other than a marginal landing in a howling crosswind.

A half-mile away, a piece of flat ground into wind seemed safer. Lack of sunlight and shadows made aerial inspection difficult but the plants looked nicely spaced. Sandy taught me well, I hoped.

With full flap and minimum forward speed, the Beaver's soft balloon tires brushed the surface. Suddenly, the left wing dipped, then angled abruptly skyward and down again, sharply enough to jolt the astrocompass from its mount. The nose plunged forward as I leveled off and collided with several hard objects before stopping.

The aircraft tilted in a frightening way with one wing tip less than three feet from masses of large, brown lumps of solid ground. As I shut off the magneto switches and retrieved my glasses from under the rudder pedals, I opened the door. Beneath the Beaver's wheels, the entire area looked like a tray of chocolate doughnuts turned side by side.

I had landed on "niggerheads," an unpleasant term applied to huge earth hummocks created by centuries of alternate freezing and thawing. Some were two feet high and all showed large, deep gaps between them, extending toward the banks of a nearby braided stream. If the Doorknob had touched its smaller wheels here, it would have been destroyed.

Because it was too rough to taxi, I walked the mile and a half to where the geologists camped. A rapidly flowing meltwater river the color of turquoise separated us as I shouted against the wind and rushing water. They would have to wait until the gale abated to allow a landing closer to their camp. With little else to

154

do, I walked back, climbed inside the Beaver and unloaded freight to make room to sleep on the hard, bakelite floor. So far, Ellesmere Island welcomed me with dangerous ground, low cloud and gusty winds.

Silence woke me. The wind had died to only enough to ripple the ribbons on my wooden takeoff markers beside the Beaver's wheels. Tendrils of feathery cirrus replaced the gloom-laden clouds. I glanced outside and saw an array of flowering plants for the first time since my hasty arrival. Afternoon warmth sent their fragrances wafting peacefully into the airplane's oily cockpit. Listening carefully, I heard flowing streams of glacial runoff sending rippling sounds across the tundra.

The Pratt and Whitney engine started smoothly. I smashed along the rutted ground and managed to get the Beaver airborne. As the speed increased, I reduced flap to climb position and pointed the nose above the level of the highest hill. The geology crew waited anxiously only a few minutes away, but I intended to take some time to absorb the beauty of Ellesmere Island.

On both sides of the airplane, sheer-sided slopes rose up from the ocean. Beyond them to the east, a gigantic white-topped glacier glimmered in the distance. Narrow valleys running in strings from north to south were mosaics of multicolored surfaces. Red, yellow and pink sandstone blended with gray, meandering channels of water oozing from gaps in brightly polished rock walls.

I saw several shades of ice, as black-edged blocks dropped from glaciers and aquamarine, snow-speckled ice floes drifted in Bauman Fjord's dark waters. Shaded, bright ivory blobs of ice protected from the bay, exposed their lacy edges shyly as swan-like patches of mist formed and vanished quickly.

British Columbia was magnificent; Northern Ontario's forests were colorful; the southern Arctic had its own distinctive beauty; but Ellesmere, with fjords, hills, and valleys, was the most breathtaking stretch of scenery I had ever seen. Circling, it occurred to me that if anyone ever gazed at John Gillespie Magee's "high untrespassed sanctity of space," I just did. Fearsome Ellesmere Island offered me its gentle side.

My private showing ended, I drifted down toward the impatient geologists. The landing taught me that the niggerheads hadn't softened during my escape into the sky as the Beaver crashed from one to the other.

While I shuttled people back and forth from Bauman Fjord to another flat area west of Vendome Fjord, I noticed two more geologists in a dried river bed. For touchdown space, their location looked to be not much more than 600 feet in length and surrounded by sloping terrain.

With the first group safely relocated and already ripping the Arctic earth with their hammers and picks, I flew up the river to finish with the remaining two men. As expected, their spot proved to be one of the worst for landing. Having been placed there by helicopter, no one looked far enough ahead to consider that a fixed-wing airplane would do the pickup. The boulders were massive and too numerous to move. Each run on the river bed required several zigzags with every angle accented by hard braking. Once airborne, the Beaver needed steep climbs followed by sharp left turns to clear the slope.

The party didn't have much gear but little as it was, I needed several trips with only 200 pounds each to do the job. They grumbled about the extra time and meager loads. With twenty-four hour daylight and a valuable airplane to consider, I didn't have any reason to rush. Each landing turned into a hit-hard-slam-the-brakes-on-stop-you-bugger ordeal.

Once I overran the end of my safe area into a cluster of boulders, but the balloon tires prevented any damage. At the drop-off point, the geologists threw their equipment outside while I held brakes and controls in a gale. On takeoff with an empty cabin, the Beaver rolled about forty feet before flying.

Most field groups working in the barrenlands assigned someone to dig a latrine. The parties generally brought a gadget resembling a living room divider to jam into the turf for privacy. As I taxied in with the final load, I noticed one man select a roll of toilet tissue and walk away from the tent.

My assignment completed, I turned the Beaver into wind for takeoff and noted the geologist crouching with his back toward the airplane. The wind briskly blew the divider flat upon the

156

tundra floor exposing the poor fellow with his pants down below his knees.

With nothing else to do but wait until he finished, I made myself comfortable while the engine idled. As the wind increased and rocked the Beaver's wings, it blew the geologist's tissue out of reach. Stretching his short arms, he forgot about the jeans around his ankles and fell heavily on his face. The wind teased him a little more as he slowly regained his balance. Without pulling up his pants, he began chasing the elusive paper by shuffling one foot in front of the other.

Down he went for the second time. Upright again—this time a little dazed from the blow—he switched to a bunny hop. His inability to crest a small pothole brought him back to earth with a thud I felt all the way to the airplane. Finally, raising himself on the edge of a frost heave, he gave one mighty leap and launched himself toward the roving toilet paper.

Successful at last, he completed the job, buckled his pants and walked briskly back to camp. I shall always remember the startling contrast between his pale pink bottom and the dark valley sides as he rose and fell across the tundra. When I eased in the Beaver's throttle for takeoff, I nearly ran into a fuel drum, unseen because of tears of laughter.

Safely in the air, I pointed the Beaver's round nose south, toward a fuel cache. In a few minutes, a large, dark musk-ox appeared on a ridge above me. I climbed a little and circled to watch him follow the airplane. I glanced back and saw him pawing the surface, sending clouds of dust swirling in the wind. Probably ostracized from his kind I felt sorry for him.

Moments later, I landed beside a row of red fuel barrels. After gouging several fingers opening them under the surveillance of a pair of white Arctic hares, I filled the belly tanks. During my first few weeks working from Resolute Bay, no amount of physical effort could enable me to stand these 400-pound fuel drums upright. Now, after moving hundreds of them, my body had become conditioned to the dangerous task.

With enough fuel for Resolute Bay, I departed. I stopped briefly at a nearby Arco Oil exploration camp. Someone in Resolute had asked me to drop off a small bag of mail after completing the camp moves. Quickly, I handed it out the door and took off southwest again. Looking ahead, I predicted that it wouldn't be long before some drastic weather changes occurred. Hopefully, the Beaver could take me home before storms swept in and forced me down.

Flying through the center of a gigantic fjord led to another stretch of ice and water. I tracked across a point where a peninsula jutted from the lower part of Ellesmere Island. Afraid to divert south across an ice cap to my left, I selected another valley as snow showers splatted against the windscreen. Turbulence increased to the point where hanging onto the control wheel with both hands became necessary.

After thirty minutes of struggling, I realized pushing further on would be dangerous and decided to wait for better weather. Selecting a flat area straight ahead, I approached nose high and throttled back, when the Beaver began sinking rapidly beneath the plateau lip. Despite full engine power, it continued downward, caught in a powerful flow. In seconds, I knew the airplane would smash into the ground like a tomato dropped from a high rise.

Easing left, I lowered the nose to pick up flying speed. Nearly in control again, I ruddered around and turned back toward Bauman Fjord, where I thought the weather would still be safe. No longer able to hold the map, I followed the river bed as the snowstorm increased. In fifteen minutes, the Beaver came out of the gorge and the blue tents of the American Arco camp appeared directly in front of the windshield.

The crew turned out to be hospitable. They let me use an empty tent and within minutes, my sleeping bag covered the floor. For three days, the airplane didn't move.

The camp maintained radio contact with Resolute Bay. While I'd been busy attempting to delay a brush with a canyon wall, Resolute's weather deteriorated to 400-foot ceilings with winds gusting to fifty knots. Now on Vendome Fjord, anyone who dared peek outside a tent flap found their nose covered in snow. When not wrapped warmly in a sleeping bag, I ventured to the cook tent to enjoy freshly baked apple pie.

Finally, a geologist from Texas announced that someone in

their camp saw a patch of blue sky. Without rolling up my sleeping bag, I threw it into the Beaver and blasted off for Resolute Bay. Halfway there, detours forced me west of an ice cap on Devon Island. At Wellington Channel, the last gap of water to cross before Cornwallis, the skies cleared and stayed that way until I was nearly home. Resolute still reported some fog but, by following shorelines, I made it into the airport.

To my consternation, the booking sheet showed another trip to Ellesmere near the spot that had held me captive for three days. During the entire flight, the same cloud, snow, and wind that hindered the previous trip still threatened my Beaver. After dropping groceries at three camps near Vendome Fjord, I made it back safely to base.

In the barracks, Art announced another charter to Ellef Ringnes Island. An insurance adjuster needed a Beaver to help investigate and photograph the upside down Door Knob. Fresh from Montreal, this character's expensive suit, shiny leather shoes and stylish topcoat looked out of place in Resolute's mud and gravel. He insisted on riding "as is" but reluctantly took my advice about borrowing a sleeping bag. He adamantly refused to leave his electric razor.

With a full load of gas, freight and mail, we left Resolute's 6,500-foot runway and tracked north to the fuel cache at Cape Ogle on the Grinnell Peninsula. Weather reports for Ellef Ringnes Island were usually scarce, but Isaachsen, not far from the flipped Door Knob, reported lower ceilings.

Another tribe of geologists who had been supported by the Dornier lived in the same tents Sandy and I visited once before. Their radio comments, "not bad, clearing," indicated the trip would likely be an easy one. With my tattered maps and a half-dozen astrocompass shots, we picked our way northward.

At Cape Ogle, six orange drums told us other aircraft had landed there before. Users turned their empties upside down according to unwritten Arctic law. Since three were full, we landed. Soon, with tanks topped again, we took off and aimed west of Table Island, a 650-foot lump protruding from Belcher Channel.

Ceilings ahead were lowering in spite of favorable weather

reports from camp. Before leaving the sunlight, I carefully took one more astrocompass shot and reset the directional gyro. Believing that Ellef Ringnes Island stayed in the clear, I decided a shortcut would save time. Besides, my passenger had used all of the Beaver's sick bags.

Past Table Island, we dropped below an encroaching rim of cloud and planned a heading for seventy miles above sea ice toward Hassel Sound. Ellef Ringnes Island, named after a Norwegian brewer, consisted of over 4,000 square miles of complex topography and shoreline with several volcanic domes of sulfur. A geologist told me later that surveyors measured one dome as high as 1,000 feet above sea level. With a Beaver, we couldn't miss finding the shoreline.

As we plodded onward, weather on all sides began deteriorating rapidly until nothing but undulating fields of car-size blocks of ice passed closely under the wheels. The adjuster stopped chattering and stared straight ahead as his briefcase slid from his lap and struck the metal floor. As I adjusted carburetor heat, the new noises made his eyes open further.

Quarter-sized snowflakes slammed silently against the Beaver's windshield. Pausing, they clung nervously to the plexiglass, then were swept swiftly away. Peering carefully through the partially opened side windows, lest I freeze my face off, I saw white slush forming on the glistening tundra tires and out along the wings. It stayed there, forming hard, draggy lumps slowing us until full throttle barely held the airplane above the sea ice.

"Good here. Keep coming. Blue sky now."

The voice, distorted in the headset pressing painfully upon my ears, came from the camp. Out of sight of land now, I held a heading above the turquoise ice and meltwater of Hassel Sound. More favorable weather reports flowed in. Greatly encouraged and anxious to get safely down, I kept pushing deeper and deeper onward. Ellef Ringnes had to be coming up on the nose soon.

Increasing fog and diminishing airspeed finally left me with no other choice. Carefully, I skidded the de Havilland Beaver slowly around to a reciprocal heading and hoped to find a piece of land. Eventually, Devon's Island's precipitous cliffs materialized through the gray mist and falling snow. Still nothing. No flat areas anywhere nor upturned fuel drums indicated a landing spot. With a slight touch of flap, we flew below the hills, searching until a tiny valley opening appeared off to our right.

Approaching an incline, I pumped down landing flap quickly and reduced engine power until the poor Beaver fell out of the sky. Its big wheels slammed onto a gravelly upslope and bounced us back into the air. We struck again and rolled several lengths of the airplane before stopping.

"God," the adjuster exclaimed, his first word since we lost sight of land.

I stepped outside and looked the airplane over. It looked undamaged but the steel disc brakes had cracked. As my passenger opened his door and climbed outside, more fog and wet snow enveloped us. Not a sign of life anywhere. Birds and seals had abandoned the place long ago. For now, we were stranded. In the days ahead, I came to know this rocky patch intimately.

I had been suckered. Weather at the camp on Ellef Ringnes couldn't possibly be clear skies and puffy clouds.

During the seventy-two hours we spent looking at each other, the insurance adjuster complained about my cooking. Odors emanated from his borrowed sleeping bag. When not talking, he snored. I had no escape.

Fortunately, a radio operator at an oil camp not far from Resolute Bay passed on my predicament to the dispatcher. At least base would be informed of our predicament. After nonstop fog and snow, I finally saw a slight break in cloud. I started the Beaver and followed a shaft of sunlight to blue sky. An estimated heading above cloud led us close to Resolute. When we landed, I learned that Art had not passed on the message concerning my position. No one knew where we were for three days.

The trip turned out to be a frustrating, expensive, fuel-consuming waste of time. Although he never saw it, the adjuster declared the Door Knob a write-off. Many years later, I learned someone salvaged and rebuilt the expensive, short-lived German import. The freight in my Beaver remained aboard until a window of sunshine broke through the clouds.

Dispatched again to Ellef Ringnes Island, I retraced the route. Before long, I landed in camp but the excellent weather did not hold. Clouds developed and dropped down so low we could barely see from one tent to the next. Trapped for over a week, I lacked clean underwear, toothbrush, soap or razor.

As the days passed, a student geologist chatted enthusiastically about airplanes and future flying lessons. Over time, we became friends. He told me it was his voice I had heard during those terrifying moments close to the sea ice. The weather, he said, hadn't been flyable after all.

"You couldn't see the top of that hill," he admitted, pointing to a low knoll outside the tent flap.

For a few moments, I reflected on how close we came to scattering a de Havilland Beaver and two people on the permanent ice of Hassel Sound. I bit my lip, sipped my soup and waited for my anger to abate. After a suitable pause, I asked politely of my new friend, "Why, then, did you tell me to keep coming?"

He explained. During that day the camp boss stood impatiently behind him. Slightly "bushed" and afflicted with a trace of cabin fever, he snapped instructions at the student geologist.

"Tell him it's good, he's got the mail."

As the week passed, the camp began running out of food. For some reason, many cases of chocolate bars had been flown in weeks before. With meat and vegetables severely rationed now, since weather showed no improvement, we enjoyed nearly unlimited access to chocolate bars and soft drinks.

By the time a pile of pocket novels accumulated beside my sleeping bag, sunlight finally returned and dried the canvas tents. After providing the party chief with a brief lesson concerning intentional misleading of Arctic pilots, I departed southbound for Resolute Bay. Over the next few weeks, I returned to the camp several times on supply flights. Curiously, someone forgot to load his mail every flight.

In my absence, Northward Aviation accepted a contract with the Chevron Oil Company to explore the oil-bearing possibilities of Banks Island. Because of the tremendous distance west from Resolute, a chartered Twin Otter went ahead to establish two fuel caches. Finding them later took considerable searching, despite the marks penciled on my map by the Atlas Aviation pilot.

Normally, air regulations didn't permit the Beaver's gross

takeoff weight to exceed 5,100 pounds. This trip would keep us away from Resolute for a week, perhaps two. Mechanic, a geologist's large, red tool box, personal gear, a forty-five-gallon drum of aviation gasoline, full gas tanks and the JICs weighed nearly 2000 pounds. In spite of the heavy load, Beaver CF-HEP left the runway easily.

Our first landing took us across the now-familiar Byam Channel between Cornwallis and Bathurst Islands. With every available cubic inch in the airplane crammed with supplies and exploration equipment, it was an uncomfortable ride. On Melville Island, we began searching for Tingmisut Lake, a small body of water where the Twin Otter pilot placed some gasoline drums.

The Atlas pilot told us a Beaver, with its exceptional short landing and takeoff capabilities, wouldn't have a problem landing at the fuel cache. Unconcerned, we crossed Weatherall Bay, spotted a flash of red drums on a distant hill and circled them for twenty minutes. I couldn't understand how an experienced Twin Otter pilot believed that landing on a narrow pinnacle of a hill over 500 feet high would be easy with our overloaded airplane.

With no alternative—we needed that fuel—we approached the ridge at ninety degrees. Hopefully, we could land on the downward slope and blast our way upwards to park on the crest. Frost ditches and boulders everywhere made me quite uneasy. With the airplane pointed at the hill, I pulled the control wheel back to plant the tires down.

Excessive speed and overzealous throttle brought us to the top of the ridge, but much too quickly. I couldn't stop the Beaver from plunging down the other side. Tingmisut Lake waited at the bottom so I slammed my left foot hard upon the brake to pivot the Beaver around. The downward momentum somehow converted to an upward force and the airplane climbed the hill. We stopped on top.

We hand-pumped the bellies full. I realized why the Twin Otter pilot didn't think his choice of fuel cache location was a poor one. For him, it was easy. Empty, light on fuel and with two powerful turbine engines, he would have been airborne in a few seconds. On landing, full reverse thrust probably stopped him in his tracks.

Leaving from the same area used for landing was out of the question. Our overloaded, fully fueled Beaver would never make it into the air before ploughing into Tingmisut Lake. Although ice-free in July, the water on Melville Island was likely to be deadly cold. Our only escape route meant a rough, uphill taxi along the humpbacked ridge. The run would have to be down-wind and downhill. Looking out over the nose, I saw the fuel drums. The mechanic pointed out another knoll we needed to clear.

Throttle open, brakes off, we began rolling down the slope, but the tail took an extraordinarily long time to rise. Past the fuel drums, the Beaver stayed on the ground. Not a flicker showed on the airspeed indicator needle. Close to the edge of the gully, the needle finally moved to 55 mph, barely enough to fly with the load we carried. At the last instant, the Beaver sailed off the cliff edge. Instead of going up, we plummeted down. I slammed the throttle as far ahead as it would go.

We continued falling until 65 mph showed on the airspeed indicator. As we waited, the nose slowly started to rise. The knoll ahead seemed to be at an even level with the airplane and it looked as if we wouldn't clear it.

We hit.

The balloon tires bounced us over the top. I looked back and saw a cloud of dust where we touched the tundra.

We flew on, map-reading from Sabine Bay toward our next gas cache 121 miles away. I swore if I ever returned to Resolute Bay, a talk with the Twin Otter pilot would be the first thing on my agenda.

Confident our escape from Tingmisut Lake would be a once-in-a-lifetime thrill, I relaxed and began enjoying Melville Island. With a land area of almost 14,500 square miles, the island had much to offer in the way of breathtaking, uninhabited scenery.

Hills up to 2,500 feet appeared on the horizon. Many short, narrow beaches lined the bay sides and channels wherever we looked. Our next stop would be at Cape James Ross on the west tip of the Dundas Peninsula. After that, I didn't look forward to crossing the sixty miles of ice floes in McLure Strait.

Judging by the contours and coloring on the aeronautical chart draped across the Beaver's control wheel, it appeared our next landing shouldn't give us any trouble. Again, we needed the stop since without the extra fuel, our chances of making it to Sach's Harbor were slim. As the Cape James Ross coastline came into view, we noticed fewer pebble beaches along the way. Rock-littered plateaus with steep, sharp cliffs ended abruptly in the ice of Liddon Gulf. Evidently the Twin Otter pilot might have placed the cache on another headland after all.

Sure enough, ninety minutes after our narrow escape back at Tingmisut Lake, I spotted two fuel drums on the top of another hill. Immense gray boulders lay everywhere. None of us could see a rock-free, level patch of ground anywhere. We picked out an area with the smallest stones.

A hard landing followed with enough brake to nearly stand the Beaver on its nose. Once down, I couldn't see any way of escaping. Potholes, rocks and upheaved lumps of earth everywhere hindered a clear takeoff run. Worse, the wind dropped as we pumped fuel into the airplane. Finally, we left everything we could behind, including two five-gallon pails of oil, and climbed back into the cockpit.

The engine started after the second swing of the propeller and we began a rough taxi to get as far away from the cliff edge as possible. Each second we accelerated on the takeoff run, I lost forward momentum because I had to tramp hard on a rudder pedal to avoid a boulder. Past the drums, I weaved and jerked in a crazy, zigzag pattern to avoid striking something. Even so, the soft rubber tires smacked into stones. One huge, lichen-covered monster appeared from nowhere. As I yanked the throttle back and pushed on brake, the Beaver began swinging out of control to the left. By slamming the opposite brake, we straightened out, but had to stop.

Disgusted, I taxied back for another try. A second near-disastrous groundloop near the empty barrels almost ended our expedition. Another throttle back and dance on the brakes stopped us. I shut the engine down and stepped outside to reconsider.

I saw no alternative but a downhill takeoff. This time, the grade was the steepest I'd ever seen. At least the distance looked slightly longer than the two attempted runs. If we made it to the ledge, we could catapult off the brim to pick up speed in the plunge toward the ice.

I asked the mechanic to ease the throttle gently forward, since I wanted to keep both hands on the control wheel. We accelerated a little quicker but the ride turned out to be the roughest in my High Arctic career. We careened past Honda-size boulders and bounced across ditches deep enough to snag a Jeep. As the airplane careened off the cliff, the engineer slammed the throttle as far as it would go. With engine badly over-boosted and propeller flashing at maximum revolutions per minute, we dropped toward Amundsen Gulf.

The Beaver's airspeed needle fluttered at 65 mph, controls became responsive and I eased the nose gently upward. We began climbing.

Banks Island lay sixty miles away. Already, a layer of fog had formed above the ice.

After more than three hours of steady, on-track flying, we located the sandy runway of Sach's Harbour and landed. Beside the airstrip, two more geologists from Chevron waited. One recently immigrated from Lithuania and the other's old-country accent betrayed him as a Welshman. With our Spanish geologist from Resolute and a Canadian pilot and mechanic, we made up an international crew. Only one rock pounder, as we called geologists, had experienced the High Arctic before.

Next morning, our contractor told us we wouldn't be flying for some time. A clerk somewhere within their oil corporation overlooked obtaining operating permits. Banks Island was a protective wildlife sanctuary, named after the ship "Mary Sachs" of a 1913 Canadian Arctic Expedition.

Our client arranged housing in a row of tracked Nodwell terrain vehicles. Occupied by a seismic crew and an excellent cook, the rooms and food on these massive vehicles turned out to be excellent.

Banks Island was a place of startling contrast. Here, grass grew nearly ankle-high. Because of its proximity to open seas, a mean July temperature of almost 9 C seemed mild. Later our first trip took us a few miles north of the coast into white fox country. Several times, we noticed fawn-colored dots in the dark green carpet below. For several days, we guessed them to be nesting geese, but we soon learned they were dead caribou. The previous winter, over 3,000 of these spindly animals suffered a catastrophic natural die-off.

In my off time, I walked the shorelines along both sides of Sach's Harbor. On a deserted stretch of beach three miles from the settlement, I came across a slowly decaying seal someone had killed. The thick, white layer of yellowish blubber that once kept the animal insulated from Amundsen Gulf lay exposed. Further on, a gigantic whale jawbone protruded from a patch of sand. Bleached dry at one end, tiny pieces of blackened flesh at the other, I had no idea how long ago the creature perished.

After four restful days in Sach's Harbor, our permit came in the form of a radiogram. We loaded the Beaver with three, forty-five-gallon drums of fuel for an exploration base 155 miles north. Steady light rain hampered navigation. Few landmarks appeared on the map but every river bend, pond or ridge had been accurately drawn. When we arrived near the camp, a distinctive lake nearby confused us. After a ten-minute search, I realized the map makers didn't miss after all—a careless lead pencil smudge hid the tiny piece of water.

The feather-light landing that evening back at Sach's Harbor felt good. As I taxied toward the Nodwells, the geologists announced another fuel haul would be needed the next day. Better yet, they wanted to explore the island's southern part, where locals reported coal seams breaking through a row of cliffs.

Early next morning, we departed for a likely looking, contoured area forty miles southeast along the shoreline of Thesiger Bay. After a low reconnaissance, the geologists selected the highest hill to start their mineral search. I examined the spot carefully and landed without damage. While I entered the flight in the airplane logbook, the passengers slipped outside and soon disappeared. For several hours, I relished the time alone.

Slipping my ballpoint pen into the door pocket, I looked outside over the Beaver's nose. As far as I could see in the unscattered dustless light, millions of multi-colored plants covered the meadows and tundra. Stepping down from the cockpit, I instinctively raised my feet to prevent crushing thousands of delicate wild-flower petals.

Conspicuous in their whiteness, dots of Arctic cotton grass towered above brown-armed saxifrage ending in bright violet flowers. Sweet green coltsfoot and mountain sorrel climbed low ridges. Not far away, a deeply eroded gully in a plateau caught my attention. Wandering closer and climbing across some rocks, I noticed a remarkable increase in temperature from the sun-warmed banks of stone.

Yellow poppies twisted out of endless boulder fields. Multitudes of butterflies and tiny bumble bees flitted by. Even the rocks added to the beauty in this Banks Island panorama. Yellow feldspars, white quartz, and dark blue streaks of sodalite-like material caught the summer light and turned it into shimmering waves.

I saw the geologists approaching. Before leaving, they decided to take a brief aerial tour of Dundas Heights. Soon we looked down on pillars, tables, and cliff sides. Yellow and red sandstones sparkled along the shoreline. At one point, the Spanish geologist gestured toward gigantic coal seams in shades of black, brown, and gray. Along the pebbly beaches, we saw whalebone glistening with fat, in spite of decades of exposure to the elements.

Several days later, our enchantment with working on Banks Island began fading as the geologists questioned my refusals to land anywhere they pointed their ballpoint pens. They wondered at my concern for running out of fuel because I rarely went anywhere without full tanks and my JICs.

Worse, they didn't understand that single-engine airplanes cannot legally fly out of sight of ground. Fog prevented early-morning flying and posed constant threats to our return once we left the airstrip.

Some exploration runs took us to the extreme top of Banks Island to a place called Mercy Bay. For more than four hours, the geologists poked the tundra and smashed rocks while I strolled out of sight from them. Not far from the Beaver, I came across the exact spot where Captain Robert McLure abandoned his 450-ton, copper-sheathed ship and came ashore in 1853. I had read a copy of his diary and had been tracing his path across the Arctic as I went. On the beaches, I discovered white crystalline sands and plucked a stick of lignite from a crumbling bank.

Cautiously picking my way across piles of rocks and avoiding millions of tiny, sun-tracking plants, a noise nearby broke the windless silence. A bull caribou stood motionless not fifteen yards away. Evidently, no human being had ever crossed his path and it seemed as though he couldn't grasp the idea of a two-legged creature. Confused, he looked right, then left, then back at me. He shook his massive antlers several times, like he couldn't believe his eyes. I didn't move.

In the gulf of silence, he again looked both ways then snapped his head back to me and stared. He lowered his antlers and licked a piece of lichen. Unblinking, he kept his eyes fixed on me and shook his head again. With one final shrug he loped over the edge of a hill and vanished.

Back at camp, we received word that federal authorities refused to sanction the aerial survey. Exasperated, the geologists called it quits, and took the next flight out of Sach's Harbor to their Calgary offices. Our return trip to Resolute Bay seemed easier because a tail wind allowed us to bypass the dreaded downhill run at Cape James Ross. Later, tracking toward Hecla and Griper Bay, we knew a strong crosswind would prevent us from using the perilous run at the gully, despite our lighter weight. We survived my landing but left behind the full forty-five-gallon fuel drum to shorten the takeoff distance.

After refueling, we perched the Beaver on the ridge and slammed the throttle forward. Like before, it seemed to take forever for the tail to rise. With an extra nudge of flap, we left the surface low and slow. For several miles, I didn't dare raise the nose. Only when a hill drew too close, did we turn. The flight to Resolute Bay lasted more than eight hours from Sach's Harbor.

Our successful, undamaged return to Resolute Bay called for

a celebration at the Arctic Circle Club. As usual, the top of our table was covered in beer cans. On both sides sat pilots and mechanics from other High Arctic airlines, as well as three Eskimo women who worked as ticket agents.

Few outsiders understood how High Arctic pilots flew. In good weather, traveling from A to B was not difficult. Weather reports, pilot reports, astrocompasses, and excellent maps took care of us. Airplanes rarely left the ground until conditions dictated more than a fifty-fifty chance of success. Sometimes, pilots went out of their way to reach a camp or crew stranded in the barrenlands. One such incident involved a geologist somewhere near Bauman Fjord who received a message from home—family problems.

Nothing less than a helicopter could penetrate the poor weather surrounding Resolute Bay to reach the man, but distance eliminated the short-ranged rotary types from leaving. Fortunately, a Helio Courier flown by one of the High Arctic's most senior pilots departed from a camp closer to Bauman Fjord. Lightly loaded, he followed shorelines, cliff sides, and open sea-water channels. Despite the marginal weather, the pilot managed to pick up the geologist and later rendezvoused with a twin-engine Dornier 28 for a flight to Resolute Bay when the skies cleared. There, the geologist connected with an Edmonton-bound Boeing 737 jetliner.

In another case, two men carried a stretcher through the door of the barracks and into our sleeping quarters. They unloaded a helicopter pilot who had suffered a heart attack after landing north of Cornwallis Island. A Twin Otter crew brought the man to Resolute Bay. The pilot had no choice but to rest until a flight to a hospital in Edmonton or Montreal.

He occupied a bunk not far from mine. Wrapped in gray woollen blankets, he sobbed hour after hour. Everyone knew he would never fly again. If he felt the same way about northern flying as nearly every Resolute Bay pilot did, he had reached the end of his life. I never knew his name and years later, still wondered how he adjusted.

Work for the short-ranged, day-only, good-weather Beaver dropped off as Twin Otters began supplying exploration camps.

For days, we thought Northward would order the airplane back to Norman Wells. Then, unexpectedly a group of geologists on Ellef Ringnes needed an airplane. Their organization couldn't afford the luxury of a helicopter. In clear weather I made the run up Cornwallis and directly across Hassel Sound without a problem.

The rock pounders didn't seem pleased to see a Beaver. Several weeks with a Helio Courier had spoiled them, but they had no other choice. Our first trip from Hoodoo Dome took us to King Christian Island, southwest of Ellef Ringnes.

Surprisingly, "KCI" as we called it, had some areas of fine, white sand resembling what I saw on Banks Island earlier. Sverdrup Basin was the target of intense oil and sulfur exploration, particularly along a lightly colored, 700-foot-high central dome. After an uneventful landing, I moved several two-man groups almost within sight of an oil rig which made world news when it had caught fire the previous spring.

While dropping off the last group, a radio call from camp demanded the Beaver return to Ellef Ringnes to take part in a search. A helicopter with a competing exploration company didn't show up and could be down with mechanical problems.

A fast Beaver trip across Danish Strait and a short search along Cape Nathorst quickly turned up the missing helicopter in a narrow valley cleft. No problem, the pilot explained. His position reports had never reached the base because of surrounding high terrain.

The party chief decided to take advantage of the clear weather and dispatched me to Amund Ringnes Island, east across Massey Sound. Beyond it, Axel Heiberg and its distant glaciers, 652 miles from the True North Pole, stood out like giant statues in the sunlight. In an immense valley where pigmented, dark tones covered the hillsides, we saw shreds of tents left by parties during the early 1950s.

We made several landings but didn't stay long. Shortly after our return to Ellef Ringnes, a fog bank rolled in and shut down flying activity for days. Winds increased and no one slept, for fear of losing their tents. Despite the stiff breeze, the fog didn't dissipate by morning.

The skies cleared after the third day of zero-zero weather and I raced away to King Christian Island to relocate the crews dropped the previous week. On this short hop, navigation meant simply aiming to the right of the burned-out drill rig. While I was waiting for the geologists to fold their tents, I got a call from the Dornier 28 pilot on the high-frequency radio. Near Eureka, fog hadhim grounded on the far side of Ellesmere Island.

While working from Ellef Ringnes, apparently someone had erred badly when selecting this patch of mud on which to live. Most camp bosses established living quarters as closely as possible to freshwater sources. Here at Hoodoo Dome, every drop of precious liquid needed to be flown in by helicopter. This was expensive for an exploration company whose owners could barely able to afford a tundra-tire Beaver.

Also, nestled as we were in a bowl created by the surrounding hills, fog tended to accumulate. This kept us grounded frequently and prevented supply airplanes from landing. Despite the many times I left and returned with the Beaver, finding the tents took much effort and extra fuel.

With prevalent low ceilings, I could rarely climb high enough to spot any landmarks until I flew almost over the cook tent antenna. Each time the wheels touched the surface, sticky mud coated the belly, struts, and tail. Sometimes, huge slabs of turf slammed against the windshield on takeoff.

By late July, weather became so consistently poor, the party chief realized the Beaver couldn't do the job. Only a Twin Otter could handle more proposed camp moves before exploration season ended. With no other choice, I settled down to wait until weather improved enough for me to return to Resolute Bay. Rain, sleet, and several inches of snow delayed my departure, but late one evening, a break appeared. I took off and turned south, leaving Ellef Ringnes Island and its horrible mud forever.

An hour north of Resolute Bay, clouds became scattered so I decided to investigate an ancient Eskimo tent ring spotted during my fuel-haul days along Devon Island. Stopping room, I knew, would be quite short, but I was alone and light on fuel. With no freight aboard, the Beaver could easily handle it. This time, I flew beneath the level of the ridge after tossing the toilet paper.

Around again, I kept my eye on it, landed, rolled a few yards and stopped quickly.

Nice one. Textbook, I thought.

Solid, the ground easily held my weight so I began walking toward the tent rings. Barely fifteen feet from the airplane, both feet sunk deeply into mud, almost to the knees. Everywhere I went, soft ground bogged me down. Somehow, I had managed to select the only dry area on the island.

A hill crest separated the Beaver and the tent ring. A few minutes later, out of sight of CF-HEP, I discovered a pile of yellowish ivory shavings left behind by some ancient Eskimo hunter. Several feet away, a bone-arrow shaft pointed from the mud. Satisfied, I decided to return to the Beaver. As I slogged across the hill top and passed some huge boulders, a string of gigantic paw prints caught my attention.

Seeping slowly to their brims with muddy water, they were fresh. A polar bear had ambled up the low side of the island and investigated the airplane while I was inspecting the tent ring. Luckily for me, the polar bear had continued on.

I started the engine, cranked down the necessary flap and took off as quickly as possible, hoping to locate the bear. Despite spending several seasons in the Canadian Arctic and northeastern Manitoba, I had never before seen a wild polar bear. After circling the island several times and searching every crevasse and stretch of ice for miles, I found no trace of the animal. Disappointed, I pointed the Beaver's nose toward Resolute.

Shortly after I refueled from our drum supply, the dispatcher told the barracks crowd that weather on Ellef Ringnes had changed drastically. Strong winds blew the small Logan tents out of sight toward the sea and only the large cook tent remained. Those who stayed behind ran out of heating and cooking naptha.

Snow fell in blankets and stopped all work until a Twin Otter could get in to evacuate the crew. Even at Resolute, winds increased day and night to 65 mph. Even though a pair of forty-five-gallon fuel drums were tied to each wing strut, I worried about losing the Beaver. In the morning, the remnants of a wrecked Parkall tent building spread across the airport property.

With the exception of a pleasant flight across Wellington

Channel for Kenting Petroleum, fall-like weather kept me in the barracks most of the time. One brief break provided by an afternoon of clear weather allowed me to hop to Devon Island's south shore. From 500 feet, I spotted new schools of white beluga whales. Young ones drifted placidly beside their parents while older animals chased each other across the wave tops. No one lived nearby so these playful "sea canaries," as Eskimos called them, had all of Lancaster Sound to themselves.

Orders finally came from Northward's Edmonton head office for us to return to Yellowknife. Above Somerset Island, all went well until just south of Fletcher Lake, when impenetrable snow showers forced us to a quick landing. The mechanic and I pushed out a gas drum and refueled, waiting for conditions to improve. Later, we landed again near the abandoned Hudson's Bay Company post of Fort Ross. Many tent rings, rock piles and tons of whale bone littered the area. After pumping in our last drum, we continued to Gjoa Haven on King William Island for an overnight stop.

The next day, forty-knot headwinds brought us close to the danger point. We lacked enough gasoline to reach Cambridge Bay. We dodged more snowstorms and landed twice on the Royal Geographical Society Islands before staggering to a Distant Early Warning (DEW) site at Jenny Lind Island. Radar operators stationed on this isolated outpost told us they couldn't decide whether we were a slow flying helicopter or an iceberg on their screens.

For three days, the Beaver rocked in windstorms. Luckily, the forty-five-gallon drums inside and cement-filled pails tied to each wing prevented the airplane from flying away without us. We made it into Cambridge Bay but freezing rain kept us there for nearly a week. One morning, we awoke to clear blue sky and quickly headed south toward Yellowknife, where my employment with Northward Aviation ended.

Soon my career as an elementary school teacher would begin, but before that I had scorned the majority of "normal" people who became "Eight-to-Fivers." Now a married man, I felt a responsibility to join them but remembering the conversation with Duncan Matheson at Yellowknife, I vowed to prove him wrong and last forever at Foley Public School in Parry Sound.

9   Little Miss Muffet

L uckily, experienced pilots with seaplane time could find
work almost anywhere in Canada during the summer months.
By January of my first year teaching, I began sending application
forms across the country. By now, I had experienced the mountains of British Columbia and had no interest in facing bone-
shaking afternoon turbulence again. Never having been east of
Ottawa, I was elated to receive a telegram in late June suggesting
a promise of new territory.

The telegram read: "THIS WILL CONFIRM A POSITION
AS PILOT WITH LABRADOR AIRWAYS FROM JULY 31 TO
AUGUST 31, 1972, SALARY 500.00 PER MONTH PLUS 5.58
PER FLYING HOUR."

Labrador Airways or "Lab Air" was incorporated in 1948 as
Newfoundland Airways, and later became Eastern Provincial or
EPA. Labradorians had accepted the salt-stained Beavers, Otters
and Noorduyn Norsemen as state-of-the-art aeronautical wonders. Before long, EPA evolved into a major eastern Canada jet
carrier while retaining its bush section. Anxious to promote an
incident-free image, the principals didn't appreciate wrinkled
wing tips and crumpled floats common to seaplanes and
skiplanes. The bush division separated from the jet branch and
became Labrador's largest bush-oriented airline.

Upon discovering that the contract would be a short one,

Linda returned to live with her parents in Toronto when I left for the wilds of Labrador.

During the flight from Toronto, I found myself forced to overnight in St. John's, Newfoundland. A promised hop to Goose Bay materialized the next day. At Goose Bay, someone led me to an upstairs office to fill out employment papers and a young hangar apprentice drove me to the pilots' summer home and left. What the company provided turned out to be unlike anything I'd encountered in western Canada.

Solid metal construction with no insulation, the "steel house" had very high ceilings despite its low square footage. In one room, an oil furnace probably pilfered from a battle ship resonated against the unbraced walls. Built on cement slabs, the house's tiles supposedly prevented grit and white dust from wafting upwards.

No one thought about a bed for my allocated room so, for several days, I slept on the floor. Three Newfoundlanders occupied the other rooms — two pilots and an airplane mechanic from Gander. The four of us lived five miles from the seaplane base without any transportation.

In spite of thousands of square miles of forest, there were no settlements in Labrador's interior. Roads were few, except a short gravel path from Goose Bay to Northwest River. Transportation in "the Labrador," as locals called this section of Newfoundland, came from the ocean. The slow, plodding movements of ships in a changing, fast-paced world encouraged residents to use the bright red airplanes of Labrador Airways and other smaller seaplane organizations.

Most Lab Air customers were transplanted settlers in dozens of picturesque fishing communities along the Atlantic coast and Strait of Belle Isle. Ten passenger Otters handled most of the work, with Beavers taking overloads. In float season, we also dealt with survey, mining, and timber companies several times a week.

Soon after my first walk to the "creek" or seaplane base, I received a nice surprise. With little else to do before a refresher training trip on a Beaver registered CF-OUQ, I began a preflight inspection of the airplane. Picking up a float pump, I inserted its nozzle snugly into the water pump-out holes. An apprentice mechanic came from behind a wooden shed where he was busily repairing a water rudder.

"By der tunderin' lard ja-zus, bye," he said. "Dim me tat."

My first lesson in Labrador flying. In this part of Canada, pilots did nothing but fly airplanes. This attitude had carried over from the company's connections with Eastern Provincial Airways.

As the days went by, I noticed ground staff doing everything. They refilled oil tanks, cleaned windshields and pumped floats when not hosing off dried sea salt from metal surfaces. Evidently, the people of Labrador thought highly of their pilots. "Labrador's about the only place left in Canada where pilots are treated with respect," explained Ken Watkins, a senior man on coastal Otters.

Chief pilot Ian Massie took me up in the Beaver for familiarization with the terrain and water between Goose Bay and Northwest River. We carried out several landings and takeoffs in a deep section of Lake Melville and returned to base. One other test flight in an Otter also helped to adapt to Labrador seaplane flying.

When Massie finished the checkout, the dispatcher said that my first passengers would arrive at dock side early the next morning. The load, he explained, consisted of two American geologists, one male and one female, to the Eskimo village of Nain, 198 miles north of Goose Bay. There, they planned to pick up their tents and a month's supply of food. From Nain, they wanted a forty-two-mile hop north to Snyder Bay on the Atlantic coast.

As I searched the wooden flight shack for the Beaver's log book, dock boys loaded the airplane. When the book turned up beneath a pile of Penthouse and Playboy magazines, I stepped outside and heard two people engaged in a loud argument. The woman geologist, judging by the tone of her voice, didn't care for her new work mate. Their voices reached us even above the noise of an idling Otter.

With match-stick arms and legs, the woman looked as if she lacked the power to pick up a packsack. Instead of heavy clothing to ward off mosquitos and early-morning chill, she sported cotton shorts and a thin semi-transparent blouse. Strands of hair poked beneath the edge of a rimless hat and nearly hid her flushed face.

Instead of the calf-high leather boots we expected of a geologist she wore white running shoes. To protect her ankles, dainty purple socks speckled with tiny pink flowers covered an expanse of noodle-colored skin.

Her male companion attempted to describe the need for Labrador-proof clothing. She sniffed, sat primly down on a stack of cardboard boxes and began writing furiously in what she later told me was a diary. Throughout the flight, Little Miss Muffet, as her fellow geologist called her, recorded every word and rarely spoke.

Loaded now, I over-primed the Beaver's engine while leaving the dock. Blue smoke billowed backwards from the exhaust stacks but the Pratt & Whitney wouldn't run for more than a few seconds at a time. After several more cranks and rapid back-and-forth movements with the mixture control and throttle, the engine steadied smoothly and we left for Nain.

Navigation was especially trying as fog developed along Lake Melville's northern edge and rolled inland shortly after takeoff. Passing the middle of Grand Lake, horizontal visibility improved to nearly two miles in haze as I carefully held a heading and map-read across the spruce. Beside me, Little Miss Muffet stopped scribbling and groped for an airsick bag.

In minutes, she filled it very properly and politely asked for another. To my horror, none could be found, despite a frantic search of the Beaver's seat pockets. Quickly improvising in true Canadian, pilot tradition, I deftly snatched the rimless hat from her head. With one baleful glance, she grabbed and placed it between her bony knees, holding the edges open with trembling hands. Wordlessly, we carried on, the sounds of her discomfort muted by engine noise.

South of the community of Nain, rain droplets began spreading backwards on the Beaver's windshield. For nearly thirty minutes, I lost track of our position and flew a steady compass heading. Odd-shaped islands began appearing everywhere ahead and on both sides. Our estimated time of arrival came due on my stop watch, but we couldn't find the settlement. Before the trip, other pilots had warned me no one ever made it to Nain the first time without becoming lost.

Suddenly, behind us and to our left, an array of white buildings caught my eye. Miss Muffet pointed a sticky finger at a small boat traveling east toward the Atlantic. Nain, in the tiny bay of a long peninsula, could barely be seen until we passed directly overhead. Dozens of colored boats dotted the tidal shore and a gigantic pier stretched far into the salt water. Huge dark slopes sheltered the village on several sides.

"The sun never shines here," shouted the male geologist.

As we landed, I realized our arrival had coincided with low tide. The top of the dock towered far above us and three men looked down from a tremendous pile of boxes, survey poles, tents and portable stoves. Our company agent handed over a message from Goose Bay requesting a side trip before proceeding to Snyder Bay. No problem, I said, for my passengers wanted time to locate equipment sent ahead by ship. While they rearranged their goods, I would fly the extra leg and return for them. Little Miss Muffet left the airplane and rinsed her hat.

Before taking the new load, everything inside the Beaver was taken out and handed upward. Cold rain increased from drizzle to a steady downpour but the wind stayed offshore and kept the fog clear of the village. Low cloud nearly touched the surrounding hill tops. I knew my low-level, map-reading skills would be severely tested throughout the trip.

Standard equipment for floatplanes during summer in Labrador included a pair of hip rubber boot, since tides and shallow shorelines made life difficult for anyone flying seaplanes. Inland, most lakes contained boulders from one shoreline to the other. On overcast days, most lakes could barely be seen by the most cautious pilots.

My newest passengers boarded happily—they had been waiting for days to contract the first available floatplane. Despite the lowering visibility, we left the harbor, flogged the Beaver across several bays and turned inland. No trees existed here. From sea level to 3,500 feet, mountains and mist-shrouded hills surrounded us as we aimed toward a pair of valleys. Tiny ponds passing underneath the floats still had traces of ice around their edges.

Ahead, sheets of ice covered parts of our destination lake. After looking the shoreline over, I landed. Minutes later, my passengers changed their minds. They wanted a drop-off on the east side of the lake, instead of the original location marked on my chart. This grounded us thirty feet from shore. Anxious to please, I donned hip waders and plunged into the water.

Unfortunately, the clear mountain lake only appeared shallow. As frigid water sloshed over the wader tops, my breath left me, my vision blurred and every opening and pore in my body slammed shut. I gasped as blood beneath my skin congealed, and my organs contracted tightly. I knew at once if I perished upon this miserable sub-Arctic lake, my carcass would be cryogenically preserved forever.

With numbed and senseless legs, I turned the Beaver's tail to shore and unloaded. The surveyors didn't want to experience the same bone-numbing cold, but I drew the line at carrying them to land. Because of the airplane's lighter load, they only had to wade through ankle-deep depths. As they splashed ashore in disgust, I finished unloading and blasted off back to Nain, quivering every minute of the way.

Nain's entire population gathered to watch the pretty red airplane and its passengers. Likely, few Eskimos had ever seen such an oddly dressed geologist. While hundreds of eyes watched, I removed the heavily laden hip waders and poured several gallons of cold, cloudy water into the sea. Giggles and titters rippled through the crowd. Even Miss Muffet, her face a lighter shade of green now, showed her teeth in what may have been a smile.

Again, we loaded and within a few minutes, left the water to track northbound from Nain. Rain showers increased in intensity. Once we passed a slice of barren rock called Igloo Island, visibility behind dropped to zero as banks of Atlantic fog rolled in. With my return route closed, we continued to Snyder Bay. The possibility of sleeping overnight on the Beaver's hard bakelite floor seemed very real.

The next landing would be my first on unsheltered ocean

water. To make matters worse, the wind dropped and, for a rare moment in time, the sea became glassy. Rain on the windshield reduced my forward view as I circled. Recalling that seaweed sometimes hid dangerous shoals and occasional weather-toughened logs, I searched for hazards and a safe, uncluttered place to go to shore.

Throttling back, I placed the airplane in a nose-high position for a standard, glassy-water approach. Descending at 200 feet per minute, I groped carefully for the surface, when a spine-jolting whack confirmed our arrival. More of a collision than a landing, our touchdown must have caused some damage. Immediately shutting off the engine, I scrambled outside on the float. No wrinkles or cracks marred the fuselage. Thank God for de Havilland's Beaver.

Someone back in Goose Bay claimed they knew Snyder Bay well. He told us we would find a sandy beach. As far as we could see, nothing but black, car-size boulders and huge kelp clumps comprised the shoreline. I guessed the next stretch of stone-free ground would likely be in Florida. We grounded on a rock shelf far from shore.

Immediately, another argument developed between the geologists concerning camp duties. As usual, Miss Muffet wanted no part of unloading, nor did she intend to stain her running shoes on the kelp. Disgusted, I threw one arm around her shoulder and my other behind both knees. Before she could protest, I carried her from the airplane and deposited her Boston-trained derriere upon a boulder.

As I unloaded, their argument escalated. I looked at the tiny two-person pup tent that would house the happy duo for the next three weeks. Mercifully, the rain stopped, ceilings lifted and with barely a goodbye, I jumped into the Beaver and left Snyder Bay. No way, I thought, would this pilot spend the night with two crackpots.

That evening, I tracked down the coast and made it as far as Hopedale, where I stopped for fuel. Enroute, the Beaver's flap mechanism sprayed pink hydraulic fluid all along the floor and down the walls. At Goose Bay, a mechanic carried out a quick fix.

While my Beaver was being repaired, the dispatcher decided to send me in another airplane south to Forteau, a Newfoundland village not far across the Quebec border. Without eating anything other than a chocolate bar and two slices of toast during the day, I did as he said. Fortunately, Bessie, the Forteau company agent and lady of the house in which Labrador Airways expected me to overnight, fed me well on cheese and crackers. Grateful for the meal, I unrolled my sleeping bag and spent the night on the Beaver's floor.

I awoke to bright, clear skies. At the seaplane dock on a small lake behind the settlement, an Otter loaded for a trip along the coast. Passengers consisted of a group of young men and women aged eighteen to twenty-two years of age destined for drop-offs in the villages. Called "WOPs" or Workers Without Pay, they were volunteers from Boston, intent on saving souls in Labrador. My role in this scenario consisted of hauling a cabin full of their baggage in Beaver CF-OUQ.

Destined for Black Tickle, my route was within sight of the Strait of Belle Isle and took me over land which explorer Jacques Cartier regarded as "….the one God gave to Cain." While some people may consider this land desolate, even the most urbanized North American would appreciate the rugged beauty of Labrador's rock-ribbed shores.

Not far from the mainland, occasional cathedral-sized icebergs drifted southward. Wind-abraded, many held turquoise meltwater as a wine glass holds wine. I saw one huge glacier rotate slowly over, toasting its load of liquid into the sea. On my right, the soft, green arm of west Newfoundland gave way to white Atlantic rollers. Below the wing tip, bright red or yellow oceangoing ships left tiny patterns in their wakes as they plunged toward sheltered coves and bays.

At Black Tickle, the Otter landed first. Since there was only enough parking space for one airplane, I shut off the Beaver's engine and drifted while waiting for my turn. As I watched, a helper opened the right-hand front door of the Otter and stepped onto the float. Like me, he was new to the region and misjudged the water depth as the huge airplane approached the dock. He stepped off the float and disappeared. The depth at this point in the clear Atlantic was almost fifteen feet.

He surfaced, spluttering and gasping, and managed to grab the dock to pull himself from the water. Luckily, he still held a rope attached to the airplane's float. He tied it securely as passengers began disembarking. When the Otter left, I pulled up and distributed baggage.

From Black Tickle, I followed the Otter to Cartwright, an American radar site and home for many fisherfolk. Nearly every building in the community wore a bright white coat of paint that contrasted with the dark coastal rocks.

Again, I waited for the Otter and as I drifted, another of the huge red bush planes took off for Goose Bay. As the days went on, I learned the company's Otter pilots worked harder than anyone on their lengthy scheduled runs. The lighter Beavers flew less than half the hours.

After the WOPs disappeared into the village, local Labrador Airways agent Frank Peters refueled my tanks. With no passengers or freight, I left Cartwright for Goose Bay. My low altitude provided close-up views of the Mealy Mountains, where the highest peak reached 3,700 feet. They didn't compare in size to British Columbia or Ellesmere Island, but these deep green mountains were cradled with spruce and dotted with tiny lakes. Their isolation seemed to issue an invitation to explore the confined silence underneath my floats.

When I arrived at Otter Creek in Goose Bay, I noticed all Labrador Airways pilots happened to be on base at the same time. Unanimously, everyone agreed to meet at the Bulldog Club.

Managed by Royal Air Force personnel stationed in Goose Bay to service Handley Page Victor and Avro Vulcan jet bombers, the place had a British pub atmosphere. Bulldog bartenders dispensed English beer and often crossed the counter tops to play a strange game called "baw-tells." Participants arranged beer bottles in rows and chug-a-lugged from one end of the line to the other. Not quite the blue-blood country squires I imagined Brits to be, many lay about the floor like slobs and slatterns by closing time. No Canadian could match the British pace.

With the early summer rush over, fewer customers called on

Labrador Airways for charter work, until a request for an aerial survey flight appeared on the booking sheet. A major lumber corporation decided to inventory land tracts where they held cutting rights. We flew for hours where every hardwood and softwood tree was harvested. Nowhere could I see evidence anyone had bothered to reseed or replant the so-called limitless Canadian bush country.

Air temperatures hovered in the high seventies and strong winds gusted every minute of the flight. Only one man didn't feel the effects of the turbulence, but his associates certainly did. They quickly filled every airsickness bag in the airplane. By the time we landed, each overflowed his hard hat as well. One hatless man resorted to unlacing his boot and filling it.

After the timber crew drove away in their green and yellow trucks, a call came from the Newfoundland Forest Service which operated a de Havilland Turbo-beaver close to Labrador Airways' dock. The failure of its turbine engine during fire fighting resulted in a request for Labrador Airways to fly in a mechanic. Smoke north of Goose Bay had been building in columns for days, so finding the camp took more time than expected. I didn't welcome the idea of mingling with swarms of black flies, mosquitos and sand flies that had saturated the air. In any case, I was asked to wait for passengers on the return flight.

The persistent insects made breathing difficult. I swallowed many while walking the sandy beach on which we parked. No matter where I turned, they clogged my nose and burrowed into the canals of my ears. Despite layers of clothing, they penetrated the tightly knit shirt weaves and found pathways down to my toes. Slapping them had no effect, other than dark hand prints and slimy palms. Retreating to the Beaver, I nearly suffocated while spraying the interior with insecticide.

At last, I heard a rap on the Beaver's plexiglass window. Two Naskaupi Indian men with packsacks on their backs had waded through shallow water to the float. Back and forth they went, not saying anything until the last fire pump, charcoal-covered fire hose, and garbage bags reached the ceiling. One climbed into the right front seat and the other made himself a cave in the freight as we taxied out. The Turbo-beaver pilot kept the mechanic with him.

Before we lifted off for Goose Bay, an orange and green Canso water bomber thundered down the lake and scooped a load of water close enough that we could see the pilots in the cockpit. Having been a crewman in a similar airplane, I wished the copilot well. Climbing above his drop height, I watched the slow moving airplane release its 800 gallons into a fire. By the time I turned final back at Goose Bay, word came over the radio that the bombers had regained control.

During open-water seasons, Labrador Airways received calls to move fishing parties to inland lakes. Commercial lodges and outpost camps needed airplanes to transport customers every day. "Day trippers" departed early morning to nearby lakes and returned before dark. Tour operators generally selected water bodies close to their main lodges so they could reach guests quickly in case bad weather rolled in. No one wanted a paying customer stranded overnight. Few tourists could handle the stress from biting flies once the sun went down.

One outfitter asked me to fly sixty-five miles southeast to a speckled-trout pond called Park Lake. As the lake came slowly into sight, I saw hundreds of glacial boulders lining the rugged shores. Only one area in the middle of Park Lake looked clear enough for landing.

Float pilots everywhere need excellent memory retention. After studying the shorelines and water, I tried to remember every pebble and shoal, for I'd have to find my way back to the same place. Once I landed, I had difficulty locating the fishermen who waved when the Beaver flew over. By throttling back and switching one magneto off at a time, I managed a slow taxi.

Out of the corner of my eye, I caught a flash of color below a stand of stunted birch. I taxied toward it, hoping to miss any hazards beneath the floats as the passengers waited patiently. Beside them, several bulging bags crammed with speckled trout flashed when sunlight occasionally broke through the overcast. Untied, the bags stood propped upright against the trees.

My passengers wore military camouflage suits and bush boots. Each man carried the same arm's length hunting knife I saw on nearly every tourist who ventured into what they considered Canadian wilderness. Neither smelled pleasant—fish scales and dried blood decorated their "Canada" outfits. Repulsive, hair-covered bellies hung over their snake-skin leather belts.

"Fishin' ain't bad," brayed one. He sucked a pair of scabby lips together and spat out a stream of yellowish brown tobacco juice. An inch of slime swayed beneath his stubble chin but fell away as he smashed a beer bottle against a rock. Chocolate bar wrappers littered the forest floor and smoke wisped upward from a near-dead campfire.

I began loading the sun-warmed bags. Sharp rocks pierced the plastic and fish slime slithered out in long, sticky stringers. Neither fisherman helped. Each time they "killed a soldier," they threw it onto the growing pile of glass beside the shoreline. As they burped and belched, strong body odors, stained the evening air.

As I hoisted the last ballooned-out bag into the Beaver, an edge caught on a cargo tie-down ring and spewed dozens of scaly captives along the floor, from the middle seats, through the bulkhead, and into the tail area. One fisherman tracked through the muculent mess and slouched in the right rear seat and the other plunked himself beside the pilot's seat. Thoroughly inebriated, they seemed oblivious to the odor. They didn't know and likely didn't care that the smell would stay with the airplane long after my return to a classroom in Parry Sound.

After thirty minutes of weaving and wriggling past boulders, I judged us clear of danger and advanced the throttle. Seconds later, a terrific bang shook the airplane. We stopped so abruptly that the control wheel flew out of my hands, slammed against the panel and hit me in the chest. Somehow, the faithful Beaver managed to find the last rock in the center of Park Lake.

At idle power, we couldn't move. The left wing tilted upward and the other cleared the water by only a few feet. Up to this point, I had never damaged a seaplane float. Now, I dared not advance the throttle further, for if we left the submerged shoal we might sink. Knowing the airplane wouldn't move, I shut down the engine and stepped outside.

I saw nothing in the deep, black water. Carefully placing my feet—boots and all—into the lake, I felt something solid with my toes. We had collided with a large, angled rock and probably caused float damage so severe we'd have to wait for help. The choice between spending the night stranded in an airplane full of slime and with two plastered dipsomaniacs or flying back to Goose Bay, crossed my mind.

Stepping deeper, I reasoned that the water didn't equal the cold of that bone-numbing liquid north of Nain. I tried to ease the airplane forward to see if it would float. Both passengers stayed inside as I jumped into the lake. Discovering the depth to be well over my head, I dragged myself out by grasping the float spreader bar. Persuading the passengers to leave their seats took more time than I'd expected. Finally, they came outside and went forward on the floats as I pushed and rocked from the rear with everything I had.

With a lurch, the Beaver slithered forward, freeing us from the rock. Quickly, I scrambled inside, politely ordering my inebriated passengers back to their seats as fast as they could move. The Pratt & Whitney started almost immediately. Before anyone fastened their seat belts, flaps came down and we turned into wind for takeoff. Everything felt normal as the Beaver cleared the water and we tracked toward Goose Bay.

Several thousand feet above Labrador's bush country, I now had an ooze-filled, sickly smelling airplane with two helpless, tipsy tourists.

Neither one carried the mental bricks to realize we might sink after landing at Goose Bay. I couldn't judge how badly the rocks had gashed the floats, but felt fortunate the floats weren't torn from their struts. Naturally, the airplane's radio had malfunctioned and our base didn't hear my calls.

At Labrador Airways, a huge, weed-covered, wooden ramp, used to change from skis to floats in the spring, looked clear of airplanes. In our situation, it made sense to touch down on the water and taxi at high speed directly onto the oily boards before settling into Melville Lake. Chances were, only the left side would have a hole large enough to sink us. "Step-taxiing" as we called it, with only one float in the water was a common procedure. Many pilots landed and took off with one float first when in crosswinds or trying to get airborne with heavy loads.

On final approach, I briefed the passengers about what could happen if we sank. They were so far into their last bottles of beer, they didn't understand a word.

With landing flap applied and engine power reduced, I raised the Beaver's nose and tightened my seat belt until I could barely breathe. The instant the floats touched, I applied near-takeoff power and raised the flaps to stay level above the water.

As we bumped across the waves at fifty miles per hour toward the dock, I saw several dock boys standing near the ramp. One casually dragged a long, black gas hose toward an Otter. He glanced at the Beaver traveling in what must have seemed directly for him. He was experienced around the docks of Labrador Airways and knew company pilots often step-taxied. A couple of seconds later he looked again and realized the big red airplane hadn't throttled back.

Everyone scattered like a handful of paychecks thrown into a Labrador gale. At the last instant, I wrenched the throttle back as far as it would go: too soon and we might sink; too late and the wings might become part of Labrador Airways' flight shack.

Both floats struck the ramp simultaneously. The airplane slammed to a stop and the tail went up as the nose went down. I expected the two-blade metal propeller to splinter the planks. Instead we fell backwards with a terrific crash, but completely on dry land and safe from sinking.

A squelching sound brought me back to my paying passengers. Both had sat in the rear seats during our wild takeoff from Park Lake. With their seatbelts loosely fastened, they had careened forward, eyes bulging, and then snapped backwards to collide with the onrushing bags of fish. Dozens of pan-sized trout slipped inside their boots and into their Canada suits.

Ignoring my passengers, I scrambled outside expecting to find a horrendous hole in the floats. There was no damage on one side; a quick inspection of the other revealed no gouges, rips or wrinkles. By now, the mechanics had returned and they, too, examined the costly Edo floats. One crawled under and beckoned me to do the same.

Somehow, the Beaver had struck the rock at Park Lake directly on the metal keel or skeg—the strongest part of the float. Miraculously, the airplane had no damage, other than the loss of a few metal shavings. My impromptu emergency hadn't been necessary after all. Years later, I accidentally ran a de Havilland Otter onto a flat rock in strangely similar circumstances and escaped without damage again.

A mechanic wrenched open the right rear door. Trout bounced out onto the planks and with them came the tobacco spitter. A pocket of his jacket caught the exit step, causing him to hang nearly upside down until the dock boys helped him stand. His friend, more steady and far more sober now, followed.

"So much for your air show," mumbled a mechanic as he began hosing the Beaver's interior. "Oh, yes, my son, you have another trip first thing in the morning."

Many Labrador flights included loads of giggling Naskaupi Indians traveling to Rigolet after shopping excursions in Goose Bay, or moribund Eskimos bound for Hopedale or Nain following hospital visits. Almost everyone who flew from the saltwater harbor was friendly and appreciative of the pilots who flew them. Not all, however, cared for the decisions we made. My worst day took place during an overcast rainy day with a crew of disgusted drillers who chartered a Beaver for a mail flight and camp move.

After a stop at Northwest River, east of Goose Bay, for mail bags and grocery boxes, I flew northwest along Grande Lake and turned right at the Naskaupi River. Following it, I found my six men and a mountain of drill rods, food boxes, tents, and an enormous green boat.

Despite the chilly air and fifteen-knot breeze, one man wore nothing more than a dirty, sleeveless T-shirt, shredded cutoffs, and badly abused leather boots. On his hands, I saw gloves so torn, fingers the size of garden hoses protruded in several different directions.

I pulled the water rudders up and let the wind weather cock the tail toward shore. The airplane sailed backwards nicely and grounded softly in the sand. As I stepped onto the float and then the beach, no one said a word. This crew had clearly spent too much time away from clean sheets, fresh underwear and flush toilets. One man brazenly asked me how long I had worked for Labrador Airways.

They all had the black hands and tattered fingernails that usually go with the diamond-drilling business. Handling greasy drill rods and machinery shredded their clothing, gouged their work-hardened skins and stooped their backs.

Evidently, someone had promised them an Otter, not a Beaver. Now, the camp move would take many short trips all day. Their baleful glares and collective groans told me no one here on the Naskaupi, was pleased.

The T-shirt handed me a wrinkled topographical map. Almost immediately, I saw his lake was too short to handle a Beaver. Another large body of water called Brandy Lake would have to do. We could likely land and leave empty from his first choice; however, the next pilot assigned to move the group would probably throttle me for subjecting him to a dangerously short takeoff run.

For a tense moment, I thought the foreman might drive me down into the earth like a drill rod. Even so, with an accident-free record to my credit, I didn't intend to risk anyone's airplane. A staring match ended with me the victor. With no other choice, the foreman blinked his pebbly eyelids and disgustedly began dragging the boat to the Beaver's side.

Hundreds of pounds of absorbed water made the wooden vessel so heavy that four men could barely raise it onto the airplane's float. Without boat racks, I used every rope on board to knit it securely to the float struts. A glance told me this would be the largest boat anyone had asked me to carry outside an airplane.

I located the company hip waders—still wet from the episode north of Nain—and slipped them on. A wave rolled against the float and I tumbled into the chilly lake. Spluttering, gasping and choking, I reached frantically for a rudder cable to steady myself. Several metal strands pierced my palms and one ripped a deep gash across my wrist. Blood ran into the water where it dissipated in seconds.

Completely soaked, I struggled upward to a semi-standing position, barely able to move. In that instant, I got a flash that the life of a pilot in Labrador might not be quite so glamorous as it seemed back in Ontario.

As I fought to regain some sense of composure and a trace of dignity even here in the "boonies," the midafternoon winds began to increasing. More whitecaps splashed against the floats.

Anxious to complete the job and get out of there, I asked the men to raise the boat so I could complete the boat-tying. They complied, but misunderstood when I flexed a finger to restore circulation, and dropped the boat prematurely on my undamaged hand. Wrenching free, I lost a fingernail and saw that my skin was scraped deeply across the tops of all five fingers. Ten minutes later, we were finally airborne. After a shaky, low-level flight below some sandy hills, I deposited the boat safely in Brandy Lake.

My next half-dozen trips consisted of whatever the drillers crammed inside the Beaver. With the right front seat removed, we carried drill rods. Some extra-long ones needed to be left behind for the first available Otter. On the final hop, the corpulent foreman sat in the middle of the floor, surrounded by cardboard boxes and holding an outboard motor. As we settled into the water off the step for the last time, he rolled over backwards toward the rear of the airplane, but didn't damage himself or the motor.

The job completed, I noticed my fuel gauges indicated barely enough gasoline to return to Goose Bay. With bulging mail bags and stacks of empty beer bottles tied behind the seats, I left. Navigation had to be in a straight line—no river following because of my fuel shortage. Along the way, I regretted the lack of cockpit heat to dry my clothing. Someone in de Havilland's Downsview, Ontario, plant long ago decreed that pilots didn't require heat in summer months and made it easy for mechanics to disconnect the system.

At Goose Bay, I rushed to the steel house for bandages to help repair my mangled hands. As I carefully taped the last shred of cotton cloth around my wrist, my two house mates arrived with several young Naskaupi women. Their party lasted long and loud as I huddled painfully in a sleeping bag on the cement floor. The noise of shattering glasses and giggling spells from beyond the room kept me awake until daylight filtered through the blinds.

No trips came in for several days. Gradually, the normal feeling returned to my body except for an intense throbbing in several swollen fingers. Before long, a call to the steel house roused me from the sleeping bag early one morning. Someone needed a flight to Big River Lodge, ninety-four miles northeast of Goose Bay.

Unlike the diamond-drilling crew, my passengers clearly looked forward to the trip. Quite elderly, neither the man nor his wife had experienced a taste of Labrador before. I assumed they came from somewhere south of the Canada/United States border, they were city dwellers and in their final years planned one last great adventure. Unknown to them, this would also be my first trip to Big River.

On a northeasterly heading from Goose Bay, Big River Lodge didn't lie on the regular tracks to Hopedale, Nain or Rigolet. Not particularly difficult to locate, its main disadvantage lay in the necessity of plotting on three aeronautical charts in the short distance. Big River happened to be in the corner of one map. To get there, we flew thirty-one miles, switched to the next unwieldy chart for twelve miles and finished the final fifty-one-mile leg on the last one.

Not far beyond Mokomi Hill off the left wing tip and Lake Melville's Mulligan Bay on the right, I unfolded all three maps. I spread them over the instrument panel, and aimed for a rapid-lined river elbow. From our vantage point in the Beaver's cockpit, we looked down on the strange string bogs of Labrador.

Framed by eskers and inundated with water, long strips of greenery reached toward encroaching gravel ridges. With cockpit instruments blocked from view, I concentrated on tracking straight across a landscape that was beautiful in its own strange way.

Most lakes were tiny ones and from 3,000 feet, I saw boulders reflecting sunlight in their centers and" lining the edges. These trackless swamps and untouched places played important roles in the sensitive northern fabric.

At that instant, the engine quit.

Earlier, I had moved the fuel selector to the rear tank to use the last few gallons in it. My plan was to switch over to a full tank before fuel pressure dropped. With the maps blocking my view of the instrument panel, I didn't see the fuel gauge's red warning light.

Instinctively, my left hand smashed through the jumble of aeronautical charts as my right hand frantically groped for the Beaver's wobble pump. The nose dropped sharply toward the bogs and gravel ridges. Pumping desperately to restore engine power, I discovered my hand had been trying to wobble-pump with the carburetor heat control. It seemed to me as if the airplane deliberately selected this moment to challenge me with my first real forced landing.

Realizing my error, I switched levers and pumped as quickly as possible. With barely 200 feet between the Beaver and the bog, the engine started sluggishly. Applying climb power, I rapidly gained altitude and continued to Big River Lodge. Beside me, my septuagenarian seat mate sat unconcerned, oblivious to my near-fatal mistake. None of us would have lasted long. The string bogs of Labrador belong to mosquitos.

We flew on, my chest pounding with each heart beat. The adrenalin in my bloodstream slowly seeped away and the tremors in my hands faded from uncontrollable shaking to normal levels. The aging gentleman leaned across and shouted above the noise of the engine.

"I know all about you Canadian bush pilots," he said. "I know you let your gas tanks run dry like that to get all the flying you can out of them."

Not one to disillusion him nor explain how close he and his wife came to premature departure from the world, I never said a word. My passengers didn't deserve to have their faith in those who fly the skies of Labrador shaken. Besides, my voice returned only when we arrived over Big River Lodge.

Back at Goose Bay, I remarked to my fellow pilots how often customers seemed to book airplanes when weather turned poor. Unable to understand the difference between day-only, good-weather Beavers and fully instrumented, multi-engine sophisticated types, they became upset when we didn't dare leave the water. For several days, I waited for rain, fog and low ceilings to lift at the creek. Finally I got away with a load of disgruntled construction workers bound for Cartwright.

Poor conditions hampered the trip, but no power lines or hydro towers lay between Goose Bay and Cartwright. Navigation at 500 feet along the shorelines of Lake Melville often proved to be a problem. This time, I noticed whitecaps increasing in size the further east we went. Turbulence above the Mealy Mountains shook the airplane so badly, that passengers began retching fifteen minutes after takeoff.

At Cartwright, agent Frank Peters refueled the Beaver and suggested parking at a floating buoy near the dock. That evening, the building in which Frank and his wife Phyllis lived swayed sideways in the gusts. Worried, I decided to ensure the Beaver didn't sink.

In the glare of truck headlights, I could barely see the airplane, as huge, saltwater rollers slammed into it. Tremendous spray clouds filled the engine cowling and the Beaver's tail dipped deeply into the ocean each time a wave hit. We could do nothing to save the airplane. Wind gusts peaked at sixty knots before the coastal storm finally loosened its grip on Cartwright.

Unable to sleep, I left the Kelly house at first light. The gale's passage left newspapers, plywood sheets, roof tiles and seaweed strewn everywhere. Occasional swells still rocked the dock, but the wind had dropped to a whisper. Much to my surprise, Beaver CF-OUQ rode calmly at its buoy.

With no trips booked, I looked forward to a leisurely and pleasant flight back to Goose Bay. Other than a salty windshield, the Beaver had somehow escaped without damage. A few puffs of bluish white smoke curled backwards from the exhaust as I taxied away. Soon I was off the water and turning westward.

Navigation to Goose Bay was easier than the day before. Finding my way home meant little more than keeping the Mealy Mountains' highest peak on my right until the white fuel-storage tanks near the airport came into sight. As I arrived, dock boys began pumping the floats of all the airplanes.

Someone in the flight shack pointed to the booking sheet. Three passengers needed transportation to Battle Harbor, about

194

an hour's ride southeast. A quick glance at a map showed their destination lay on the open-ocean side of an island. Unable to land in the sea, I hoped to find a sheltered area.

Before long, a narrow stretch of water called Lewis Inlet took shape on the horizon. Winds stayed light, although rolling ocean swells prevented landing at the village. Luckily, a tiny cove not far away would suffice, and we touched down easily. The problem now became a long, boring taxi as the airplane skirted over the top of one swell and down into the trough of another.

My civil-service passengers, all native Newfoundlanders, understood why I landed so far away from Battle Harbor, and sat patiently waiting to disembark. I busied myself by setting the elevator trim, checking fuel and completing the logbook as we slowly whacked from wave to wave. Suddenly, someone in the rear seat gasped.

On the airplane's right side, a gigantic, billowing wall of water welled up out of the depths. Only a few arm lengths away, I thought the tidal wave would swallow the airplane and plunge us into the ocean so far that none of us would ever surface again.

Helpless, I snapped my hand toward the throttle. As quickly as it appeared, the hillside of greenish water receded back into the Atlantic, like a strumpet settling on a silken sheet. In seconds, no trace of it, save for a few whirls and curlicues in the wave tops, existed.

We had just witnessed a phenomenon Labrador fishermen frequently saw along the coast. Some fisherfolk explained that swells and currents frequently follow the contour of the ocean floor. Unseen from above, these lifelike water masses strike a flat rock or climb sloping terrain and ricochet upward to the surface. Usually harmless, unless a boat or, in this case, an airplane happens to be near them, they last a few seconds and fade to nothingness.

A fishing boat chugged slowly from behind an island and turned toward us. A passenger recognized the crew and knew they'd be docking at Battle Harbor. Shutting off the engine, I stepped outside and beckoned the boat closer. The captain didn't object to taking my load, although the transfer required several sailors holding the wing to prevent it from smashing their radio antennae. After completing the move, I started the engine and watched the water nervously as I retraced the taxi route before taking off for Goose Bay.

Near St. Lewis Inlet on the homeward leg, a message on the HF radio ordered me to St. Anthony on the northern tip of Newfoundland. Labrador Airway's scheduled Otter couldn't carry an extra five passengers who needed transportation to Goose Bay. Turning around, I soon began crossing the Strait of Belle Isle. Off to the left, I saw the island from which the famous strait obtained its name. Tremendous icebergs and white water flickering from the tops of swells reminded me that forced landings here meant an unlikely chance of survival.

St. Anthony, home of the International Grenfell Association, contained a well-sheltered harbor. The landing would be my first on the island of Newfoundland. Carefully picking a path between a flotilla of fishing boats and net clusters, I eased the Beaver's nose gently down after retarding the throttle. Off to my left, a group of people stood watching on a dock. My passengers, I assumed.

Despite hundreds of landings in all kinds of conditions and a logbook full of flying hours before arriving in St. Anthony, I misjudged. The Beaver's right float struck the water first and bounced the airplane back into the air. It hit seconds later on the opposite side and glanced off a wave churned up by a motor boat. On the third whack, the airplane struck hard enough on both floats that it stayed down. Red-faced, I taxied toward the crowd who witnessed the entire escapade.

Three women about my own age and two older men waited with suitcases neatly arranged for loading. Floating parallel to the dock, I tossed a rope toward a small post. It missed.

With me standing outside on the float, the Beaver went sailing past the audience. I climbed back in, restarted the engine and came around again. This time, I parked successfully.

Judging by their bemused expressions, these Newfoundlanders understood seaplane flying more than most Canadians. Anyone can fly an airplane, they knew, but true pilot skill manifested itself in proper docking. They realized I'd "blown" it.

Nevertheless, they didn't have a choice of pilots. The next

scheduled Otter wouldn't return until late the following day. They climbed inside and settled in for the long haul to Goose.

As I pushed away from the dock, I felt something break and realized the water-rudder cable had broken. Steering to a boat-free takeoff area took more time than I had anticipated. As breezes sifted into the harbor from across St. Anthony's rooftops, I applied many blasts of engine power to taxi in a straight line.

Twice, I applied takeoff power and both times retarded throttle quickly, as the nose swung around in the wrong direction. Finally, with enough propeller slipstream over the tail to keep straight, we thundered along the harbor, left the water and tracked to mainland Canada.

No matter how high we climbed, afternoon turbulence followed us and refused to dissipate. At least scenery across "the Straits," as locals called the Strait of Belle Isle, made the trip enjoyable. Seasoned travelers, my passengers marveled at the vast watery expanses spreading out from the Gulf of St. Lawrence.

I planned the Goose Bay landing carefully and contacted the surface nearly three hours after leaving St. Anthony. As each person left the airplane, they thanked me for the pleasant journey. By the time their taxi's taillights disappeared, a mechanic repaired the broken water rudder and another passenger waited with a duffle bag.

This time only one person booked the flight: the captain of a boat involved in oil exploration not far from Saglek. He wanted to be dropped off at Cartwright, where a helicopter would pick him up for transfer to his vessel. After another easy hop high across the Mealies, I took time for a coffee break with the agent. With enough daylight left to get back to Goose Bay, the day ended nicely with over ten hours of flying time in the logbook. To top it off, one of my house mates returned in the Cessna 180 with fresh salmon from Rigolet.

Sadly, the bountiful summer flying predicted by Labrador Airway's management didn't materialize. The three red Beavers sat idle most of the time while the airline's Otters did most of the work. The owners agreed that the chances of extra work before the end of summer were unlikely. If I left, they saw no reason to hire a replacement and suggested I return in better times. They added that if I decided to leave teaching, I would be welcomed back.

I parted friends with Labrador. Although I never had the privilege of working for Lab Air again, I visited the area years later and saw how much the airline had changed. A solitary Beaver and three Otters handled the water work. From the airport, spotless turbine twins carried the company's new logo.

10 Les Ailes du Nord

During a telephone search for a short-term Beaver job, persistence paid off when Les Ailes du Nord in Sept Iles, Quebec conceded they could use my services. One of their pilots had left without notice to work for a major airline.

Les Ailes du Nord, or Northern Wings, operated several different types of airplanes from the airport and from Lac Rapide. In earlier days, they flogged Noorduyn Norsemen along the north shore of the St. Lawrence and inland from dozens of tiny fishing villages. The company moved up to de Havilland Otters, Beavers and Dornier 28 seaplanes purchased from Wheeler Airlines—a rare type in Canada, especially on floats.

Chief pilot Roly Ferguson picked me up as promised. As he drove along the sand roads toward the water base, he gave me some bad news. The promised de Havilland Beaver wouldn't be available for almost a week. Stationed at Gagnon, 118 miles northwest of Sept Iles, a mining exploration contract kept it busy in the bush.

"Instead, you fly a Cessna 185 until the Beaver's free to come here," he added.

Until then, I'd never flown a Cessna 185. Most of my first employers had assigned me to slightly less powerful Cessna 180s. I knew I would need plenty of flying time and a thorough type checkout in the 300-horsepower 185 before feeling completely comfortable. With longer floats, the 185 carried an incredible load for its size.

Ferguson decided to combine the checkout and training with a revenue trip. Dock hands loaded naptha cans, groceries, and gasoline kegs to the ceiling and we taxied away. About twenty-five miles east of Sept Iles, a group from the Ontario-based University of Waterloo managed a salmon research station. They contracted for regular supply runs to keep their equipment functional and members fed. The flight with Ferguson in the pilot's seat felt rough as afternoon sunlight heated the ground and the rising air stopped only at the cumulus clouds.

Tall trees and steep-sided hills surrounded Lac Rapide. After landing, Ferguson stressed again how much of an incredible load the Cessna 185 carried from confined spaces. To prove his point, he taxied a slight distance from the dock. As I watched, he selected a touch of takeoff flap and pushed the throttle in as far as it would go.

We looked close—too close, I thought—to clear the trees. I expected him to throttle back and settle into the water. He slammed the control wheel hard against the stop and staggered into the air at such an angle the tail nearly touched the lake.

Instead of losing the lift from our wings and falling off to one side, the Cessna 185 climbed at a fantastically steep angle. The stall warning horn blared loudly as the airplane kept going up. We cleared the trees by a safe margin and leveled off.

Ferguson landed again to switch seats with me. After repeated takeoffs and landings, I couldn't do anything except bounce across the water on every touchdown. Turbulent air and gusting winds didn't help, and each approach ended far from the preselected point Ferguson wanted. Nevertheless, he pronounced me safe to fly the 185. It was apparent I needed many hours before coming close to wringing top performance from this airplane. For the first few days, I thought of nothing but returning to the Beaver.

With a new assortment of aeronautical maps, I began serious flying for Les Ailes du Nord. One of the first trips took place shortly after the checkout. A retired medical doctor from Philadelphia arrived in a taxi loaded with sacked potatoes, fishing poles, and every expensive liqueur known to mankind. He wanted a flight to a private salmon fishing camp on the Moisie River.

Our destination lay in a deep, steep-sided valley with tops marked on the map as 2,500 feet. Although Quebec's hills didn't compare to the mountains I had seen before, they looked just as formidable because of the narrow nature of the valley floor and the nearby bankless river. Our first attempt to reach the camp wasn't successful. As we arrived overhead in bright blue sky, we barely saw the river because fog blotted out the valley. Unable to find a safe way to land, we returned to Lac Rapide to wait for clearer skies.

By noon, an overflying Otter reported that most of the fog had dissipated. A few remaining patches here and there forced us to select a landing spot further south than the camp. Descending to a few feet above a channel of white-water rapids, I flew as slowly as possible a few feet above the surface until a calm spot appeared. Closing the throttle, we plopped onto the river beside a rock I had memorized when looking down through a hole in the mist.

Immediately, the doctor knew we had landed many miles from his favorite fishing lodge. Taxiing into current lasted an appallingly long time. Not once did we bump bottom or smack a shoal.

Every few minutes, my passenger pointed out, "My, my, we are so far away."

After hearing this more times than I could possibly bear, I nearly forgot he represented a paying customer and told him to shut his mouth. The strain of watching for water hazards and the ever-present possibility of hitting a rock had made me testy. At the instant my patience reached its limit, the fishing lodge appeared around a bend.

Shutting off the engine at the last second, I managed to throw a rope to a waiting passenger on the dock. As baggage, the new customer brought four of the largest newspaper-wrapped Atlantic salmon I had ever seen. Moments after we taxied away, he informed me that the camp owner didn't appreciate visiting pilots roaring past the lodge at full takeoff power. The engine noise might disturb the fish, he believed. With little wind, light load, and low fuel, the Cessna 185 didn't stay on the Moisie River very long anyway.

Much to my regret, flying hours weren't any more plentiful with Les Ailes du Nord than with Labrador Airways. Fog from the St. Lawrence River kept us parked many days at a time. In general, business dropped off everywhere in Quebec. Mineral exploration companies reduced their charter requirements and airstrips along the St. Lawrence's north shore encouraged residents to travel by wheelplane.

Only one drill camp kept active not far from Sept Iles. We carried out regular runs to a small lake northwest of Lac Rapide with groceries and returned with core boxes fastened with razor-like wire. Once, another pilot flew in a happy cook who won a small fortune in a lottery the day before. We envied him for his good luck and wished him well. He planned to complete one last work session before opening his own expediting business.

Flights for injured miners or tourists with fish hooks snagged in their fingers happened regularly for most float-plane companies. Some organizations occasionally hauled orphaned bear cubs, moose calves and other animals. A most unusual rescue occurred during a warm Sunday morning when the St. Lawrence Fishing Club called the office. A group of members needed to move six men up the Moisie River.

Somehow, a school of migrating salmon was trapped in a pool beside some rapids. Unable to escape upstream to spawn, they would die unless they could be transferred into flowing water. The fishing club took on the costly task of rescuing them. After a hop from Lac Rapide to a pickup spot closer to Sept Iles, they loaded dip nets, lunches and maps into the Beaver.

An hour's flight placed us down-river from the rapids. Parking proved tricky because of swift currents and large rocks. Using every available length of rope, we tied the Beaver to some spruce trees and walked twenty minutes along a well-traveled bush trail. At first, the quiet in the forest unnerved us, but as we drew nearer the rapids, sounds of rushing water became louder. For the balance of the day, we shouted over the roar of the river, and came home that evening with sore throats.

Beside the main channel, we found the gigantic gully holding the salmon. A few feet deep and stagnant, the pool didn't have much oxygen and the fish moved sluggishly searching for escape routes. Two men jumped into the water, dipped the fish out and passed them one by one along a line formed by the others. Instead of being released directly into the river, each salmon required artificial respiration.

Offering to help, I plunged in. To revive them, I grasped the tail and gently moved each one back and forth in fresh running water. Slowly I felt their energy return as they tried to escape. All I had to do was lessen the pressure of my fingers and they slipped away to continue the upstream push to spawning grounds.

After the last salmon, we walked back to the Beaver, untied the ropes and started the engine. While we had been working, surface winds had increased and changed direction across our original landing path. We would now have to negotiate some sharp bends in a strong crosswind. On the takeoff roll, I left the water rudders down to help follow the river's curve. Unable to climb straight ahead and over the valley's steep sides, I banked left and right several times before reaching a safe altitude.

Back at Lac Rapide, weather forecasters predicted dense fog and heavy rain showers for the following morning. With little prospect of flying anywhere, I joined a group of pilots led by contract Cessna 185 pilot Roly Merrien in the investigation of Sept Iles' colorful drinking establishments. Late that night, I returned to the hotel and anticipated sleeping until late the next day.

At 4:00 A.M., the telephone woke me from a sound stupor. Base manager Monsieur Paradis needed a pilot to leave Lac Rapide at daylight for an emergency flight to a drill camp. His other pilots apparently had removed the telephones from their cradles or wouldn't answer.

"Can't," I whimpered. "Weather's out. Weatherman told me."

"Yeah? Take a look outside, mon ami," he suggested.

I groped to the drawn plastic curtain and pulled it back. Clear, black skies dotted with millions of tiny pinpoint stars spread from horizon to horizon.

203

Sunrise took place an hour later as I stepped from a Les Ailes du Nord sponsored taxicab onto the dew-moistened seaplane dock. Before long, a doctor arrived and we soon cruised above the trees as the sun peeped over the eastern horizon behind us. No rain or fog grounded us this time, much to my regret.

Enroute to the camp, the doctor explained that a man lighting a gas vapor lamp inside a tent received serious burns when it exploded. The dried, oily canvas enveloped the victim in flames as high as fifty feet. Before he could escape, several aerosol cans burst, injuring him further. His work mates radioed for an airplane but they couldn't do anything for him except basic first-aid until the doctor arrived.

Locating the lake and landing on it was easy. A makeshift dock in front of the camp held the Beaver. Not anxious to see anyone so badly burned, I stayed behind while the doctor went to the scorched remains of a tent frame. Black soot and ash marked the tents beside it.

A crew of weary men emerged from a cook tent. Four held the corner of a green sleeping bag as they walked very slowly and carefully toward the Beaver. When one stepped into a pot hole, I heard him curse in French from fifty yards away. The victim screamed despite the efforts of his friends to carry him as gently as they could. As they came closer, I opened the Beaver's left rear door.

Unable to avoid seeing the burned man as we hoisted him into the airplane, I saw that rolls of bandages swathed both his arms. At one end, blistered feet lay exposed and at the other, tremendous patches of skin hung down in flaps from his uncovered face. Swollen ears dripped yellowish pus on the sleeping bag. He raised what remained of his eyelids and looked at me. His lips were nothing but puffed globs of reddened flesh.

Shocked, I recognized him as the lottery winner I had congratulated only days before. He tried to nod but the effort was too painful. The doctor injected him with a pain killer and thankfully, he slipped into a painless sleep.

The return to Lac Rapide seemed to last forever. Fortunately, smooth air prevailed. As I approached the seaplane base, we were assured that an ambulance would be standing by. When we landed, however, it hadn't arrived. Frantic that his patient would die on the seaplane dock, the doctor grabbed the telephone and screamed in French to some hapless dispatcher. We learned that the driver, on the job for only a day or two, had taken a wrong turn.

After the ambulance arrived, the burn victim was whisked away to hospital. I thought the man would need far more than a winning lottery ticket to live a normal life if he survived.

Pilots rarely flew business-suited passengers from Lac Rapide. Once, however, five smartly dressed executives, loaded with incredible amounts of baggage, showed up at the seaplane base without an airplane booked. All top management of a car-rental chain in Montreal, they needed a ride to a private lodge on Lac Kegashka near Kegaska, a fishing community 232 miles east. For this trip along the North Shore, the Beaver would needed full belly tanks. By the time everyone climbed into the airplane, the overload caused the float heels to submerge.

With the extra weight, I tried starting the run with a reduced amount of flap. As the airplane slowly ploughed water and made it onto the step, I added more flap to help the Beaver stagger into the air. Before long, the seven islands from which Sept Iles derived its name faded behind us in the haze. The dispatcher suggested refueling at Havre St. Pierre.

We landed north of the community, filled up and soon took off again to track past another village called Natashquan and then on to Lac Kegashka.

Several buildings took shape on the far shoreline as we flew closer. Much to my surprise, the lodge lacked the amenity of a dock. Despite high winds and huge waves, we unloaded without damage beside a slippery, half-submerged boulder. One executive stepped onto its mossy surface and slid into the water. A guide, hearing his shouts, rushed outside to help pull him out.

One of the party suddenly decided his group couldn't survive in the Canadian wilds without fresh, saltwater clams. He told me he knew some were available a few miles away at the village of Kegaska. With the guide aboard, I took off again, pointed the nose south and aimed for the Gulf of St. Lawrence. Over open water, dangerously high swells looked far too hazardous for landing. Behind some shoals, I saw strands of kelp wrenched upward from the sea floor. One moment they surfaced on the crest of a wave; the next, they vanished in the frothy water.

In spite of the stormy ocean, calm spots occasionally appeared in herd-like groups between the rollers. Selecting one as closely as possible to an island near Kegaska, I approached with the Beaver's nose held high. Unfortunately, I misjudged the proper moment to retard the throttle and slammed into the face of a wall of salt water.

Greenish white liquid flew up over the propeller and onto the windshield as the floats dug in and pitched us forward. We rose again in time to strike another swell. Between slams, I managed to reach my left hand toward the water rudder cable and drop it.

High winds made taxiing arduous but luckily, the water-soaked Pratt & Whitney engine didn't miss a beat. Without question, the sea conditions behind the island would not allow a safe takeoff back to Lac Kegashka. A friendly fisherman in heavily accented English led me to the town's only telephone. After several tries through a French-speaking operator, I contacted the office staff at Les Ailes du Nord. Now, they wouldn't have to worry about the airplane.

I planned to stay the night, but incoming fog blankets looked as if they might settle in for an indefinite stay. Coastal weather often kept floatplanes grounded for weeks at a time. Instead of waiting for blue skies and calmer water, I decided to take a chance and leave Kegaska for the lake.

The guide stayed behind. After spending nearly a month back in the bush, he needed a break. Besides, a long-haired village beauty led him away to somewhere far more pleasant than a camp full of demanding, whining tourists.

With light fuel and only the clams stowed behind the seat, I taxied out. Thankfully, the only available takeoff space faced into a strong wind, which shortened the run. The trickiest part was missing many fish nets spread across the cove. Waiting for waves to subside in hopes that a calm patch might come my way strained my limited patience.

At last, the moment arrived to advance the throttle. Not quite fast enough to provide lift over the Beaver's fat wings I struck a tremendous swell and bounced into the air, then fell back toward the surface. I was out of the sheltered area now; one touch of a float could cause an upset.

Instinctively I jammed the throttle as far into the quadrant as it would go. I staggered slowly along, waiting for the heels of the floats to snatch a wave. With one last gasp, I cleared the water and airspeed increased. Safe now, I reduced flap and engine power, and climbed away.

Most pilots dread carrying external loads on their airplanes. Affluent bush airlines or government air services usually have specially designed canoe or boat racks attached to the aircraft sides. Others depend on creative knot-tying skills. If anyone does a poor job fastening objects to an airplane, the load rarely breaks away cleanly. Many pilots have perished when a canoe or boat beat the tail end of an airplane to pieces.

The owners of Les Ailes du Nord didn't have racks for Beaver CF-GCX and expected pilots to secure their own loads. Monsieur Paradis called to advise me that an Indian family of five with a giant, square, stern canoe would be my next trip.

At the time, my external load experience included a few aluminum or canvas, lightweight canoes at Georgian Bay Airways and one or two heavy boats in Labrador. The Cree family now expected me to move not only their square stern but also the entire tribe with enough groceries to last their children to adulthood. They expected a lift to Lac Grandmesnil, sixty-eight miles northwest of Lac Rapide. Dock hands Danielle and Tio helped load the Beaver, but I had to tie the canoe myself.

It took all of my strength to secure every knot of the thick manilla ropes. Although the finished product still wiggled and rocked slightly when I shook it, the canoe seemed solid enough that it wouldn't break loose. With everyone aboard, including a large Labrador retriever, we taxied away with the canoe's far end trailing in the lake. Once takeoff power pushed enough air backwards over the tail to raise us onto the step position, I expected the canoe to lift clear. Despite an unbelievably long takeoff run, the Beaver left the water cleanly.

As we approached the shoreline, the airplane suddenly began shaking. A quick glance outside showed the canoe had slipped backwards several inches in spite of the ropes. A cushion of shock waves kept it suspended above the float struts as if it were on a flight of its own. Violent vibrations traveled from the outside into the control wheel and to my hands as we barely cleared the trees of Lac Rapide.

I dared not turn because of the slow airspeed but continued straight ahead with the engine at maximum power. No matter how I handled the controls, the oscillation didn't change. Yelling above the noise, I asked the passenger in the right front seat to grab the map from between the seats and unfold it. Instead of turning around to land, flying straight ahead would be the only, and the wisest, move.

Ahead, the deep Marguerite River valley led to flatter terrain. Below, no lakes or clear, rock-free spots existed. We dragged on, searching for the first landable spot. Never far from critical stalling speed, I couldn't relax as the miles passed slowly by. Thirty miles from Lac Grandmesnil, it looked as if we'd make it. Finally, thank God, I saw a glimpse of dark water ahead.

Standard procedure, when landing in unfamiliar areas, meant conscientious, unhurried aerial inspections for shoals, floating logs or hydro lines. Now, white-knuckled and exhausted, I simply cut the throttle and pointed the nose down. So far the canoe hadn't moved backwards any further but kept fluttering and threatening to break loose. Since leaving Lac Rapide, I hadn't made a turn more than a few degrees either way.

Closer to the surface, I increased airspeed and drifted to the center of the lake before the floats skipped several times. At each touch, the canoe shook violently, but the airplane stayed down.

Elated that we had made it, I shut the engine off immediately. Because I could not examine the lake for hazards, I decided to unload far from shore where it was less risky. The canoe barely held my five of passengers, but no one complained as they paddled toward a sand beach a mile away, their Labrador retriever swimming behind. On takeoff, I yanked the Beaver into the air toward a safe cruising altitude.

The last day of August meant my final day with Les Ailes du Nord. After returning from a trip east to Lac Manitou, I caught a company Douglas DC-3 to Montreal via Mont-Joli and Quebec

City. In Toronto, I noticed an attractive woman in the arrivals area searching for someone in the crowd. Easing past her, I saw no sign of my wife. Moments later, someone tapped me on the shoulder. It was Linda—the woman I had admired moments before.

During my second year of teaching, it became clear I had to choose either a classroom or a cockpit. Working with children aged eight to twelve was enjoyable but as the months went by, I began pacing the floors. Ambivalent thoughts of spending my life between four unchanging walls began bothering me.

The lure of untrod places, different cultures, and new experiences won out. Unlike many pilots' wives we had met over the years, Linda encouraged me to stay in aviation. Despite our fondness for Parry Sound and the friends we had made, I handed in my resignation at Foley Public School. Somewhere, we thought, the perfect flying job must exist and we would find it. If that special place didn't turn up within five years, I would return to the classroom.

11 Big Yellow

Shortly before leaving Parry Sound, Linda arranged to board with her parents. It wasn't long before she located a secretarial position in Brampton, Ontario. I contacted Perimeter Aviation in Winnipeg, Manitoba, which specialized in instrument flying training. Having "flown the bush" for years, I realized the changing industry demanded that pilots fly by more than their seat-of-the-pants instincts.

To me, maintaining an airplane in level flight had always meant keeping the ground in sight. According to a government publication I read pilots going into cloud without proper training rarely lasted more than a minute before entering the dreaded "graveyard spiral." For many, it turned out to be fatal.

In Winnipeg, Perimeter's instructors subjected me to many frustrating hours in a blue cage called a Link Trainer. Loaded with instruments, the device was bolted to a cement floor. After many drills and discipline, I finally learned instrument landing procedures, in spite of my natural tendency to depend on ingrained survival instinct.

After the Link trainer, Perimeter assigned me a light, twin-engine plane called a Beechcraft Travel Air. Patient flight instructors explained that higher-time pilots, almost without exception, didn't find transitions from seat-of-the-pants styles to rigid instrument procedures easy. One instructor pointed out that commercial pilot graduates, with 150 to 200 hours, needed approximately half the training as ex-Noorduyn Norsemen or Beaver pilots.

After a lengthy period in the Travel Air, and three times as long studying, I left Perimeter Aviation with a Category II instrument rating. At almost the same time, I received word of another earth-shattering event that changed my life. Linda and I named our child Rhonda.

Armed with the fresh instrument rating, my search for a job in which to spend the rest of my flying days began. To log a few more hours, I accepted work with Georgian Bay Airways to fly a Piper Aztec on fire patrol in Timmins. At the end of the season, a flying club near Toronto needed a flight instructor to teach basics on "Wichita Wonders." These tiny, tricycle-geared Cessna 150 trainers, in which two people barely fit shoulder to shoulder, didn't appeal to me. Nevertheless, I endured three weeks on them and a variety of other light trainers, when I got a call from Red Lake, Ontario.

Ontario Central Airlines needed a Noorduyn Norseman pilot. Although my expensive instrument rating would be useless in this pug-nosed floatplane freighter, my diminishing money supply left no alternative. The company seemed interested in my bush background, and the work sounded exciting. Besides, I had never lost my fascination for the yellow, wood-winged wonders that had roared down Chapleau's Kebsquasheshing River so long ago.

One of the busiest Canadian aviation centers during the gold rush era of the 1920s and 1930s, Red Lake was paradise for airplane aficionados. Several airlines based huge floatplane freighters, such as de Havilland Otters and Beechcraft 18s, at nearly every dock in the downtown section. Large numbers of smaller, private planes added to the traffic.

At the far end of the main street, I found Ontario Central Airlines' main base. In the office, I met chief pilot Roly Heinl who immediately decided to begin my Norseman checkout.

Norseman CF-BHU was one of the biggest airplanes I had ever flown. Its wingspan was more than fifty-one feet and it had a maximum take-off weight of 7,400 pounds. It wore yellow fabric covering and a gigantic Edo 7170 seaplane floats. Previous pilots, who had heard the ear-shattering roar of the powerful CF-BHU on take off, affectionately called it "Big Yellow." The huge airplane's gas tanks held up to 242 gallons of fuel.

After my introduction to the outside of the Norseman, Heinl pointed me to the left front seat and then climbed aboard. A dock boy turned us toward open water. After a flick of a switch and quick action on a wobble pump to boost fuel pressure, the huge, three-blade propeller turned over several times. Bluish black smoke burped from the edges of a soot-edged exhaust pipe.

We taxied out into Howie Bay as the chief pilot pointed out various instrument limitations. He suggested a pair of earphones over my ears would do wonders for noise protection but I ignored his advice. Seconds later, we turned for take off and, as the throttle went in, I regretted not heeding his warning.

The vibration became so severe my vision blurred, and both ear drums shook so much I could only lean into the agony. In desperation, I gestured at Heinl to grab the control wheel while I frantically groped for the earphones. Flattening them against my ears, the nearly incapacitating pain diminished. Next time, I would heed an experienced pilot's advice.

At 1,000 feet, we leveled and headed northward. Comfortable now, we settled into the business of learning to manipulate the Norseman. After several take offs and landings, we returned to Red Lake. The ride went well, but Heinl didn't feel the checkout would be complete until he rode as an observer on my first revenue flight.

The next morning we left Howie Bay for a fishing lodge on the west side of Vermilion Lake, north of town. The owner needed a big airplane to haul a load of "turkeys" (tourists) to the airport for a connecting flight somewhere into the southern United States. As we approached to land, a bank of leaden rain clouds slowly moved toward the lake. By the time we reached the lodge and docked the Norseman, rain came down in torrents. The wind had increased so much that the remaining guests didn't dare leave the lodge.

Our turkeys climbed aboard and we carefully threw in their fishing poles, ice coolers and sleeping bags. The Norseman started easily. We taxied from shore as I reached for an overhead flap handle, similar in shape to an automobile window crank. Ready to go, the water rudders went up against their stops with a clink as the airplane weather cocked into the wind. A second or so before I eased the throttle forward, the chief pilot reached over and stopped my hand.

"Uh, uh," he said. "Do it down wind."

Normally airplanes, especially fully loaded ones, began their take-offs into the wind to enable the air flowing over the wings to obtain better lift. With the freight we carried, downwind runs in strong winds would usually be considered a no-no in the aviation business. It didn't matter now. Heinl insisted, so I dropped the water rudders to turn around.

The take off turned out to be the longest one of my life. With a probable overload—weigh scales didn't exist in the bush—the run exceeded anything I had experienced before. White caps jolted the Norseman as solidly as if we had run across a field of granite boulders. Designed for such conditions, and probably tougher than any airplane ever produced, the Noorduyn Norseman withstood the battering as we lifted slowly into the air.

I looked back and saw that our baggage-tying job didn't fare too well. Every piece of freight lay scattered around the airplane. Much of it was on the turkeys' legs or in the center of the floor boards.

After we returned to Red Lake, only two short trips showed up on the books in several days. One took me to a lodge ten minutes east on Trout Lake. Another introduced me to the Cree Indian village of Poplar Hill, where I flew in a compartment full of propane cylinders and lumber. Human excrement lay everywhere despite the presence of outhouses. Unimpressed with the lack of help from a crowd of Indians watching me dock alone in a strong wind, I left the smelly place.

September meant quiet times for the pilots in Red Lake except for a brief flurry of activity before freeze-up when moose hunters besieged every northern Ontario operator. They wanted quick trips into the bush and out again to transport bloody animal carcasses. Although the few trips I had were enjoyable, I regretted my decision not to wait until a job turned up in which my instrument rating would be useful. The present position looked more limited than I had realized.

Shortly after I finished scraping frost from the Norseman's wings with a rope, Ontario Central's dispatcher thrust a written telephone message into my nearly frozen hand. "Call Ray," it said, referring to a friend from the Canso days a few years before.

Ray Simcoe worked for a well-known oil company operating airplanes from one side of Canada to the other, and into the High Arctic. His flights in Douglas DC-3s or de Havilland Twin Otters took him to Fort Nelson, British Columbia, the main base for an airline called Arctic Air. While stopping on his way to oil fields east of the community, he overheard someone remark that the company needed pilots.

Ironically, the mounds of application forms I mailed from my home in Parry Sound had included a detailed one to Arctic Air. Few prospective employers bothered answering my queries, but Arctic Air responded with an offer. I declined since moving from Ontario to northeastern British Columbia would be an expensive proposition. With a family to support, a cross-Canada move seemed illogical.

After heeding Simcoe's suggestion to work for Arctic Air after all, I learned the company reimbursed new employees for moving costs. My basic salary in September, 1973 began at $400 per month and $6 per flying hour as a Douglas DC-3 copilot.

12 Footprints on the Ceiling

My opportunity to enter the esoteric world of multi-engine transport airplanes had finally arrived. Arctic Air operated Piper Aztecs, DC-3s, a Twin Otter and a Beechcraft Baron at Fort Nelson in British Columbia and at Fort Simpson in the Northwest Territories. They also used several single-engine airplanes to carry out light charters.

The chief pilot carefully examined my pilot license as he talked airplanes and outlined the virtues expected of Arctic Air's DC-3 copilots. Now and then, as he thumbed through my logbook, he asked me what held my interest over the years. I told him. He listened.

"Well, we'd like to have you on the Three," he said. "We'll provide the training and endorsement, but would you mind doing a few trips now and then for us on our Cessna 185? You won't be on it long—just until we get somebody else checked out."

No escape from single-engine bushplanes, I groaned inwardly. I had no choice but to trust the chief pilot's assurances that I would soon fly a twin. Besides, credit card debts now amounted to hundreds of dollars and my wallet contained nothing more than air.

Except for the classic Noorduyn Norseman, few airplanes appealed to me as much as Donald Douglas' elegant creation, the Douglas DC-3. Each of the graceful ladies that crossed my camera lens went into a cherished photograph album. I kept every word printed about the venerable airplanes in storage on my bookshelves.

Never did a DC-3 pass by when I didn't stop and gaze longingly, until the last whisper of its radial engines had faded away. As pleasurable as the Cessna 185 was, my goal was to occupy the right seat of an Arctic Air DC-3. In time, I hoped the captain's seat would be mine. That the Douglas company, in Burbank, California, produced only 10,655 of these magic flying carpets didn't make my quest any easier.

Despite my unbridled eagerness to copilot the DC-3, my first flight with Arctic Air took place on the Cessna 185. Having never flown the airplane on wheels, my landings became progressively smoother until a check pilot pronounced me safe to fly the only single-engine piston airplane at the Fort Nelson base.

Registered CF-YIF, my latest steed didn't have a pilot available for over six weeks until I came on the payroll. The blue and white 185 stared at me from under the tail of a shiny Twin Otter and showed many marks of heavy usage. Abrasions along both sides embellished a beaten fuselage and unsecured seat belts had pounded deep gouges into the metal framing behind both doors. Any trace of finery this elegant bird may have possessed when it rolled out the factory in Wichita, Kansas, had long ago departed.

Inside, it looked worse. Sometime during its inactive phase, a mechanic had borrowed most of the instruments. The remaining few showed cracked glass and scratch marks in their corners. The fluorescent radium in the turn-and-bank indicator lay heaped in a tiny pile at the bottom of the instrument. Behind the windshield, a nearly dry compass rocked unsteadily; its supporting liquid long ago dripped into radios that hardly represented state-of-the-art avionics, even for a place like Fort Nelson.

Long tears in the upholstery held together by oversized safety pins, arched steadily toward the ceiling. Several distinctive footprints directly above the front seats really caught my attention. The airplane had flipped upside down on a mud airstrip the previous spring. The "it's on order" headliner never arrived.

I remembered British Columbia and its frightening mountain peaks well. To anyone who absorbed the lore propagated by tourist associations, British Columbia signified tall, magnificent peaks dripping with startling mountain sunsets, and verdant, unpeopled valleys teeming with near-exotic wildlife. My not-so-hazy memories also focused on teeth-jolting turbulence when oil cans hovered six inches from my bulging eyeballs before slamming into my knees, leaving deep concave valleys of their own.

Short airstrips and dead-end canyons waited to snare suckers soothed into complacency by occasional mist-stilled mornings. In the northeast corner, where B.C. joins Alberta and the Northwest Territories, endless acres of flat, mountainless country soaked in deceptive mud, waiting to grab the wheel hubs of an airplane. Suddenly stopped airplanes turned upside down quicker than the most devout pilot could fire off his first Hail-Mary-Jesus-Christ-shit. Those days and hazards, I remembered well.

My first Cessna 185 flight into "the Rocks," as Arctic Air pilots called the western mountains, occurred shortly after the wheel checkout. A pile of burlap bags stacked by the hangar door required delivery to Horseranch, a hunt camp seventy-five miles southwest. As I marked out my route, charts for the trip showed pronounced color changes. Pale green, grassy lowlands gave way to solid brown, stone mountains. The airstrip, snuggled coquettishly into the bottom of a narrow valley, could only be approached from one direction.

After loading the 100-pound, fetid sacks, measled by tiny, black spiders and sun-dried sparrow manure, my departure from Fort Nelson became a hurried one. The haste stemmed from the unbelievably dank odor in the cockpit, not because Arctic Air paid pilots hourly. Flying with a side window unlatched helped little.

In the foothills, turbulence released clouds of dust from the sacks every time a jolt shook the defenceless Cessna 185. Eventually, I spotted a patch of relatively level ground with wheel marks down its center. A previous rain squall made the airstrip glisten in the afternoon sunlight.

On my overhead visual inspection, I spotted three horses strolling exactly where I intended to land the airplane. Attempting to buzz them off with a low, full-engine power pass was a fruitless waste of time and gasoline. They didn't even bother raising their heads. As I burped the engine by easing the throttle in and out, someone rode out from a row of buildings and waved the horses away.

Apprehensive about landing in such a short, muddy spot, I wanted to make my first approach into Horseranch as slowly as possible. The Cessna 185 thudded heavily into the mire slightly beyond the airstrip's halfway mark. Horse manure splattered over the propeller spinner and onto the engine cowling and windshield. The nose curtsied toward the dark, brown earth, nearly touching it with the propeller before dropping back.

After shutting down the engine, I dragged the sacks outside and dropped them on the ground. The cowboy who herded the horses out of range sat astride his mount and watched me work. He finally withdrew a dirty, hand-rolled cigarette from between his lips. "Annie, getcher gear," he spit. "D'airplane's leavin'."

A young, Chipewyan Indian girl, carrying the standard cast-iron suitcase all northerners seemed to own, crossed the ruts toward us. Her long, black hair flowed off to one side in the crosswind and under her arm she carried a beaded, deerskin jacket. The cowboy pulled a wagon loaded with fatty animal hides, blood-smeared sheep horns, elk antlers, and dripping red meat to the left-hand door.

I hesitated, wondering about an overload. "New on the job, ain'tcha?" he sneered, as I sized up my chances of leaving Horseranch with a solid airplane. "Guys before you always took moren' that."

"The guy before"—the same line I had heard in Labrador, Quebec, Ontario and Manitoba.

I forced everything inside the Cessna 185. The girl tossed her suitcase beside the door and planted her blue-jeaned bottom on top of a meat quarter.

As we dip-taxied across potholes and furrows, Annie shyly asked if she could be dropped off at Fort Nelson's airline terminal. With two notches of takeoff flap and throttle to the wall, the overloaded airplane bored through the mud and manure. With 300-horsepower on wheels, skis, or floats, not much could stop a good Cessna 185.

Despite our bumpy return to Fort Nelson, my passenger

didn't become airsick. I parked the mud-covered airplane under the giant, silver wing of a Canadian Pacific Airlines Boeing 737 jet. As I watched Annie disappear into the confines of the giant transport, I realized that Cessna 185 CF-YIF and I would become good friends. The hell with the way the airplane looked.

Between Cessna 185 flights, the chief pilot suggested a course of study and assigned a check pilot to give me sessions in a Douglas DC-3 registered CF-HBX. Before the ink dried on the license endorsement, Arctic Air wound up with an exceptionally enthusiastic copilot raising and lowering the landing gear in northern British Columbia, the Northwest Territories, and sometimes into the fabled Yukon.

The building of a British Columbia Railway spur kept us over the Rocks almost daily. When the valley filled with fog and the peaks disappeared, plenty of flatland charters made up the slack time.

West of Fort Nelson, construction camps with several hundred men did the ground work, pushing railway tracks through the mountains. Every item needed to be flown across the Rockies, and almost every pound went in the Threes. Rhoda, wife of the construction camp foreman at Mosque on the Skeena River's east bank, transmitted weather reports several times daily to our base. Her encouraging words usually launched a trio of DC-3s. When Rhoda said go, we went.

Standard procedure for a Mosque run, once the wheels settled into the wells after take off from Fort Nelson, involved long cruise climbs to 12,000 feet. At our pre-calculated arrival time, if no breaks in the cloud deck appeared, we would descend cautiously to 10,000 feet. This left 1,000 feet between us and the highest peaks. Rarely did we fail to find recognizable landmarks. A valley, peculiar-shaped rock formations, or sometimes a lake told us our exact position.

After regaining visual contact with "earth"—for our world above the clouds often seemed surreal—valley crawling followed. In clear weather, lack of enroute, low-frequency navigation beacons forced us into map reading along the ridges, valleys and glaciers. Every trip in spring or fall meant plenty of instrument-only flying. Hundreds of flights before us boiled down to some nearly perfect methods of finding Mosque. "Not to worry" became our theme.

Rhoda expected us. We carried a cabin full of tractor parts, cable reels and cartons crammed with steaks, all tied securely toward the airplane's front end and along its sides. Parallel to our load were two passengers. One, a portly type with blue and red tattoos on arms that dangled from a sleeveless T-shirt, snored loudly. The other, a suit-and-tie from Edmonton head office, spread sheets of paper before him and worked quietly. Both sat on locked-down seats.

Our flight planning showed the estimated time over the Mosque camp to be one hour and thirty-five minutes after Fort Nelson. As usual, we saw solid overcast below. In the west, the sky turned a yellowish color, frequently an indication of strong winds aloft.

"What's our estimate?" snapped the captain, a husky Ukrainian who later stepped down to smaller twins for a company in Whitehorse, Yukon. I checked our take-off time and verified some speeds.

"We're over Mosque," I replied. "Guess we look for a hole, eh?"

With our time up, we began searching for breaks in the cloud deck. After circling over an opening in the stratus, we discerned a piece of land marked by a twisted, tiny river. The edges of a huge lake flicked by. It had to be Thutade Lake, which was only a few minutes from the camp. This flying DC-3s in the mountains is a picnic, I thought.

"Throw out the gear!" the captain ordered, as he eased the throttles back and changed the fuel selector to full tanks.

With wheels down and locked, flaps full down and throttles back to the stops, we verticalled into a white-walled tunnel that ended at the dark-brown valley floor. We raised the nose, selected gear and flap up, and applied barely enough power to keep us staggering along a few miles per hour above our critical minimum speed.

As the Pratt & Whitney R-1830 engines crackled and banged, the hole slammed shut behind the tail, committing us to freezing rain, snow squalls and intermittent fog. We picked up a tree-lined water course leading southward along a series of jagged rock outcrops, the tops of which disappeared into the murk. Not one mountain slope or twist of the river matched what we read on the aeronautical charts.

"Oh, Jee-zus, oh-Jee-zus, that ain't Thutade," mumbled the captain.

Corners became sharper. Rain droplets froze to the windshield in sheets, then flicked backwards and disappeared at the same time the pungent odor of de-icer alcohol permeated the cockpit. Ice chunks, cast off from the propellers, slammed against the fuselage. On the right wing, a section of rubber de-ice boot malfunctioned, causing build-ups of coffin-shaped areas of clear ice on the leading edge.

Windshield de-ice fluid ran out as we wheeled around a corner, almost slapping a wing tip on the ground. Waiting for us directly ahead as we rolled level stood one of the most solid fog banks I had ever seen. With no escape route on either side to save us, we barged into it, not knowing whether that innocuous-looking mist held a mountain.

"Power! For Chrissake! Power!" yelled the captain.

My two hands slammed into each other and both pushed pitch, throttles, and mixtures to the wall. I also raced desperately to adjust carburetor heat and synchronize the screaming propellers.

Now began the longest climb in the world. Nothing existed for us in those terrifying, please-let-me-live moments, as we focussed intently on the vibrating instruments in front of our faces. Holding a heading, we watched and waited for the altimeter to move from 4,800 to 10,000 feet. We saw nothing, but knew that out there somewhere, solid British Columbia granite waited, perhaps only a few inches away on each side of the laboring, over-boosted Douglas DC-3.

All sound seemed obliterated in the cockpit, although we both knew that a pair of R-1830 engines at full bore could make a bloody racket. Even the smell of alcohol disappeared. The windshield stayed opaque, seemingly sealing us into a white-curtained casket.

After what seemed like centuries, that incredibly beautiful

airplane popped through the vapor into brilliant, blue sky with sunshine and pretty, white-topped mountain peaks all around us. We survived.

"Holy shit, that's as close as I ever want to come," croaked the captain. At that instant, I resolved to someday seek new employment anywhere east of British Columbia.

Marvin, our cabin attendant for the day, came forward to ask what time we planned landing at Mosque. The business-suited passenger, he explained, was an accountant on an audit, and was demanding explanations about why we accumulated flying time and burned gasoline at the expense of Arctic Air.

For many weeks, the company kept me busy alternating between the humble side of the DC-3 and the pilot's seat of the Cessna 185. The company had only one "little airplane" pilot in Fort Nelson—me. Westbound trips usually meant horrifying mountain flying with accompanying thunderstorms and few emergency landing places. Trips east were almost all oil-related because of the province's waning energy exploration boom. Tall, easily identifiable oil rigs and plenty of long runways made flying into this area more like a picnic than real work. Names like Tattoo, Pacific Pettitot, Commonwealth Rig #3, and Sierra became tiny Xs on my maps.

Early one fall morning, three men from the Workers' Compensation Board booked the Cessna 185 for several consecutive days. They intended to inspect safety standards at every oil rig within reach of Fort Nelson. Arrival procedure at these isolated locations meant buzzing derricks at low level with the propeller in full fine-pitch position to create as much noise as possible. Machinery inside usually prevented the workers and their supervisors from hearing the Cessna's engine.

Landings at the nearest Caterpillar-hacked airstrip followed. Most oil people treated us well, but few invited visitors into their drilling platforms. After we were welcomed to the trailers or tents where the roughnecks lived, inspectors donned their white hard hats while I passed time by flirting with the female cooks, if the camp had any.

Northeastern British Columbia oil companies routinely rotated personnel once a month. Top-level management learned

222

long ago that lengthy isolation caused some people to do bizarre things. Once at a DEW line station on Jenny Lind Island, I met a manager who lacked an ear on one side. During a long, black Arctic night, he told me, a technician, convinced of his resemblance to a Samoyed dog, decided to try his teeth on a living creature. He caught the manager unawares.

On one of our first oil rig stops, a morose crew barely acknowledged our presence—a sure sign of underlying tension. Their cook could hardly be described as feminine. Weighing, by conservative estimate, at least 250 pounds, and less than five feet tall, she had the sex appeal of a flattened football.

Despite her appearance, I learned a few weeks later that a group of berserk, woman-starved drillers chased her from her pen at midnight. Wearing little more than blue tennis shoes and a shard of fabric in -37 C, our company medevaced her out with a Turbo-beaver. She had frozen both feet by the time anyone at the rig came to their senses.

Oil country had many emergency calls. The complex machinery used to penetrate the earth for oil and gas could be dangerous. During late fall, a well-dressed company representative from Vancouver pleaded with us to carry a large, metal box of critical equipment to his rig. Outside the wooden, white-washed window panes of Arctic Air's office, I studied the falling wet snow and occasional precipitation-free periods.

The non-pilot base manager relented and "volunteered" the Cessna 185 and me to do the trip. With full fuel and holding my wheel/skis a few yards above the spruce and balsam, we bored low level along a pipeline and turned sharply left at a yellow-topped rig. With one eye on a stopwatch and the other staring through the nearly opaque windshield, I timed twenty minutes and held the wings as level as possible. We found the strip and landed straight ahead, barely stopping before sliding off the end into a drainage ditch.

Wet snow turned to freezing rain, which clung tenaciously to the wings after we landed. The time seemed right to wait overnight and blast off in the morning when the weather cleared. Without wing or engine covers, I couldn't do anything except attack the ice tomorrow with a snow scraper.

After unrolling a sleeping bag on an empty bunk bed, I found myself with an evening to kill. To pass the time, I strolled into the office trailer to see what Arctic Air's base manager decided matched the value of a high-priced airplane and its pilot. The oil company rep's box was open on the table. Inside were video tapes for a television set, hardly worth risking an airplane and its pilot.

My favorite Douglas DC-3 happened to be the sorriest looking collection of metal in the fleet. Built in 1945 as a troop transport for the Royal Air Force, it later became the property of the Royal Canadian Air Force. Almost all of its military flying took place in Canada. Now, with Arctic Air, it carried the Canadian registration CF-PIK.

No one had ever intended CF-PIK to be an opulent passenger liner. Inside, shredded, khaki-colored headliners exposed the sweet-smelling, zinc chromate undercoating. The cockpit contained the bare essentials. Wires, taped in black, hung from empty holes in overhead switch panels. Sometimes these wires snagged the pilots' hair as they slipped into their thrones.

The cracked side windows barely closed. Behind the copilot seat, pink streams of hydraulic fluid dripped from a broken glass tube. The floor was littered with cigarette butts, sawdust and crinkled flight manifests. Near the tail stood a five-gallon can stuffed with a plastic bag, which served as a lavatory. God help any pilot caught without a seat belt near the so-called toilet. Replacing the bag always became the duty of newly hired copilots.

Outside, lift-truck forks had stabbed several holes beneath the DC-3's door sill. Someone had spilled a pallet of paint, leaving long garish streaks and splotches dribbling rearward toward the tail wheel. On the fabric-covered elevators and ailerons, an uninspired apprentice used mismatched green tape to hide the rips and tears. Underneath the cockpit, battery acid overflow whitened the faded, metal skin.

Despite the Three's forlorn appearance, every captain at Arctic Air asked for the "Garbage Truck." It started and flew like a dream. Being the oldest, shabbiest airplane on the flight line, dispatchers usually relegated the dirtiest assignments to it.

Greasy drill rods and slimy, commercial lubricating mud left their trademarks. Ceiling-high lumber loads and rusty, sharp-edged steel planking punched the walls. Fuel hauls with rubber bladders roped to the floor destroyed electrical wiring and ate rubber boots.

One contract called for a regular run to Pointed Mountain, a drill rig seventeen miles west of Fort Liard, where the borders of British Columbia, Northwest Territories and the Yukon joined. The limp bags of charcoal we carried didn't deserve a place in the spotless, corporate Hawker Siddeley 748 of Amoco Oil, the company that owned the rig. By the time the captain and I rolled out the last bag, we looked like a couple of Mississippi River sailors instead of two pilots flying the antiquated but regal DC-3.

13 Rhoda Said

Fort Simpson, at the junction of the Liard and MacKenzie rivers, held no claim to fame as far as Arctic Air's pilots were concerned. Two airstrips, numerous squalid shacks and trailers, and a two-story building representing a hotel/restaurant provided the only breaks in sub-Arctic river country. Higher authorities in the company decided to allot a trip to Fort Simpson, one of the places in the Northwest Territories DC-3 pilots despised the most.

After landing on the 3,000-foot, dirt airstrip, we ventured toward the hotel in the hope of finding a meal. Glaringly obvious in our zipper-laden flight suits topped with the company's Husky dog crest, we entered a dark hovel containing a half-dozen tables and broken chairs. Draped over one table, a wizened old man with a beet-red nose snored wavelets loudly into a bowl of tomato soup. Parked a few feet away, in the corners of the small room, solemn, rubber-booted Indians with baseball caps stared sullenly.

Debris littered the floor. Cigarette stubs chewed to the filters, wrinkled bottle caps and broken glass crackled and crunched under our feet. Stained serviettes stuck to the floor tiles. Dust and grime covered everything.

We sat nervously by the window. Spying a mass of dead and dying flies between the panes, we quickly moved. The captain,

Al Findall, knocked over a greasy, finger-printed salt shaker containing several nibbled toothpicks. A waitress, resembling a nail keg with legs, grumbled through the folds of her filthy, fat face when we ordered coffee.

She returned in thirty minutes, waddling toward us with two cups in one hand and the fingers of her other performing facial hygiene above her hairy upper lip. She spilled the steaming liquid on the table, shrugged and walked away. We decided on a rapid departure and bolted for the door to settle our queasy stomachs.

Our Fort Simpson load consisted almost entirely of walk-ons, that is, a volleyball team with overnight bags and camp followers. As players slipped aboard in the glare of yellowish truck lights, several liberally dispensed remarks that we, as DC-3 aficionados, considered derogatory, uncalled-for slurs. Our grand dame Douglas DC-3 may not have been the most perfect, pristine flying machine in the Northwest Territories, but we resented their insults.

The Fort Simpson-Hay River leg turned out to be a picnic. Both points depended on directional radio beacons, a luxury pilots working from Fort Nelson rarely enjoyed. Enroute back to Simpson after dropping our passengers in Hay River, the lights of Fort Providence slid slowly by the wing tip in the pitch black night. I had little else to do but reflect on my career in a Douglas DC-3.

No Douglas product ever carried such an enthusiastic acolyte. The easy-to-fly Threes lacked any treacherous vices. No matter what airplane was parked nearby, the Douglas DC-3 always won when it came to graceful lines and elegant stance. The problems, however, came from within the company and not the airplanes. As hours increased in my pilot's logbook, the general theme of "we can't go broke" manifested itself in many ways.

Flights scheduled for 0900 departures often left as late as 1200. More serious, those who never understood the terrifying turbulence found near most of British Columbia's grasping peaks became careless in their loading. One airplane taxied to the end of Fort Nelson's Runway 25 and returned moments later—the cargo of lumber and steel plating had shifted toward the tail because of poorly tied hold down ropes. Without question, a fatal accident would have taken place after take off. Ambitious pilots became disillusioned, and far too many mechanics became lackadaisical in caring for the airplanes we flew.

At Fort Simpson, a radio operator told us the outside air temperature dropped to -28 C. We were told to spend the night and get up early for a dawn trip to the north. After landing, we diluted each engine by holding a toggle switch on the copilot overhead panel for two minutes. We followed up by exercising the propellers to ensure the gasoline-oil mixture traveled into the hub. After shut down, we stepped outside into the cold air to unroll yards of stiff extension cord for the oil heaters on both engines.

Exhausted, we struggled with gigantic, greasy canvas tents in the rear of the airplane and dragged them onto wings and over cowlings. We buttoned the canvas up with fingers stiffened by frostbite and called it quits. An apprentice directed us toward a company house for the night.

Shortly after making ourselves comfortable in the heatless building, a loud pounding noise woke us. A light flickered on downstairs, and a tall Indian stamped into the room. Evidently, he learned from someone where we stayed and came to "shoot the goddamn white man."

At first glance, his reddish face made us believe we were both about to enter the next world, but in the low light from the single, overhead bulb, we saw our visitor start to laugh. Seeing the horrified expressions on our faces, he laughed harder and then slipped back outside. We later learned he was a fellow employee who had a weird sense of humor. He often greeted strangers by terrorizing them.

At first light, we trudged through the snow toward the DC-3. From the cockpit, I noticed an idling Cessna 185 on wheel/skis at the gas pumps. The young pilot refueled his gas tanks by standing on the wheel between the wing leading edge and whirling propeller. Bright, I thought, but he told us he saved time on engine warm up. One slip on the ice or snow and he would have destroyed the propeller.

Our airplane started well after we undressed it, repacked the canvas covers, and rolled up the electric cords. Clouds of blue smoke belched backwards from the engines and almost made the airplane disappear. With oil pressure off the clock, the R-1830 radial engines idled smoothly as temperatures edged slowly into the green markings of the instruments. With no heat in the cockpit, our breath quickly fogged the windows. My glasses also became opaque. As I reached to clean the lenses, my mittened hand knocked them to the floor.

After refueling from stiffened gas hoses, the loaders threw a pile of Hudson's Bay Company freight inside for Wrigley, 110 miles down the MacKenzie River. The first airplane to take off that day—a Piper Navajo—roared away, causing decreased visibility in ice fog. Everyone who followed did so by watching their directional instruments carefully. In most parts of the Northwest Territories, instrument take offs became routine winter procedures.

At Wrigley, the local Slavey people helped unload bundles of dusty gyproc sheets. When I flicked on the high-frequency radio after engine start, the dispatcher in Fort Nelson radioed that a bush-clearing crew expected us at Nahanni Butte, a village near the legendary Headless Valley of the Yukon. The strip measured sixty feet wide by 2,500 feet long. When we arrived, the strip turned out to be much shorter because of unploughed snow. Scrub trees lined both sides.

Eleven men and their gear greeted us. As they piled aboard, we knew the soft surface would lengthen our take-off run. The captain kept both hands tightly on the control wheel and his feet on the brakes while I ran the engines up to full power. When the wheels began dragging, he released the brakes and the Three slowly accelerated.

Sluggishly, we gathered speed, but still didn't become airborne until past the runway's midway point. Seconds before the end of the airstrip and the beginning of a poplar and aspen forest, the captain hauled hard back, staggering the thirteen-ton airplane into the air. We quickly retracted the landing gear to keep the wheels from ploughing a trail through the trees.

Again, we escaped with damage to our beloved Douglas DC-3, I thought. Back in Fort Nelson, Arctic Air's mechanics called me out of the pilot's room. One showed me a six-foot length of tree branch they had found speared through the fabric of the elevator.

Many weeks later, "Hooby" Hoobonoff as captain and I as copilot received an assignment to fly a load of construction workers from two mountain camps to Dawson Creek at Mile Zero on the Alaska Highway. The first stop, we were told, would be Eaglesnest, 102 miles north of Mosque. The second stop would be Mosque itself, with a return to Fort Nelson late the same night. As we cruised westbound by the Rocky Mountain Trench, I called ahead. Weather on the horizon didn't look favorable.

"...below limits here...heavy snow...go to Watson Lake," Rhoda said. "Your passengers will meet you there."

Fine. Watson Lake in the Yukon Territory would be a new stop for me. Luckily, it had a published instrument approach if we needed it. We tuned in a navigational beacon, identified the Morse code signal of Watson Lake, and pointed ourselves up the Trench. Relaxed now, we placed our maps in the rear seat pockets since the valley led directly to Watson Lake. Finding the town would be simple.

Ten minutes from landing, Rhoda notified us the snow squalls had passed. "Can you turn around and come back?" she asked. "Stop at Eaglesnest first."

We had been sailing complacently along in unrestricted airspace, enjoying the British Columbia scenery. By smugly following the needle pointing to the airport directional beacon, neither Hooby nor I had any idea of our actual ground position. Turned around and re-established on an approximate heading, we unfolded every map we could find but couldn't agree on our location. After two hours, I glanced down and recognized a rock formation not far from Eaglesnest. Seconds later, we spotted the long, yellow trailers near the Stikine River.

The squalls had deposited several inches of heavy, wet snow on the airstrip. Fifteen minutes after the huge, black wheels bounced onto the surface, a school bus loaded with the construction workers arrived. Instead of ten men as manifested, I counted twenty-eight big ones, each with heavy packsacks and tool boxes. The altimeter read 4,100 feet on the ground.

No pilot at Arctic Air considered Eaglesnest a pleasant place because of its short length and an enormous dip just past the runway's center. Beyond the midway point, clearing crews didn't have the equipment to remove a large earthen knoll. At the end, a huge block of granite required a sharp right turn seconds after leaving the ground.

With excess fuel, unexpected passengers, and a soggy runway, we had zero wind to help us. On the roll, reaching suitable lift-off speed seemed to take forever. We weren't airborne until the airplane struck the hump and staggered sloppily aloft, shaking badly as first one wing dropped, then the other. A sharp bank put us around the rock outcrop, but we flew down the valley at least a dozen miles before either one of us dared to move.

"What about Mosque?" I asked. "Rhoda said..."

"Turn the god-damn radio off," came the reply.

Dawson Creek, 340 miles away, would be a long, monotonous haul. On top of cloud at 12,000 feet, we plugged in the hot cup, made coffee, and again drifted to lassitude. We soon tuned in and identified the Fort St. John beacon and made a slight heading correction. Now on track, we had nothing to do but look forward to an uneventful trip.

Suddenly, several sharp jolts shook the airplane. Nothing else happened for a few minutes, and then more shaking in the direction of the tail had us both sitting upright. The metal door separating the flight deck from the passenger compartment slammed open and bounced against the radio rack. Our flight attendant, Jennifer, staggered in.

Jennifer, a former bartender from Whitehorse, hadn't exactly been hired for her delicate form and adroitness at mixing martinis and Singapore slings. At 170 pounds of muscle, she could usually handle herself in almost any situation.

This time, however, our passengers managed to bring with them considerable quantities of their own "hooch," and were happily enjoying a private party over the Rocky Mountains. One, Jennifer said, became quite boisterous, careening around the airplane, slapping backs, spilling drinks, and making a dangerous nuisance of himself.

Jennifer smiled demurely between her cavities and coyly asked our husky Ukrainian captain to settle the inebriated catskinner. A captain of any airplane two miles above the earth carries as much authority as the commander of a ship at sea. Expecting him to put down his styrofoam coffee cup, unfasten his seat belt, and use the omnipotent power Arctic Air vested in him to deal with the cave man, I was aghast when he pointed at me and said, "You."

In my high-school days, the nickname "Spider Legs" aptly described my physique and I had not gained a pound since then. Being characteristically meek, mild, and obedient, I had no choice except to follow Jennifer into the cathedral-like spaciousness of the DC-3's passenger compartment.

The captain, carefully measuring more sugar into his styrofoam cup, promised to climb to 15,000 feet. Most people with alcohol in their systems, he reminded me, tended to fall asleep at high altitudes.

Near the two-piece cargo door a solid, substantial creature rummaged through a brown canvas backpack. Using a mental picture of an acquaintance of mine as a scale, I estimated his weight at 300 pounds and his height more than six feet. He withdrew something out of the bag, and leaned against the handle of the left rear door.

In his paw, about three inches of clear liquid remained in a dirty, glass bottle. His coveralls, in contrast to my freshly laundered, robin-egg blue flight suit, was nearly black with slimy lumps of grease glistening along the forearms. Later, I learned he had barely finished lifting the mud-coated blade of a Caterpillar tractor before someone informed him of the flight to Dawson Creek.

Blood, from a cut acquired when he fell upon a metal suitcase in the aisle, streaked across his unshaven face. While wiping his crusted lips, he smeared the gore from cheek to cheek and deep into the furrows of his slanting forehead. Most of his teeth were missing, except two yellow stumps on each side of his prognathous jaw. A pair of wide, myopic eyes tried to focus as he shuffled toward me. Occasionally, tent-sized eyelids swept down to clear the haze through which he peered.

The engine vibration lessened as the captain, up front in his cozy cockpit, leveled the airplane at 15,000 feet. The giant standing before me reached down and placed his log-size arm on my shoulder for balance as the Three collided with a patch of turbulence.

Over a dozen bottles of alcoholic beverages were stilled as twenty-seven members of his herd, each identical in size to the creature before me, craned their necks in our direction. Imperiously gathering every last reserve of authority and fortitude within my physical being, I squeaked, "If you would, sir, please take your seat, sir. If you don't, sir, we will have to drop you and we don't intend to land."

He seemed not to have heard so I added another "sir." His hand remained heavily on my shoulder, but the bottle slipped from his other hand and shattered on the metal floor. The flow of garlic breath pumping from his flame-red throat became so overpowering that I tried desperately to breathe through my ears. Now that his hand was empty, his great, hairy arm groped upward and settled beside my neck. Oh God, I thought, if he claps his dirty hands, my head will pop like a watermelon seed.

The pressure increased, and then slowly lessened. Both hands slid off unsteadily, leaving a pair of tread marks on my flight suit. The altitude must have finally affected the part of his brain that dealt with night and day. The eyes clouded, eyelids drooped, but before he fell backwards through the latched lavatory door, I heard a rumbling undercurrent of grunts that sounded much like "...nice kid."

"Org" regained consciousness after the directional needle swung abeam Fort St. John. Jennifer dragged him to his seat, clipped his belt across his girth, and fifteen minutes later we landed in Dawson Creek. We stayed only long enough to refuel for the return to Fort Nelson.

Each time the company hired new, low-time staff, our chief pilot pulled me off the DC-3 because the newcomers couldn't handle the Cessna 185 on wheel or ski landing gear. "You're more valuable to us on the 185," became the standard reply when I checked the booking schedule. As a result, I found my name inked on the sheet for the day before Christmas.

Luckily, since I thought it would be enjoyable spending some holiday time with my wife and daughter, low ceilings in the mountains canceled the trip. However, weather improved and the next day, while normal people were spreading Yuletide joy, I rolled Cessna 185 CF-YIF from the hangar.

A few Indian families lived between the Selwyn and MacKenzie mountains of northwestern Canada. They preferred traditional, living-off-the-land lifestyles rejected by most of their North American contemporaries. Frequent sources of revenue for Arctic Air included flights to deliver native trappers back to wilderness or tuberculosis victims to hospitals. Often the load consisted of a stack of sleek animal pelts gathered during frigid, sub-Arctic winters.

Less than an hour after leaving Fort Nelson, I greeted a bush-booted Roman Catholic priest at Fort Liard, Northwest Territories. The province of British Columbia was sixteen miles south of Fort Liard and eighteen miles west, the brown-dappled hills of the Yukon Territory dominated the skyline.

The priest had booked a flight to transport someone across the territorial border to a trapline seventy miles from Deadman Valley. Standing beside him, a middle-aged Locheaux Indian man stared solemnly at the Cessna 185. He wore the only hand-stitched, moose-hide parka I had ever seen. His skin matched the color of the muddy banks along the Liard, and the deep recesses of his face held a pair of coal-black eyes.

What instantly commanded my attention was the man's bearing—not obsequious, not overbearing, but proud. His manner reminded me of some figures depicted in a collection of Paul Kane paintings in a museum back home.

His name was Harry Fantasque and his lake was Fantasque Lake. He couldn't speak a word of English. The priest told me this short, wiry man had walked from a cabin deeply ensconced in the winter wilderness across the river. He had somehow made his way to Fort Liard, a distance of fifty-two air miles, pulling a toboggan load of furs and earning his living from the land. Back in a valley somewhere, Harry's family waited. It was Christmas and he wanted to go home.

The freight load was a light one. Several bags of groceries were topped with colorful, plastic toys for his children—it was their Christmas too. Without a word, Harry climbed into the

Cessna 185, and we blasted off toward a bank of clouds that began obscuring the nearest mountain range.

As we bored onward, lowering ceilings forced us to divert toward the winding Beaver River where snow squalls soon turned to impassable curtains. Turning north, we chased several narrow, frozen water courses. Finally, not far from the Nahanni Valley, we turned south to seek better flying conditions. After what seemed like a lifetime, a large limestone ridge ahead showed a spot of blue. Through the break, the airplane shot up and over a row of gargantuan, reddish boulders.

What waited for us on the other side in the blue sky, was a sight unlike anything I could possibly imagine. Even Harry gasped, for he had probably never approached his valley from such an angle. A bowl-like depression, resembling a white Shangri-la, spread before us. Nestled in the spruce and shaped like a giant teardrop, we saw Fantasque Lake in startling contrast to the dark green forest encircling it. No breaks in its snowy surface could be seen, except two rows of tiny trees placed as markers at the far end.

Aiming directly at them, I spotted a trace of bluish wood smoke wisping straight up through the stone chimney of a log cabin. We circled, drawing out four figures who waved excitedly as the blue and white Cessna streaked low above their heads.

After touching down on the soft surface, the snow depth forced me to run a race-track pattern for nearly fifteen minutes before I dared stop. We parked in front of the rustic shack as three lightly clad Indian children came rushing through the powdery snow to greet Harry Fantasque. Some say that northern bush Indians feel no emotion, but that day on that Yukon lake, you could have fooled me.

In the background, I saw a woman clad in an ankle-length skirt. Possessing the same proud demeanor as Harry, she stood waiting until the children finished. Her husband walked slowly and silently toward her. The three children stopped chattering and watched their parents greet. They stood together and embraced.

Suddenly, the family dog shattered the special moments as he tried to jump into the airplane cockpit. The children, on their father's command, trudged through the snow to unload the freight. Just as I will never forget the silence of the greeting moments before, I will have forever imprinted on my mind the surprised looks on the faces of the little kids when they discovered their Christmas toys.

No one said a word to me as I watched. Harry returned to the airplane and extracted several large bills from a roll of money in a plastic bag. Smiling now, he placed the exact price of the trip in my hand. Then, with his family, he disappeared into the tiny cabin. I stood alone in the snow.

The Douglas DC-3s proved ideal for the short, rough airstrips of British Columbia. The captains I flew with knew how to land and stop them in remarkably short distances. Despite the pilots' skill and willingness to go wherever the company needed them, business began declining. When the provincial socialist government chased the oil exploration corporations from the province, many people found themselves collecting unemployment cheques.

The chief pilot informed his copilots that chances of becoming captains in less than two years looked slim. Each time we approached him about a promotion from right to left seat, he expounded his "pebbles-on-the-beach" theory: many younger unemployed pilots would do nearly anything to seize our jobs for less pay.

In March, the airline owner, complete with expensive fur hat, impeccably laced shoes, and short-skirted, blond secretary, arrived from Edmonton, where he also owned a construction and river barge company. He made a grand entrance with the base manager several steps behind him. The secretary smoked a filter-tip, kicked off her high-heel shoes, and sprawled on the pilots' leather couch. After a lengthy lecture about pulling up our socks and flying more, (his managerial subordinates obviously neglected to tell him we were paid by the flying hour) the chief pilot stepped forward.

He announced his cancellation of all days off and holidays until further notice. The future looked grim for those of us with low multi-engine time. Before long, most of the staff resigned. As the company approached bankruptcy.

To my relief, a business envelope with Ottawa company letterhead arrived one morning. With the offer of a copilot position on a Frobisher Bay-based de Havilland Twin Otter in my back pocket, I, too, handed in my resignation.

Like many of Arctic Air's pilots, I fastened a "Last One Out of B.C. Please Turn Out the Lights" bumper sticker to my Ford. Lucky to have found new work, I hit the road with my family and belongings.

Driving down the dusty Alaska highway, and across the wind-swept prairies, I could barely keep the sounds and the feel of the Douglas DC-3 from my thoughts. Years later, I re-read my pilot logbook and felt the nostalgia understood by those who have experienced that magnificent airplane.

14 Orange Bird

After getting Linda and Rhonda settled in Toronto, I traveled to the headquarters of Survair's office in Ottawa. The organization ran aerial survey airplanes around the world. My assignment, however, didn't come with promises of exotic travel. Instead, my place would be the right-hand seat of a de Havilland Twin Otter owned by Bell Canada in Baffin Island's Frobisher Bay.

From "Frobe" the airplane carried installers and repairmen and sometimes traveled as far north as Grise Fjord on Ellesmere Island but normally they considered Baker Lake their western limit. Other trips included long hauls south to Fort George, La Grande and Paint Hills into Quebec along Hudson and James Bay.

After an intense study of flight manuals provided by Survair chief pilot Don Reynolds, I began understanding why the Twin Otter had earned a reputation as a magnificent STOL or Short Takeoff and Landing airplane. First flown in 1965, it carried up to twenty-two passengers. By the time the last rolled out twenty-three years later, each was equipped with powerful, 620-horsepower turbine engines. Smaller than the Douglas DC-3, the Twin Otter nevertheless proved enjoyable to fly and became my first turbine airplane.

The thought of living in Frobisher Bay didn't sound inviting at first. More than 1,200 miles north of Montreal, the Inuit/white community supported a population of almost 2,500. Not a collection of igloos, as many people thought, it contained a high school, hospital, high-rise apartments and other amenities common in the south.

As the Eastern Arctic's regional headquarters, pilots described Frobisher Bay as a place of perpetual poor weather and low temperatures. After several hours of Twin Otter flight training in Ottawa, I caught the first Baffin Island-bound Nordair jet.

My arrival coincided with one of the most severe spring windstorms the locals could remember. I waited an hour in the terminal hoping head office had remembered to notify someone I would be reporting for work.

On the snow-blown asphalt ramp, I saw no Twin Otter that might belong to a telephone company. An airline clerk told me the airplane had left earlier that day for Pangnirtung but she couldn't be sure of a return time. Everyone in the Eastern Arctic knew the airplane well, since it had flown from Frobisher Bay for many years.

Before long, a taxi driver helped lug my baggage up the steps of the Frobisher Inn and I checked into a room. Expecting to spend my first Eastern Arctic evening alone, I turned on the television. An hour later, the telephone rang.

"Hello there," a male voice with a French-Canadian accent said. "You are the new copilot for Survair?"

"Yes, who's this?" I asked.

"Well, we're having a party and thought you'd like to join us," he asked. "Sorry nobody met you but everybody's here now and you'd be welcome."

The voice, I learned that evening, belonged to Jerry Leblanc, the aircraft maintenance engineer for the Survair-operated Twin Otter. His welcome proved typical of Bell Canada's staff who depended on Survair pilots to fly them around the Arctic. Almost all were Quebecers who worked well together. A few brought their families to Frobisher Bay, but the majority left wives and children behind in Ontario or Quebec.

Everyone—from the newest rookie to the highest level of management—seemed loaded with what I came to know as a "joie de vivre." Rarely, in spite of long working or flying hours, did arguments break out between work crews and Survair staff. My six months in Frobisher, as things turned out, became the most enjoyable of my life.

Much of the flying took place on instruments, a field in which I lacked extensive experience. Almost every trip from Fort Nelson meant climbing blind through clouds with little practice in the complicated procedures needed to carry out airport approaches to landing. Leblanc assured me that captains assigned to Frobisher knew every trick in the book. I looked forward to learning from them and soon returned to the airport to see the Otter.

As the tail came into view, a startling flamboyant orange caught my attention. The Twin Otter wore the most bizarre coloring I'd ever seen. Besides looking as if someone had dunked it in apricot juice, a large bell-shaped black logo devastated the elegant contour of the nose. Even black speed lines couldn't detract from the hideous scheme. Ostentatious as it appeared, the design could prove practical during a forced landing in either winter or summer. The outstanding paint would help searchers find it quickly if we ever had a forced landing on the tundra. Locals knew the airplane as the Orange Bird.

This Twin Otter was the most famous of its kind in the world. Used as a demonstrator on tours to many countries, it appeared in dozens of international magazine advertisements and reports. Earlier, CF-YFT or Your Family Telephone, as pilots called it, served as a flying test bed for a fire-bombing system designed around a membrane-bottom water tank. First of the powerful 300 series, the telephone company ran it from Frobisher Bay without benefit of a sheltering hangar.

In the next six months, Survair assigned me to a half-dozen Twin Otter captains. Nearly everyone showed his willingness to pass on the secrets of successful Arctic instrument flying. Only one or two tended to ignore the person sitting on the right. Fortunately, the selfish ones didn't stay long.

The first flight from Frobisher Bay became a memorable one, shortly after I discovered an unfamiliar device called a Global Navigation System, or GNS. Below the instrument panel, this

240

electronic navigation aid took advantage of very low frequency or VLF waves to display our exact location. Depending on signals from ground stations as far away as Greenwich, England or Lima, Peru, accuracy was amazing. Sometimes, atmospheric disturbances rendered the system useless, but we could usually depend on it. As a backup in bad times, we monitored with standard navigational radio beacons.

On the GNS face, a counter read in tenths of a nautical mile. Nothing could be so accurate, I thought, as Urban Murphy, the captain, started the Pratt & Whitney turbine engines. As we taxied out, he advised me the first hour would be a familiarization flight. "Sit back and enjoy the scenery—just observe," he said. Near the end, I could begin my copilot duties.

I was surprised we were going in the first place, considering the blowing snow, low ceilings, and high winds. I watched "Murph" push some bright little white buttons on the GNS to insert latitude and longitude. Seconds later, we left Frobisher's Runway 36 and the ground disappeared almost immediately. In the murk, we flew steadily southwest using instruments to find a destination at the tip of Arctic Quebec.

Asbestos Hill, a mine a few miles inland from Hudson Strait, depended on a gravel runway for communication with the outside world. Workmen stationed there produced five ship loads of asbestos per year to keep a factory fully occupied somewhere in Germany. The place offered nothing in the way of navigational aids except a low-powered beacon. I felt certain that locating it in the gloom would be highly unlikely.

A mine operator called to say that low cloud and snow squalls obscured the hills and camp. Occasionally, a break or two in the clag allowed us a glimpse of barren rock or blocks of sea ice flashing beneath the balloon tires. I watched our mileage counter tick off the final mile in tenths until the glow of the digital numbers read zero. No airstrip.

"See, I told you. Nothing's that good." I said.

"Yeah?" said Murphy. "Just wait."

We began sinking at 500 feet per minute through the clag, maintaining track, counting and waiting, as pieces of ice snapped loose from the three-blade propellers. Each piece slammed against the fuselage, when suddenly the yellowish tint of Asbestos Hill's tiny runway lights along the runway edges appeared below. Murphy leveled the wings, brought the overhead engine power levers back and dropped underneath the cloud. As copilot, I completed landing checks, slipped our propellers in full fine pitch and awaited his call for flaps.

"Full," Murphy mumbled, his voice barely audible in the earphones.

In seconds, the tundra tires touched the stones and we swept by colored tar-paper cone runway markers. Ahead, I saw a frightened Arctic hare scamper quickly from behind a light. We slowed to taxi toward a small silver shed and shut the engines off. Now, I believed in the accuracy of the GNS.

The load, Murphy said, was typical of ones handled by our Orange Bird. Besides the telephone men, we carried monstrous reels of black plastic cable, climbing spurs, Princess telephones or grocery orders needed to support installers in the communities. We rarely enjoyed the luxury of an empty airplane. Each time we struggled into the air from limited-length runways, I marveled at the Twin Otter's remarkable capabilities.

Nearly as rugged as the Douglas DC-3s of Arctic Air, the Twin Otter's weak point, Murphy pointed out, centered on the nose wheel. Supported only by a few bolts and tiny struts, it could be snapped off easily in deep snow or ditches. Nevertheless, landing on unprepared airstrips rarely hurt the airplane, mainly because of techniques developed by pilots during operational flying. Strange touchdown sites rarely surprised me after the first few weeks.

On one trip with another captain named Rod Poitras, we over-nighted for several days in Fort George, a Cree Indian settlement later known as Chisasibi.

Our flight from Fort George took us to communities on the coast of Hudson Bay and down along James Bay. Paint Hills needed a work crew to raise and wire telephone poles delivered by barge weeks before. With several reels tied snugly in the centre of the Twin Otter, we left the soft sand runway of Fort George and pointed south.

A short hop of forty-nine miles, we quickly located Paint

Hills. To my surprise, I couldn't find an airstrip anywhere. Unfamiliar with the area, I kept silent as Poitras circled the village and then leveled. He called for a slight touch of flap, reduced power settings and asked for landing flap. I looked at him, then outside. He nodded.

Worried now, I saw nothing resembling a patch of ground on which to place a multi-million dollar de Havilland Twin Otter and its pilots. With the village off to my left, I looked everywhere for the strip. I desperately tried to understand what Poitras had in mind as we drew close to the spruce tops. Seconds went by, but still nothing.

Ahead, a hole in the bush took shape and a thin ribbon of road passed through it. The road was far too narrow for the Twin Otter's wheels. Trees on either side would rip the airplane apart if we landed there. The edge of the hole moved closer now.

"Full flap," Poitras snapped as he yanked the power levers back to their stops.

My God, he's lost his mind...he's landing in a gravel pit, I thought, preparing for my first accident. Down over the trees and into the hole, the wheels slammed down hard and Poitras stomped the brakes. He smoothly slipped the power levers backwards through their rearward stops for full reverse. The Twin Otter came to a shuddering halt sharp enough to fling me forward in the shoulder harness. We stopped in an overwhelming cloud of dust, spruce needles and other debris. Our "runway" was a gravel pit.

When the wind blew away the dust, I noticed a yellow truck waiting patiently, facing the nose of the Twin Otter. Unfazed, Poitras backed loudly off the road to a small, level patch in the bush. The truck driver waved when he passed by.

We carefully rolled the cable reels from the airplane and let them thunk into the gravel. Our four installers moved them away from the propellers as another half-ton truck drove up. We walked into the village to pass the afternoon while the crew went to work. With little else to do, I wandered among the houses then down to the nearby river. As I stepped across a dormant snow machine, I saw a huge congregation of Cree people watching a float-equipped silver gray de Havilland Otter land and taxi to shore.

Children by the dozens stood ankle deep in water. Behind them, others watched the pilot step onto the float. Behind this group, more people, much older, sat on timber piles, canoes and overturned fuel drums. Curious, I joined the throng.

A man told me many children were leaving Paint Hills for boarding school in Fort George. One boy, about nine years old and dressed differently from the others in a new jacket and pressed pants, stood rigid, trying to be a brave little soldier. No tears coursed from his eyes but from several feet away, I saw a trembling lower lip.

A woman wearing a dark blue skirt so long it covered her ankles walked with him to the Otter. She carried a small canvas backpack in her hands and wore a blood-red kerchief on her head. They stopped together as a man by the airplane's tail reached down to shake the boy's hand. He said a few words and stepped aside to let the woman hand the boy his packsack. The pilot made a move to boost the boy onto the float. Another figure approached from the crowd—a wizened old man who supported his thin, trembling frame with two wooden canes.

The boy looked into the man's eyes. Not a word passed between them. I noticed a movement and shifted my stare from the elder's face to his hand. He fastened a white-edged feather on the rim of the boy's hat.

I later learned the feather came from a Canada Goose. The people of Paint Hills depended heavily on these winged, life-giving creatures. To them, the feather represented a bond between family members, a link passed from generation to generation. Evidently, I had witnessed a special moment. Considering the elderly man's physical condition and age, he was likely the boy's grandfather. Chances were, I thought, it might have been their last moment together.

The Otter's side doors clunked shut. As the huge propeller blades turned slowly over and settled into a noisy idle, low wailing sounds began to build into a dirge. I watched the water rudders raise onto the backs of the floats and the engine steadied into the characteristic "pocketa-pocketa" sound of Otters. Soon, only its silhouette remained above the spruce, and then it too disappeared.

Many families had watched their sons and daughters fly away that day. The laughter of these children wouldn't be heard again for several months.

At dusk, we returned to the Twin Otter. Strong winds had dressed our Orange Bird with a fine coating of whitish dust. Most of it disappeared in a swirl when we fired up the turbine engines. Light now with only four installers and no cable reels aboard, the airplane leaped out of the pit easily.

Odd landings took place often with CF-YFT. The next day, we received word about telephones that didn't work at Payne Bay, 130 miles northwest of Fort Chimo. After another hop across Hudson Strait and parallel to Ungava Bay's west shore, we circled the village. Like the day before, I didn't see an air-strip. Poitras knew the place. This time, I kept my thoughts to myself. After a gravel pit landing, nothing could be surprising. He pointed to the side of a hill north of the village.

"That's it," he said.

I still didn't see anything that looked like a landing area. By the time he called for final-approach checks, a pair of orange, five-gallon pails caught my attention. Someone had placed them on the hill top to represent a runway threshold. No wheel marks indicated the strip had been used. We bumped and slammed to an uneven stop. The surface was so hard and dry that we barely raised a speck of dust.

Copiloting the Orange Bird had some fringe benefits. Most companies that previously employed me had kept their pilots in the air as much as possible. With Survair, crews had time to explore the Eskimo or Indian communities while waiting for telephone installers. Places like Payne Bay looked interesting from the hill top, but a long walk downhill and an exhausting climb back to the airplane didn't look appealing.

We heard a diesel engine start from somewhere in the village and soon watched a front-end loader chug slowly up the slope. At first, I thought the driver planned to improve the so-called run-way. To my surprise, it turned out to be Payne Bay's airport limousine. When the big, yellow machine jerked to a halt, the telephone men threw their equipment into the shovel and hopped aboard. We also climbed over the rust-edged lip and settled in for a downhill journey to town.

At such a steep angle, I feared a brake failure would end with us piercing the nearest house, or the machine would topple, crushing everyone beneath its bulk. My fears were unfounded; we arrived safely and enjoyed a walk in Payne Bay. The front-end loader went back to moving earth on the waterfront, so Poitras and I trudged uphill to the airplane. My recently purchased Eskimo stone carvings made climbing more difficult. Our departure took place in the opposite direction and seemed more like a carrier launch than an airplane takeoff.

During my Resolute Bay epoch years before, astrocompass usage was routine in the High Arctic. Back then, most newcomers quickly reached the stage where they could calculate a heading within minutes. In the Orange Bird, we carried enough electronic navigational equipment that nothing else was necessary. Nevertheless, the company insisted we carry an astrocompass but relegated it to semi-permanent storage under the copilot seat. Only once during my months with Survair did I bring it out to pass the time.

After departure from Southampton Island's Coral Harbour, we tracked east for a return trip to Frobisher Bay. Fifteen minutes later, a cloud deck obscured the rocky barrenlands, but at 11,000 feet, we flew comfortably in blue sky. Although we lacked an autopilot, the Twin Otter needed little more than a nudge now and then to keep the wings level. Since the captain flew this leg, I had little to do after bringing the logbook up to date and ensuring our passengers were comfortable.

To break the routine, I brought out the astrocompass. It had been since I last used one and I didn't want to lose the skill. We knew our approximate latitude and unlimited sunlight everywhere provided the shadows as I fed in the necessary numbers.

Strange, every time my figures showed a heading, it failed to match what registered on the airplane's instrument panel. I tried again and again but each answer came out the same. Thinking I might have forgotten some vital steps, I reviewed my arithmetic, but still no change. Apparently, the Twin Otter's instrumentation could be wrong. Before bothering the captain, I turned on the radar.

Designed to portray islands and shorelines, radar proved helpful near Arctic settlements during poor weather. Communities showed on the screen as bright, greenish, oval shapes as we drew closer. Knowing we still had much barrenland to cover before Frobisher Bay, the absence of color on the screen came as a surprise. The unit remained dark, indicating the airplane flew over water.

I mentioned this to the captain but he believed in infallible cockpit instruments and wasn't concerned. Both our radar and navigational aids couldn't malfunction simultaneously. Impossible, he said. It never happens. I must be wrong.

Chagrined, I sat back in the seat. Airplane captains didn't make mistakes, I remembered. Since the fault must be mine, reviewing my astrocompass after landing at Frobisher Bay would be a wise move.

Suddenly, a glow appeared at the top of the darkened screen as the shape of an island slowly slid into the center. Now, the captain agreed that something didn't seem quite right after all. The airplane heading may have wavered slightly, but we knew the approximate wind speed and direction at our altitude. According to our timing, Twin Otter CF-YFT should have been dead on track. From beneath the seat, I extracted a topographical chart and quickly identified Charles Island, a few miles north of Deception Bay in Arctic Quebec. We were definitely far off our intended route.

"Call Frobe," he said. "See if they can pick us up yet."

Weakly, the voice of a radar operator confirmed our position as ninety-five miles south of the published airway. Somehow, our directional indicator had developed an error of more than sixty degrees. If we hadn't noticed and continued, expecting to land in Frobisher Bay at our predetermined time, we may have been in serious trouble.

Out of sight of ground, we would have dropped below cloud as planned, probably in terrain higher than expected. No question, Survair would have lost an airplane and its crew. At the least, we would have had a forced landing somewhere, once we ran out of fuel. To this day, I wonder at the coincidence that made a bored copilot practice astronavigation.

Standard policies in most companies that had hired me as copilot either on DC-3s or Twin Otters, involved a 50/50 split of flying duties. Safe captains considered any suggestions copilots might contribute. Some quickly forgot that they, too, started their multi-engine careers from the right seat.

Other airmen told me that one pilot nearly ran out of fuel in the Orange Bird while flying to Great Whale, Quebec, from Frobisher Bay. This pilot decided not to bother refueling after landing at Povungnituk, though the company had arranged several gasoline drums beside the runway. He didn't need it, he said, as Great Whale was only a mere two-hour hop south.

At the former mid-Canada airport on the east coast of Hudson Bay, gas attendants simply inserted a hose into the Twin Otter's tanks. Too impatient and not wishing hand pump at Povungnituk the pilot decided to wait until Great Whale. Unfortunately, weather turned extremely poor. In spite of two instrument approaches to minimums, he and his copilot couldn't locate the runway. With no other choice, they turned toward Fort George, another ninety-eight miles south.

Halfway there, the red fuel low-level warnings began flashing. Before long, the captain decided to shut down one engine to save fuel. Off to their left, they saw the lights of La Grande, the main airstrip for the massive James Bay project. The copilot spotted more lights to the right, which they knew would be Fort George.

After an engine restart, they turned toward the slightly closer dimly lit airstrip of Fort George when fuel starvation caused an engine failure. The captain made the landing, but as they turned around near the fuel drums, the remaining engine quit. Few pilots could bring themselves so close to losing an airplane and live to tell about it.

Now, I rode with this captain and knew of his reputation for cutting things too fine. Weather west of Frobisher Bay reportedly grounded a large number of airplanes, including one flown by an experienced RCMP Twin Otter crew. A rare Arctic thunderstorm passed Coral Harbour and topped at 35,000 feet—far beyond our legal ceiling. Despite the likelihood of meeting this monstrous storm somewhere enroute, we left Frobisher Bay for Coral Harbour.

Cruising west at 12,000 feet, dark clouds on the horizon suggested a rough ride ahead. Radio operators in Coral Harbour confirmed that the thunderstorm still hovered within sight of their airport. A few lightning flashes indicated the massive cell stayed clear of our intended landing area.

On our final approach at Coral Harbour we depended on instrument flying to find the runway. As we taxied in, the pilot of an airplane passing overhead radioed that severe snow squalls followed the thunderstorm and blanketed the west coast of Hudson Bay, including our destination at Rankin Inlet.

Coral Harbour, I knew, offered a luxury that we rarely encountered away from main airports. Like Great Whale, aviation fuel at Coral came from electric pumps. We would be spared the back-straining effort of rolling forty-five-gallon drums to the Orange Bird and laboriously pumping smelly kerosene into the airplane's belly.

A quick trip to the weather station told us that low visibility and snow ceilings still dominated Rankin Inlet. With limits at legal minimums, it made sense to take as much extra fuel as possible in case they lowered further. Our next logical landing place or legal alternative was Churchill, beyond our range from Frobisher Bay.

"Nope, we don't need any," the captain announced. "We'll get by."

Astounded, I dropped the papers on which the weatherman had written his Rankin Inlet forecast. To pass a fuel pump in the Arctic struck me as idiocy. Evidently, he hadn't learned anything from his close call over a year before.

Still a green copilot, I knew that no one would defend me if I refused to step aboard. Also, our company might be forced to answer questions from the owner of the Orange Bird.

"Well," I said, trying to stall as I racked my brain for some way to get the fuel aboard our airplane. Then I remembered.

"Fuel's cheaper here at Coral than at Rankin Inlet," I said. "By at least a nickel a gallon."

249

"Oh," the captain replied. "In that case, fill it up."

Relieved, we now carried enough extra fuel to reach Churchill, if necessary. I watched the snow fall heavily, but it was dry enough that none stuck to the wings as we taxied out. After an instrument takeoff, we ploughed back into the gloomy cloud. Rankin Inlet, if my calculations proved correct, would take us one hour and forty-five minutes.

In Canada, pilots depend on "approach plates" to find a runway when they can't see the ground. Printed on eight-by-five-inch sheets of paper, the plates show headings and altitudes to which aircrews must adhere. If pilots descended underneath the published minimums, they placed themselves in grave danger. Rankin Inlet's plate showed an absolute minimum final approach height of 460 feet above sea level. If ceilings dropped below that, legal landings wouldn't be permitted. In our case, a missed approach would be followed by a flight into improved weather at Churchill.

Many Arctic companies designed their own illegal procedures which sometimes were practical, if not dangerous. At Povungnituk, for example, I knew that no federally approved methods existed but pilots, desperate to get down, selected headings that placed them over the sea free from obstructions. Dropping into cloud with radar and special altimeters to measure height above the surface rather than sea level became routine. Once at ice or wave-top level, pilots flew slowly east until the village came in sight. Beyond it was Povungnituk's raised airstrip.

Ahead waited my first instrument approach into Rankin Inlet. I was familiar with the former mining community from my days on Lamb Airways' Cessna 180. With the proper plate in hand, I did exactly what the captain expected and called out altitudes, times, and airspeeds.

He passed the navigational aid and continued toward Hudson Bay, then slowly turned around to a land-bound heading. Simultaneously, we dropped below the minimum legal altitude on the altimeter. At least we might perish close to the runway, I thought, or perhaps a hole might appear in the swirling snow through which we could grope toward the surface.

Without warning, the captain brought the power levers further back and began descending lower. We flew deeper into the snow, and came closer to the ice of Hudson Bay and to the rocks of its rugged shoreline.

"Watch that radar altimeter close, real close," the captain snapped. "Call me when we're fifty feet above and let me know if you see anything."

From the corner of my eye, I spotted an ice ridge flash by not much lower than our big, black tundra tires. "Got the ice," I yelled, nearly shaking the earphones from the captain's head.

Beyond the windshield, visibility picked up to almost a mile. In the distance we saw the tall, wood head frame of the abandoned Rankin Inlet Nickel Mine. Seconds later, the litter of the mine passed on my right and we touched down on the gravel runway.

Another lesson: rules could be broken and the pilots could survive. With a radar altimeter, ridged sea ice and the tall mine shaft, airplanes could make it into Rankin Inlet when approved practices didn't work. Had we followed the approach plate precisely, our next stop would have been Churchill. Nevertheless, I resolved to carry as much fuel as possible, in the airplanes I flew.

A few weeks later I found myself bound towards Pond Inlet with another captain. At the top of Baffin Island across from Bylot Island, moisture and high winds slamming into the sea ice made landings tricky. At the time of our flights, the airstrip consisted of a narrow patch of land on a hill. After a stop at Clyde River from Frobisher Bay, we arrived in time to greet a full-scale northern blizzard. Straight down, we spotted the red and white buildings of the Hudson's Bay Company.

Movie makers like to portray Canada's north as a land of constant snowstorms and whiteouts like this one at Pond Inlet. On final, winds and snow hit us with an unbelievable violence. The world we'd seen from the cockpit seconds before vanished completely in a screaming white fury. Rarely has any Arctic storm blown with greater severity and rocked an airplane so violently. We continued down, hoping to see the ground as winds gusted to forty knots and ninety degrees across our intended landing track.

Someone from a parked airplane on the airstrip radioed us that the exposed section we saw consisted of glare ice. A slip could place us in a snow bank, but Captain Urban Murphy kept the Twin Otter perfectly aligned. His reputation as one of the best in the business proved itself as he came up and over the runway threshold.

To keep straight, he advanced power on one engine and reduced it on the other. Murphy gently touched the rudder pedals to keep the nose in line and occasionally adjusted the control wheel. Closer to the runway now, buffeting increased so much that I wished I had taken time to tighten my seat belt even more. The airplane settled onto the ground with barely a bump.

Still in control, Murphy applied gentle braking. He kept considerable power on the left engine to prevent us from being blown off the side. By the time we parked, visibility dropped so low, we could barely see our wing tips. Parking into wind, Murphy shut the engines down as a Volkswagen station wagon backed to the side of the airplane.

Murphy deserved the respect he brought to the Arctic. Unfortunately, after this trip, the company transferred him south and I never flew with him again.

The arrogant captain who replaced him conveyed nothing in terms of skill and claimed to know the Arctic well. After the first flight, it became obvious he had spent little time in the barrenlands and far less on Twin Otters before Frobisher Bay. While on approach in a strong crosswind at Asbestos Hill, I noticed he retarded power on the wrong engine.

As we approached, the captain began having a hard time keeping the Orange Bird's nose pointed along the imaginary runway center line. He struggled, slamming the controls one way, then the other. The nose pitched down and speed increased beyond the recommended limit. Before he drove us straight into an accident, I decided to speak up.

"Shut your fuckin' mouth," he snapped.

Far too fast, the Twin Otter slammed heavily onto the gravel surface, spraying tiny stones upwards into the propellers and along the belly. It darted right because the captain forgot he still carried power on the incorrect side. He yanked the levers back hard and hit the brakes so sharply, the front end snapped down. For a moment, I thought the nose wheel strut would break.

We stopped. Aghast that anyone could treat an airplane in such a manner, I was speechless.

"I don't have to answer to you," the captain snapped again, this time from the corner of his mouth. "I know what the hell I'm doing."

At this point, my time on the airplane had been accumulating for over three months. The near disaster took place during his first four days on the job. Happily for all, Survair kept him in Frobisher Bay for only a short time before mechanic Jerry Leblanc told us that CF-YFT needed special maintenance. He asked the captain to make the flight to Montreal for final adjustment and replacement of electronic gear—the same that nearly caused our crash weeks before while returning from Coral Harbour.

Having been in the Arctic for so long, I welcomed an opportunity to see my family, no matter how brief. We loaded Leblanc's tools and two drums of scrap copper he planned to sell in Montreal. Our first stop took place in Wabush, Labrador. Next, we planned landing at the French-Canadian community of Lac La Tortue to drop telephone company staff whose work terms in Frobisher Bay ended days before.

As we neared Lac La Tortue we saw several private airplanes flown by weekenders for pleasure. Although they weren't professional pilots in the sense they didn't earn their living in the air, most long ago learned safe and courteous flying. They obviously enjoyed their evenings aloft as winds died and turbulence subsided. Although no radio control existed at the airport, these pilots practised proper procedures and spaced themselves correctly when landing and taking off.

Before landing, I removed a flight information manual from the door pocket on my side of the airplane. A cautionary note for Lac La Tortue suggested broadcasting our intentions on a special frequency called unicom. As I began tuning it in, the captain stopped me.

"Don't bother," he said. "We don't have to talk to those puddle jumpers."

Perplexed at his blatant disregard for safety, courtesy, and

253

common sense, I said nothing and did as he directed. Ignoring the standard entry procedure to the rectangular traffic pattern, he barged in front of a Cessna 172. We touched the narrow asphalt smoothly and taxied to a grassy area to unload.

As I stepped outside, a forgotten smell immediately caught my attention. It took a few minutes for the idea to sink in that the fragrance wafted upward from freshly cut grass beneath my feet. A lawnmower was parked a few yards away. Its owner and some local pilots came over to have a look at our Orange Bird. Friendly people, they asked about the turbine engines and the reason for the gigantic balloon tires. Suddenly, an angry voice broke in.

"Who the hell's flying this airplane?"

I turned to face a very irate man. In his hand, he carried a green airplane logbook and looked as if he intended to hit me with it.

"Over there," I said, pointing to the captain who stood underneath the Twin Otter's tail, calmly urinating. The presence of several young children and their pony-tailed mothers nearby didn't faze him. The enraged man stomped over to the captain.

In the parking area, a white, tricycle-geared airplane sat with both doors open. Someone must have left it in a hurry, I thought, and then realized it was the airplane we had cut off during our landing approach.

As I listened, the private pilot delivered a long, harsh lecture on aerial courtesy. The red-faced captain couldn't deny his rudeness and stood listening. Our passengers and other local residents including the young mothers who had turned away when he piddled on the grass moments before, gathered around and listened to every word.

Ashamed for not speaking out more strongly before we landed, I retreated to the cockpit and brought the logbook up to date.

Empty now, we left Lac La Tortue and proceeded along the St. Lawrence River to Montreal. As I watched the long, narrow fields passing by, the captain said nothing. At Montreal's international airport in Dorval, he planned to catch a flight to Ottawa for assignment somewhere else. I drove him to the terminal after handing over CF-YFT to the avionics company, thinking we would probably not meet again. As he hoisted his last suitcase from the car, he turned to me.

"I owe you an apology," he said.

"What?" This guy, I already knew, was never sorry for anything. Surprised, I waited.

"Back in Asbestos Hill, you were right. I nearly lost the airplane," he said. "Also, today in Lac La Tortue, I acted like an idiot. Sorry."

Somewhere long ago, I learned that only big men admit they are wrong. With new respect, I realized his apology took plenty of effort. Now, I hoped we would fly together again someday, but we never did. Survair later dismissed him and he disappeared from the aviation industry.

Two weeks later, Rod Poitras replaced the previous captain and soon we found ourselves circling Povungnituk to announce the Orange Bird's arrival. We had flown from Asbestos Hill and expected to wait a day for the telephone installers. The short runway east of the community looked barely adequate for the loaded Twin Otter. In the left seat on my leg of the trip, I landed at the strip's northern end.

The airplane didn't go far in the soft sand. Taxiing to a parking spot took plenty of engine power. After shutting down and stepping outside, the sand sucked the boot from my right foot. Leaving Povungnituk might be a problem, we thought. The soft runway surface would probably quadruple our takeoff distance.

After refuelling from drums sold to us by Austin Airways of Moosonee, I walked the area carefully. Close to the runway, I saw a badly damaged Piper Navajo, a ten-seat airplane manufactured in Pennsylvania. An Eskimo who drove us to the village explained the airplane had crashed on takeoff. Its pilot landed the night before in a heavy snowfall and the next morning, stranded and unable to leave, he decided to be resourceful.

No runway-clearing equipment existed in Povungnituk, so he located some wood toboggans to rope under the wheels. His takeoff plan might have worked but, according to our driver, one toboggan broke loose and swerved the Navajo into some rocks. Later, more experienced pilots told me the technique can be used, but the toboggans must not be tied in place. They had to be left loose to drop away after the airplane became airborne.

After an interesting day in P-O-V, as pilots called the community, we managed to talk our way into another ride back to the Orange Bird. On the way, we passed two young Eskimo boys who had shot a beautiful, white, swan-like bird moments before. They would probably eat the unfortunate creature but it always saddened me to see Arctic wildlife destroyed. Another time, I saw the putrefying, maggot-filled carcasses of murdered beluga whales littering the beach at Koartak on the northwest tip of Ungava Bay.

The captain allowed me to do the take off, despite the shortness and poor condition of the airstrip. I slid into the left seat, started both engines and slithered in the sand to the threshold. Besides the softness and lack of length, our run also pointed uphill. Beyond that, a stagnant slough of water waited to snag the Twin Otter's big, black tires.

"We can't do it," I said.

The captain knew the place well, having spent the early years of his career servicing Povungnituk from Great Whale. "No problem, you make a normal takeoff and I'll take care of the flaps."

Flaps, the low-lift devices on the trailing edge of the wings, normally helped an airplane become airborne at lower speeds and in shorter distances. Standard procedure for the Orange Bird called for ten degrees.

Deferring to the captain's experience and my lack of it, I eased the power levers to maximum settings and we began rolling, slowly at first. In the passenger/freight compartment, we carried four men and two cable rolls—quite a load, considering the strip condition. Airspeed increased but we still lacked enough to leave the ground.

"Watch," the captain said.

This man, who enjoyed teaching, always insisted I learn the most practical techniques in Twin Otter flying. Now, he selected full flap, a setting normally used only for landing. To my surprise, the airplane jumped into the air shortly past the halfway mark. It wouldn't climb so I kept the nose level and barely skimmed across the uphill end of the runway. The captain watched the airspeed indicator closely while keeping his hand on the flap selector. Seconds later, he retracted them and we climbed away for Great Whale. I had gained more experience in taking an airplane to its limits.

The airplane owners handed down a strong rule before my assignment as copilot in Frobisher Bay. Absolutely no non-company passengers rode in the Orange Bird, except in emergencies. Commercial organizations didn't appreciate a telephone company delving into their meager sources of passenger revenue. Baker Lake, a village in the western section of our territory, happened to be a place where airlines served the settlement of 1,037 white and Eskimo residents and charter airlines arrived nearly every day. A prosperous lodge, offering fishing tours or wildlife walks, also operated full-time.

Frequently, our schedule demanded overnight stops in Baker Lake, when we spent time along the Hudson Bay coast and south to Churchill. One evening, a breathless man dressed in a khaki-colored, government-issue parka arrived at the lodge. We had already checked in and planned leaving in the morning.

A technician at the weather station, he told us his child seemed seriously ill and had no way to hospital until the next scheduled flight. The last Transair DC-3 had left Baker Lake hours before. Distraught, he asked if we would take his baby daughter to Churchill where better facilities existed. When we suggested he contact the telephone company head office in Frobisher Bay for approval, he left and returned twenty minutes later.

The lodge soon received a long-distance message authorizing the flight. We checked out and went back to our Orange Bird. Moments later, the man and his wife stepped aboard with their daughter. The child didn't look ill, although she slept during the entire flight. The mother, we thought, was in far worse shape. Frantic that her baby had become sick far from modern hospitals, she held her tightly while the father rode solemnly behind them.

The trip was a routine one. Skies stayed clear, winds calm and no atmospheric electrical disturbances bothered our navigation equipment or the Global Navigation System. Fifty miles from Churchill, I radioed for a taxi. After we landed, the family climbed into the waiting cab and sped away.

That night we investigated the night spots in the port community. In one bar, we watched as a tiny woman stopped an altercation between two huge men, one her father and the other, her uncle. Two more fights broke out before midnight and an unconscious drunk blocked the door to our hotel floor.

I forgot the Baker Lake mother-baby incident since only the more exciting flights above the barrenlands tended to stay in my mind. A few weeks later, we returned to Baker Lake and checked into the lodge. With little else to do while the telephone installers worked, I walked to the Hudson's Bay Company store. Like most retail establishments in the Arctic, this one sold the usual plastic southern goods, rifles and lethal-looking animal traps.

While at the cash register, I heard a loud gasp and felt a hand on my shoulder. Turning around, I recognized the woman whose child we had taken to Churchill. Tears rolled down her cheeks and she threw both arms around my neck. For a moment I feared her child had died. I was embarrassed and at a loss for words, as other patrons watched the scene.

"Thank you," she said. "Thank you, thank you."

She told me her baby slept safely at their home in Baker Lake. Evidently, the child was far more seriously ill than anyone had thought. Without the trip to Churchill weeks ago, the little girl probably would have died. Our Orange Bird had made the difference. As I left Baker Lake behind the next day, the captain and I felt that someone appreciated the value of airplanes and the pilots who flew them.

Crisscrossing Arctic barrenlands day after day was never monotonous. Periodically, incidents took place to add to the excitement of northern flying. On a trip to Great Whale, we overheard a harried radio operator desperately trying to contact a doctor in Frobisher Bay. At the time, a mysterious radio blackout weakened ground communications, but midway between two stations and at 10,000 feet, every word came across clearly in our earphones.

A young miner had become seriously ill so we volunteered to relay his symptoms over the air to the doctor. After a few moments of chatter, we passed word back to Asbestos Hill—it was probably acute appendicitis, the doctor thought. The pilots of a passing Nordair Short Skyvan airliner overheard the conversation and quickly offered to divert for Asbestos Hill. They could get the man quickly and move him to hospital in Frobisher Bay. We continued south but during our return sometime later, Asbestos Hill's radio operator recognized CF-YFT's letters and called us.

"He made it and is doing well," he said. "Thank you."

After landing at Povungnituk, we went on to Great Whale via an Eskimo settlement called Inoucdjouac, which meant leaving the relative security of land beneath our wheels. As we passed over Hudson Bay west of the Nastapoka Islands, sky conditions became scattered before we spotted the dark gravel of "the Whale's" 4,000-foot runway and landed.

Before long, a gangly lawn rake of a gas attendant, who worked as a diesel mechanic, noticed the Orange Bird. At the end of a night-long bender, his beltless pants slipped halfway down his rump and long slivers of slime drooled from the corner of his mouth as he stumbled toward the airplane. Twice he fell on his face before reaching us. Unimpressed by the way he handled the gas hose when he dropped it into a puddle of foam-flecked water, I took the thing away from him and finished refuelling without his help.

During my Frobisher assignment, no crew members damaged the airplane and no one was injured or badly frightened. One occasion proved to be an exception. Our passengers and pilots received quite a surprise after a long instrument descent through cloud above Chesterfield Inlet, north of Rankin Inlet. After groping carefully down, we broke from the overcast directly into white-out. Snow flurries and occasional freezing drizzle made judging height above the ice nearly impossible.

Our only reference points were faded snow-machine tracks with battered gasoline drums spaced too far apart to be of much help. As the airplane thudded into the slush, we skidded sideways across the runway, despite the captain's application of full reverse on one engine.

The nose wheel ploughed through a snow bank, sending

clouds of snow and crystals of ice up and over the Twin Otter's windshield. As we slammed to a stop with both PT6-27 turbine engines at maximum reverse, the Orange Bird surprised us again. The airplane shot backwards across the strip, its tail barely missing a fuel drum.

Concentrating on finding our way down, tracking accurate headings and monitoring the radar altimeter had so absorbed our attention, crosswinds completely slipped our minds. Unbelievably, we escaped without a dent or broken landing gear, but the telephone men in the back of CF-YFT were rudely shaken from their reverie. A few moments later, as we taxied toward some gray church buildings on a rocky shoreline, they broke out in a round of applause.

Many flights lasted more than two hours. Day or night, we rarely saw signs of life, except occasional pinpoints of light or snow-machine tracks reflecting the sun's warm rays—possibly Indians or Eskimos living off the land, we thought. In later years, I learned that few non-natives, other than exploratory geologists, showed much interest in the area, especially between Fort Chimo on Ungava Bay, and Wakeham Bay near Hudson Strait.

Wakeham Bay, 260 miles northwest of Fort Chimo, held no surprises when I made my first trip into the settlement. Before working for Survair, I had viewed a documentary on the Hudson Strait expedition of 1927-28, when a group of brave, resourceful men and airplanes went into voluntary Arctic exile to chart a water route from Churchill to open seas.

Six short-ranged, open-cockpit, fabric-covered airplanes flew in that storm-lashed land during the survey. A fragile de Havilland D.H.60 Moth made the first flight in Canada's Eastern Arctic, until gale-driven seas and an irresponsible ship captain sent it to the bottom of the bay.

As a historical aviation nut, I contrasted our own "expedition" to Wakeham with the undertaking over fifty years earlier. We tracked across a series of well-mapped, salt-water bays—Burgoyne, Whitley, and others—before sighting a track packed smooth by hundreds of snow machines. Our on-board navigational package, especially GNS, made arrival simple: follow the needles and watch mileage readouts.

The pioneers flew with little more than hope and 100-year-old Admiralty charts. In our state-of-the-art Twin Otter, communication meant the effortless push of a button on our 280,000-channel radio. We could speak to anyone in North America and, if conditions held, the world. Pilots of the wood-framed Moths and Fokkers carried heavy, tube-filled radios. They considered themselves lucky to contact their base at Wakeham Bay while taxiing for takeoff.

Modern airplanes in the Arctic traditionally handle rough or wet terrain with ease. Equipped with tundra tires, airplanes rarely stopped because of structural damage. Film clips of the Hudson Strait project illustrated the fragile structures of the Fokkers and Moths. Wooden propellers were standard then. Our precisely balanced, three-blade Hartzells could slam us to shoulder-jolting halts with reverse pitch.

After landing at Wakeham Bay, yellow, orange, or blue snow machines flooded out from the village and surrounded the Twin Otter. In warmer months, motorcycles greeted us—a far cry from the kayaks and dog teams that probably met the wind-burned faces of the expedition pilots. However, I felt certain that the smiles of the Inuit children who stared, noses dripping, at our Orange Bird, matched the ones of long ago.

Wakeham Bay trips meant long waits but I didn't mind. Affable Eskimo people and their children held my interest. So did semi-wild Husky dogs, cream-colored polar bear hides draped over wooden poles and seal skins stretched on plywood walls of tiny frame houses. A fringe benefit of working along the northern coasts included the awareness that the Eskimo people didn't resent the "tingmuit" or pilots. Those who flew CF-YFT gave them a link with the outside.

Unlike most Survair copilots before me, I enjoyed the work tremendously. Many from Ottawa head office completed their three-month terms and returned south as quickly as they could. In my case, Frobisher Bay was not just a place to live: it was a base from which to learn the art of realistic instrument flying.

Near the end of my six-month stay on Baffin Island, my instrument rating renewal came due. Now, before promotion to full-time captain, Survair expected me to upgrade to a Category I. Ottawa head office brought me south for training.

Since passing the initial flight test months before, all my instrument flying had occurred as a member of a two-man crew. In the Arctic, most procedures I became accustomed to were quasi-legal ones, like the never-miss method of getting into Rankin Inlet. In Ottawa, however, published protocol must be followed when dense traffic and crowded skies prevailed.

Survair checked me out on an airplane called an Aero Commander. An earlier-model, high-winged type, it lacked the Orange Bird's sophisticated electronic navigational devices. Nevertheless, a senior pilot insisted I use it to pass a pre-booked flight test with a Montreal inspector. Despite my protests that I wasn't ready for any test, especially in an unfamiliar airplane with stone-age avionics, we flew to Dorval.

After the paperwork, the inspector and I taxied toward the departure runway. Having never flown from Montreal and after six months in Frobisher Bay, the acres of asphalt seemed like a confusing jumble.

When I outlined my experience as a crew member and asked if he would act as copilot, the inspector haughtily refused. Legally, he was correct but like many inspectors, this one was out of touch with the real world of commercial flying. Surly, he refused to do anything.

We passed by a taxiway leading to the active runway.

"Guess I missed the turnoff," I remarked in a friendly manner. I was determined not to match his rudeness as I eased on the brakes and began turning the Aero Commander.

"Of course," he snapped. "You had your head in the cockpit."

Before stopping at the end of the runway, I thought about returning to the ramp. Judging by this man's attitude, I knew I would never pass the test ride. Less than ten minutes after takeoff, he told me to return. I failed.

Hardly surprised, I returned to Ottawa, where the chief pilot insisted I take another flight test the next day. The company desperately needed a copilot for a survey-equipped DC-3 in Quebec City for two weeks. This Transport Canada inspector had worked for Survair and was an old drinking buddy of the operations manager. As I feared, the test went poorly. Now, the humiliation of two consecutive failed instrument proficiency rides in two days went into my record.

That evening, I reviewed my aviation progress and decided that wasting more of the company's flying time would be useless. Somewhere back in Frobisher Bay or perhaps Fort Nelson, the basics of instrument flying had slipped away. Unless I regained proficiency, the chances of moving into a captain's seat were nil.

My employer allowed me a short-term break with pay in which I returned to Perimeter Aviation in Winnipeg. It didn't take long. A few hours in the Link trainer and another two in the Beechcraft Travel Air twin trainer and owner Bill Wehrle recommended a government flight test.

The Winnipeg inspector was a cordial ex-military pilot who had spent some of his civilian life working for northern airlines. In a few minutes, we completed the paperwork and taxied toward Runway 36.

"So," he said, warmly. "Tell me what you've been doing."

I was surprised, considering the experience in eastern Ontario and Montreal. I responded by letting him know that my duties in the last two years consisted of copilot teamwork.

"Fine. Today, you're the captain, I'm the copilot," he said. "You tell me exactly what you want and I'll handle the radio work and copy clearances."

Because of his attitude, every exercise he assigned went perfectly, both in instrument techniques and emergency procedures. In less than an hour, I met the standards for an airline transport rating or ATR, the highest grade of Canadian pilot license.

As soon as the federal inspector wished me well and left the flight school, I made a quick call to the operations manager in Ottawa.

"Now what?" I asked.

"You have the Class I? Excellent. You're captain on a Twin Otter," he said. "It's undergoing some modifications for a few weeks and won't be back until after the New Year. Why don't you take some time off?"

Ecstatic about my promotion and increase in salary, I asked about my future with Survair. The company's plans included three months on a Twin Otter modified for geophysical survey work and then to Great Whale, where another Twin Otter flew charters. In the Whale, I would alternate as captain and copilot and then return to Frobisher Bay as captain on the Orange Bird.

When I returned to Toronto to visit Linda and Rhonda I realized how lucky I was doing exactly the type of work I enjoyed in one of the world's most challenging environments. Decent salary, a place to which my family could eventually come and a superb airplane—few pilots dared ask for more.

While spending time with Linda and Rhonda in Toronto, I received an unexpected telephone call in mid-December. Survair's operations manager, in the city on business with another survey branch of the company, asked me to come to the office as quickly as possible. After flogging my Ford through early-morning, rush-hour traffic, I entered a tall brick building where he waited in a spare office.

I felt loyal to Survair. They had allowed me to stay the extra three months in Frobisher Bay and paid my family's airfare to join me. Survair's management stood by patiently while I worked out my instrument flying problems and completed the ATR. Few employers would have bothered. At the time, pilots of all ages and levels of experience could be found by a quick telephone call.

The operations manager opened a black, leather attache case and withdrew a narrow, white business envelope and handed it across the desk. He waited as I opened it. Inside, I found a large pay cheque. It must be a Christmas bonus, I thought, since the holiday season began soon.

"It's a separation cheque," he said.

"Separation cheque? The survey contract fell through?"

"No, I had no choice. You've done good work for us but we have to let you go."

Let me go? My God, not from this job, I thought to myself.

Evidently, the aviation inspector with whom I'd failed the Ottawa flight test still socialized with Survair's management. A drunkard, who talked too much when drinking, he had attended a

Survair party and asked what became of Robert Grant. On learning I had recently returned from Winnipeg with my ATR, he seemed surprised. He blabbered, "Oh, we'll get him. He can't go to another region. Those guys in Winnipeg are too easy."

Hardly a winner himself, I knew his history. Before becoming a civil servant, he had tried to take off in a high-performance survey airplane while inebriated and, according to a Survair mechanic, he damaged the machine badly. This upstanding epitome of a power-hungry civil servant was hardly qualified to judge anyone's proficiency.

Until that moment, I believed that flight-test standards across Canada didn't vary, nor had anyone ever suggested that an ATR in Winnipeg differed from one in Ottawa. Nevertheless, the operations manager decided Survair couldn't take a chance on someone for whom federal inspectors planned a "we'll get him" campaign.

I pocketed the cheque.

The operations manager thanked me for coming and claimed he could do no more. Too shocked to retort that perhaps the company should stand by employees who proved their abilities, had accident-free records and committed no wrong-doings, I left the room. It was the beginning of the holiday season. Finding winter work wasn't going to be easy. Merry Christmas.

Immediately, I called Transport Canada in Ottawa. After several "please holds," the head of the organization came on the line. He listened to my story about why my job evaporated and then curtly interrupted.

Government inspectors worked under the strictest principles, he said. Yes, flight test standards in Ontario matched Winnipeg's. He coldly pointed out that no one under his authority drank to excess. His highly trained virtuosos never threatened legally licensed pilots. Never, he snapped, and slammed the telephone down.

Trying to convince myself the incident never took place, especially when payday arrived and no cheque came my way, proved fruitless. Despondent, I called across Canada for work. For the first time since entering commercial flying, I stood in line at an unemployment insurance office.

Months into the New Year of 1975, I continued sending applications and followed up on whatever tips anybody passed on. Once, I contacted Toronto Airways at Buttonville where an acquaintance had become head of flight instruction. He needed no one and pompously sneered that freelance instructors didn't know how to teach properly anyway.

Not bad, I thought, coming from someone who never left the traffic pattern at his airport.

15 Watching High

By late February, my self-esteem dropped to an all-time low and my bitterness toward the inspector hadn't decreased. When Linda reminded me that the situation had to improve, I received a call from Aero Photo at Ancienne Lorette airport at Quebec City.

The operations manager said he needed a pilot right away. His pilot had broken his arm and couldn't work. The idea of living in Quebec City appealed to us. Although not fully bilingual, I knew much of the language and speaking two languages at an early age would be an asset for Rhonda. I accepted a position as pilot and left for Hamilton to pickup and deliver a newly painted Cessna 310.

The flight went well, until winds shifted and snow showers cut the forward visibility. After passing Kingston along the ice-bound St. Lawrence River, I began feeling tired. Near Brockville, turning on the automatic pilot seemed like a way to take a break.

Until then, I'd never used automatic pilot. Unsure of how to engage it, I looked around for an operating manual, but found none. The apparatus revealed no clues so I flicked a small switch marked "on."

The instant the switch made contact, the Cessna 310 went straight up. I slammed into the seat cushion and my eyeballs sunk so deep into my sockets I could barely see. Unable to raise my arms, I couldn't turn the runaway device off. Afraid to enter the cloud ahead in such an unusual attitude, I forced one hand upwards to turn the system off and made a mental note to report the autopilot's reliability.

At Quebec City's airport, Ancienne Lorette, I signed some papers and found myself hired at an annual salary of $13,000 per year. The work ahead consisted of flying either the Cessna 310 or one of three Aero Commanders. Each airplane carried a huge camera that exposed eight-by-ten-inch negatives.

Almost all assignments involved long waits at nearly every airport in the provice. Aerial surveys, map making and ice patrols above the St. Lawrence River called for clear skies to produce quality photographs from high altitudes. Sometimes contractors wanted photos at lows of 6,000 feet for pulp log inventories at paper mills. The accuracy expected was unbelievable—calls for half- degree heading corrections took place every trip.

Aerial photography demanded an instrument-rated pilot and a camera operator or navigator. In front, the pilot used a topographical chart on which Aero Photo staff at head office had drawn colored lines. The navigator kept the pilot on track by peering through a periscope in the airplane's belly.

Most flights went to 21,000 feet, where the crew needed oxygen masks. Although I respected the organization for its sophisticated camera equipment and quality maintenance, the breathing apparatus they used came as a surprise. While reading about aviation before World War II, I saw a bomber pilot wearing the same unit we used decades later at Aero Photo.

My first photo work took us along the St. Lawrence to Mont Joli and then inland, with a long climb to 21,000 feet above Edmunston, New Brunswick. Never before had I flown so high or been so unfamiliar with the precision expected in this trade. As a result, I was anxious from the moment of takeoff. At almost five miles above the earth, the world looked strange.

The oxygen mask began chafing the sides of my face and chin as I unfolded reams of maps. With everything in place, I prepared for the first line. Behind me, navigator Gary Stapledon checked equipment and measured drift angles. The Aero Commander's engines already ran at full throttle and wouldn't advance further in the thin air.

After thirty minutes of concentration to stay in position, the tension I felt didn't ease. We carried on to the end of each line, turned left forty-five degrees, then came around to the reciprocal heading. Stapledon, a veteran in the business, seemed pleased with my flying. However, I began feeling an overwhelming claustrophobia. Nothing looked amiss on the instrument panel but the sensation wouldn't leave. Sometimes, the altimeter dropped a hundred feet and headings wandered.

For no logical reason, I lowered the wheels to maintain the altitude, which is the worst possible way to keep a sinking airplane in the air. We kept coming down and still dazed, I selected flap down. We lost more height.

Everything I did was the reverse of the proper procedure. Nothing worked and it felt like somebody had sealed us into a dinky, little metal box destined for an abrupt stop in the New Brunswick spruce trees.

"Your oxygen's cut off!" I felt, rather than heard, Stapledon yell. He had left his station at the camera to come forward when he saw the landing gear and flaps go down.

Through what was becoming a gray haze, I realized a red warning indicator had appeared in my air line. Neither of us knew how long I had felt the effects of anoxia.

I reached for the throttles, yanked them back to the stops and pushed the control wheel fully forward. The Aero Commander plummeted down so rapidly the altimeter unwound like a clock spring. A solidly built airplane, the airspeed needle never passed the maximum exceed speed. At 5,000 feet, we leveled so that I could settle myself in breathable air. In a few minutes, the claustrophobic feeling of impending doom left.

One navigator with Aero Photo seemed to have what his previous pilots euphemistically described as a personality problem. The operations manager pointed out that, in spite of the man's irascible nature, he was the company's best navigator. A new assignment to photograph plots near Sept Iles and Baie Comeau found me teamed up with the troublemaker, who had found himself in a situation where every Aero photo pilot refused to fly with him.

We first worked from Sept Iles, on a half-dozen lines before finishing a stretch near Baie Comeau. Miserable weather grounded us for weeks until finally a forecast suggested a clearing trend. The next morning, we cruise-climbed north for three short plots. We landed in Sept Iles for fuel, then took off to do the Baie Comeau lines. After finishing the assignment, both of us could go home.

We leveled at 21,000 feet. Clear, cloudless weather for more than half a day didn't come often, so we had to take advantage of every minute. Although I knew the navigator wasn't the most congenial character in Quebec, I respected his abilities and depended on him to finish the job quickly.

At the end of each line, the navigator called out the turn and when to roll the wings level. Each time I heard "camera on," I maintained as straight a track as I could. At "camera off," I began turning again. He never missed aligning the airplane with the plots on his chart.

We completed two lines near Baie Comeau and started another. This time, we missed and I heard him call to go around. Unusual, I thought; he may be good, but nobody's perfect. I banked left, held a heading for a few seconds then came right to find the line, but the navigator called another miss.

I looked to the rear but saw only his back as he spread the maps on the floor. On the third run, he again yelled that the Aero Commander wasn't in place. This time, I trimmed the airplane, loosened my safety belt and stretched back as far as I could.

Instead of red lips, his matched the purple of bituminous coal. He groped forward, eyes wide open, and placed his hands on the right, front passenger seat. His fingertips were blue-black.

This time, I recognized oxygen starvation. I ordered him to the back to turn on another air tank. During the journey to the bulkhead behind the camera, he stumbled twice. Lacking enough clearheadedness to let go of the clipboard and maps, he looked lost and confused.

I yelled at him to drop them. When he finally did, he shut off my air instead of adjusting his own.

Throttles came back; the nose went down; so did landing gear and full flap, like the day over Edmunston weeks before. As we descended with the vertical speed indicator off its peg, I raised the nose slightly. Slight engine power prevented the engines from backfiring, and saved the cylinder heads from rapid cooling.

After leveling a few thousand feet above Baie Comeau's airport, we flew until the navigator recovered. With one line to finish, we climbed back up and then, contract complete, we flew directly to Quebec City.

Later, my partner told me he couldn't remember shutting off the wrong air tank, nor could he recall his actions until we reached the lower level. The bag of his oxygen mask had somehow ripped, so he had nothing to breathe.

The monotony of waits for clear skies took a toll on Aero Photo's pilots and navigators. The Aero Commanders and Cessna 310 were not difficult to fly; however, lack of flying hours prevented us from maintaining the skills we had gathered before coming to the company. A good flying month with Aero Photo meant thirty hours, and that within a period of a few days. An occasional trip or two back to our homes in Quebec City provided welcome breaks.

Once I returned to Loretteville, a few miles northeast of Quebec City, where Linda and I purchased a house. I looked forward to a weekend at home. However, thirty minutes after I closed the door behind me, the telephone rang. Aero Photo wanted me to go to Mattagami, 165 miles northeast of Timmins, as quickly as possible. Later, while counting days away, I discovered I had spent eight months out of twelve from home and family.

Approaching Mattagami, I watched for the green lights indicating wheels down and locked but the Aero Commander's nose wheel stayed red. Raising and lowering the gear again caused a sharp, metallic, breaking sound. We would have to land without knowing for sure whether our airplane would collapse on its belly once we touched the runway. I asked Stapledon to sit as far back in the rear as he could to place more weight toward the tail.

271

Remembering the Canso incident in Victoria years before, I hoped to delay nose-wheel contact.

Aero Commanders normally didn't fly comfortably at slow speeds, but with full flap and plenty of engine power, I managed to hold the nose in a surprisingly high attitude. As the main wheels touched, I stayed off the brakes. With the nose still up, we slowed nearly to a walk as Stapledon jumped quickly out a rear passenger door and threw his 180 pounds on the tail. We stopped and he lowered the nose. Nothing collapsed and we re-started the engines to taxi to the terminal.

I discussed the situation with the chief maintenance engineer in Quebec City. He asked us to bring the airplane home for repairs. We could take off safely, he said, but shouldn't raise the wheels. Our airspeed was slower than our normal 145 knots, but we had no handling difficulties or excessive engine temperatures.

Aero Photo held a contract with Quebec Hydro, a low-level photo survey at 6,000 feet, to be completed before first snowfall. The chief mechanic and his crew worked through the night and into the next morning to send us back as quickly as possible. They had ordered parts before we left Mattagami.

I returned to the airport as a group of volunteers pushed the Aero Commander from the hangar. Spotless now, for someone took the extra effort to wash it while the mechanics worked, it looked dazzling in Aero Photo's paint scheme. The replacement navigator climbed in for a test.

As usual, both engines started almost instantly. With necessary checks completed, we taxied to Quebec City's active runway and made our takeoff. After retracting landing gear and watching the airplane's long legs swing into the space below the engines, we confirmed that warning lights indicated wheels up and secure. All looked well.

For ten minutes we cruised above the city, and took a look at the historic Plains of Abraham, where France's General Montcalm and England's General Wolfe battled in 1759. Since accepting work with Aero Photo, I had little time to explore my new home.

Back to work, we raised and lowered the wheels several times and watched three green lights appear. We could now land, refuel and load our baggage for the return to Mattagami. Weather maps showed a high-pressure area with clear air moving that way. We needed to meet the system to complete the contract.

On final, with landing gear lever down, flap selected and airspeed on target, we prepared for landing on the runway's huge white numbers.

"Sierra-Romeo-Golf," said the tower. The controllers knew we had planned a test flight. "Check gear down and locked."

The navigator laughed and pointed at the three lights between our seats.

"In the green," I confirmed.

We passed the threshold, and held the Aero Commander's bulbous nose off until the main wheels touched. A smooth landing, I thought and held the control wheel back to reduce wear on the nose-wheel tire. Finally, we rolled on all three wheels and our test was over.

Suddenly, as the wings lost their lift and the weight settled onto the wheels, we heard a metallic snap, louder this time than in Mattagami. The front end of the airplane plunged further down and the metal nose-wheel doors bored into the asphalt.

With a sound like a thousand steel plates scraping a thousand chalk boards, we slid down the runway. Smoke billowed out from our nose and flashed backwards by the windows. Above the high-pitched scream of the grinding nose-wheel doors, we heard a thunder-like rumbling reverberating through the airframe.

Slewing sideways, we came to a halt. Smoke stopped tracking behind us and enveloped the airplane. I opened the door and ran. The navigator stayed behind and struggled to unfasten his seat belt. As I raced back and reached inside to help him, several fire trucks pulled up beside us, their sirens nearly breaking my eardrums. Other vehicles joined them by the time the navigator jumped out.

A wisp of bluish vapour whisked upwards from an inspection panel on the nose. Making sure Aero Photo's valuable airplane didn't perish, I jumped into the airplane to snatch a screwdriver and fire extinguisher. After a few quick turns of its fasteners, the inspection hatch popped off, and I emptied the extinguisher inside.

While watching the firemen check the airplane over, I remembered the fuel shut-off switches in the cockpit. On the ceiling between the pilot and navigator seats, the Aero Commander had two toggle switches for emergency shut-offs. One for each engine, they stopped all fuel and oil from moving beyond their respective tanks to reduce fire hazard. To prevent an accidental selection, a small loop of wire secured a guarded red switch.

During training, I had wondered if a pilot had the strength to break the wires. Now, with the airplane slumped ungracefully on its nose, it seemed that I had overlooked proper procedures in the rush. Disgusted, I stepped into the cockpit to flick the switches. Much to my surprise, both had been selected down and a broken wire hung from each.

I looked at my fingers and found two perfectly parallel scratch marks glistening with fresh blood. Sometime during the crisis, training and instinct took over. Without realizing it, I had carried out the step-by-step emergency procedure drilled into me by check pilots. A quick scan around the cockpit revealed that all other necessary switches were also off.

Aerial photography demanded that crews take advantage of every minute of blue skies. To do so often meant flying airplanes until just enough fuel remained to land. Winds, closed airports, and other factors sometimes made it necessary to land elsewhere besides pre-planned destinations.

Our incident at Quebec City caused a three-day delay during which time the forecasted clear skies passed by Mattagami. By the time we got there in early fall, occasional snowstorms covered the airplane during the night, but melted when sunlight hit the early-morning bush country. Constant cloud kept us grounded for weeks.

At last, strong upper winds cleared the moisture above our photo lines. The assignment specified following a proposed hydro cut through the coniferous forests. The coverage would take us to the famed James Bay Hydro Project, where fuel could be taken at La Grande, a staging area for construction activity.

We worked diligently north from Mattagami. Our Aero Commander carried enough gallons of aviation gasoline for six hours at reduced engine power settings. By the time we finished, the navigator expected us to be almost overhead La Grande's 6,500-foot paved runway. We weren't eager to visit this place because of the surly security guards. Worse, I'd read in *Maclean's* magazine that construction crews staged a violent strike a few months before our arrival. The aftermath resulted in a xenophobic attitude toward anyone not employed on the massive project.

As each line ended, I took a mini-break, breathed easier and let the airplane fly itself as much as possible. We both carried soft drinks and snacks to pass the time. Even the vast wilderness crawling by underneath us lost its luster, although I marveled at the activity taking place. Floatplanes and helicopters had opened up the area before a single drop of tar covered any runway. Many still worked supplying work camps.

I enjoyed listening to the radio conversations of the working pilots below. They carried everything, lumber, gasoline and diesel engines, wherever a Beaver or helicopter could go. A scheduled Boeing 737 jet used the paved La Grande airport for construction worker shift changes. Its pilots also contributed to the repartee.

With only two lines to do, I noticed the light-hearted chit chat on the radio had dropped to almost nothing. Unusual, I thought, as I studied the wind-scudded lakes below. Gigantic, white-capped rollers swept across most of them. I realized that gale-like winds grounded almost every airplane and helicopter.

We depended on La Grande as a fuel stop and didn't have enough gas to fly anywhere else. A quick call to a radio operator gave us good reason to worry. Winds increased to forty knots and gusted higher across our runway, at ninety degrees. I rechecked the fuel gauges. We had used our reserve to finish the last line, and couldn't get back to Mattagami.

The navigator shut his camera off, secured what objects he could in the rear and climbed into the seat beside me. We lacked shoulder harnesses and depended on lap belts to hold us. This would be my first severe, crosswind landing in an Aero Commander. Judging by the trees bending below us, we would have a rough ride.

On final, I eased the throttles back and held the nose up until airspeed dropped to ninety knots. Unable to point directly down the runway's white center line, I turned into wind, flying side-ways across the surface. Low-level turbulence rocked the wings so badly that I needed both hands on the control wheel. One second we descended at 3,000 feet per minute; the next, a gust pitched us upwards. Alternating engine throttles back and forth, we maintained a crab angle so sharp, it appeared as if the runway would come through the navigator's window.

Uprooted bushes blew across the nose, as ferocious air blasts ripped them from the rocks. Swirling, tornado-like currents lifted sand from runway edges and plants with widespread root systems flattened against the ground. I saw that little more than a few tatters remained of the airport windsock. Debris from the camps flew everywhere.

A foot above the runway, I abruptly kicked the airplane's rudder pedals to centre us down the runway. Before the wind could drift us sideways, the main wheels touched. Quickly, I pushed the controls forward to lower the nose wheel. As we slowed, a gust erupted from a gap in the trees. The blast spun the airplane on the spot.

We stopped ninety degrees to our original direction with the nose facing into the hurricane-like gale. By the time we taxied to the gasoline pumps, the radio operator told us no airplanes and helicopters within a hundred miles moved. Almost before his words faded away, the pilot of a Province of Quebec Douglas DC-3 announced his intention to land.

We watched the huge airplane battle its way down. Landing a tail-wheel airplane in such conditions would be far more challenging than our Aero Commander. As the huge freighter taxied in, I accidentally dropped a can of oil on the pavement and watched it blow away into the sand.

Job completed, we left for Mattagami when winds diminished. With full gas tanks, we then aimed for Quebec City. A low-pressure area would shut down eastern Quebec for days, a weatherman told us. For us, it looked as if the photo season had finally ended. Several hours later, we landed at Ancienne Lorette and, bags in hand, I went home.

One hour after walking through the front door of my house, the telephone rang. Not again. The chief pilot explained that

Hydro Quebec needed more lines flown not far from Lac St. Jean, north of Quebec City.

"What about the snow?" I asked. "By the time we get there, it'll be winter."

"Don't matter," he replied, "you're the only pilot I can find. Everyone else has gone on holidays."

Chances of this assignment being short-term were almost nil. Fall weather around Lac St. Jean rarely brought clear skies.

Our accommodation in the Chateau Roberval consisted of small rooms in a very old but clean hotel. Downstairs, a three-stool bar with a half-dozen tables provided entertainment. A friendly community, Roberval became one of my most favored locations from which to work. With little else to do, I improved my French.

In the stay there, I heard English spoken only once, when we met another survey crew ferrying a Douglas DC-3 to West Africa's Ivory Coast. They decided to overnight because of forecast icing. The moment I saw their airplane, I knew why they landed. They flew the only DC-3 I had ever seen without rubber de-icing boots on the wings.

With a different navigator along with me for this assignment, I waited for photo weather. It finally happened and we climbed quickly to 21,000 feet. Each line brought us closer to going home. We flew a different Aero Commander than our customary airplane. Having frightened myself at La Grande, I monitored gasoline gauges closely.

After running on our auxiliary gasoline tanks, I switched to the main ones. We continued crisscrossing the sky west of Roberval, as a few puffs of cumulus began forming. We knew they would soon hamper our photography. Sure enough, navigator Gary Stapledon called camera off. I noticed fifteen gallons showing in the auxiliary tank and decided to switch back and use every drop. Minutes later, I reached for the microphone to obtain clearance for descent from Montreal air-traffic control.

Without warning, the left engine stopped. No twitch, stutter or gradual die-off from declining power, the propeller simply stopped turning. I realized the auxiliary tank fuel gauges must have been wrong. Instead of fifteen gallons, they didn't have a drop.

"No problem," I reassured Stapledon. "We'll just switch tanks and it'll start."

As I pushed the starter button, the three-blade propeller rotated several times, but refused to start. Surprised, since Aero Commanders rarely gave us trouble I tried again and continued descending from 21,000 feet. Our lines had taken us well east of Lac St. Jean toward the Saguenay River.

At 13,000 feet, the remaining engine held us. Now, we felt we could easily make it to St. Honore's triple runways and land with one propeller stopped. Our main concern centered on our inability to complete more photo lines. The chances of another clear day before Christmas were slim.

As St. Honore came into view, I noticed the temperature of the remaining engine creeping toward the red danger line. Bringing the throttle back allowed a gentle sink and increased cooling air over the cylinders.

In a few moments, I would be making my first, "for-real," single-engine approach and landing at an airport that lacked emergency vehicles. We landed without difficulty. Taxiing with one engine proved to be a problem until we stopped on a taxiway. One touch of the starter and the recalcitrant engine started instantly.

Later, the mechanics found no faults, and concluded that vapour lock or air entered the fuel lines and caused the engine failure. They replaced a corroded fuel gauge and theorized that my touchdown probably jolted the system clear.

The operations manager suggested we work from St. Honore near Chicoutimi, since it placed us closer to the remaining photo lines. I felt badly about leaving Roberval, for it had become my second home in a friendly community. Residents there seemed to appreciate an "Anglais'" attempts to speak the language. Despite the political problems between French and English we were treated well wherever we went in Quebec.

A one-day compulsory inspection brought us to Quebec City for a brief stay. Returning home for the few hours was enjoyable, although it astonished me to see how much my two-year-old

Rhonda changed. I thought we got along well as father and daughter. Shortly before the navigator arrived to take us to the airport, I heard her say to Linda, "When's that man with the moustache leaving, Mommy?"

On the way to St. Honore, the navigator mentioned that we'd likely be there a long time. He also said that Aero Photo received another foreign contract, one the operations manager mentioned at the time of my hiring. He had promised that I would be the first company pilot to work in Haiti, but a more junior pilot had already been told that he would be doing the trip.

During our last sojourn in Mattagami, a three-engine airplane with antennae and wires protruding from wings, nose, and tail parked beside the Aero Commander. We met the crew who flew nearly every day while we waited for blue sky. One mechanic told me the pilots worked thirty days, and had thirty days off and could live anywhere they wanted. It sounded ideal for someone who enjoyed flying, traveling, and spending blocks of time at home.

When we finished in the St. Honore-Chicoutimi area, the operations manager sent us to Montreal for several weeks to cover a contract near Sherbrooke. A call from there to Toronto put me in touch with Questor Surveys which owned the odd airplane in Mattagami.

16 On Line

The survey platform operated by Questor looked less like a flying machine than anything in my pilot logbook. Called a Britten-Norman Trislander BNA-2A Mk III, it needed three small Lycoming engines of 260 horsepower each to stay aloft. The center engine in the tail was often troublesome to start in cold weather. A mechanic told me that keeping fuel pressure in the lines from the cockpit to the tail was a problem.

Considering the weather in which the Trislander operated, it seemed ludicrous that the airplane lacked fuel primers. These devices injected gasoline into the engine cylinders for quicker ignition. Without primers, starts involved heavy throttle pumping—a common cause of fires, especially on cold days.

Questor's Trislander had been modified with long, square, booms from the nose, and another from the tail. Cables several inches thick linked the booms, and a device resembling a yellow bomb, called the "Bird," trailed a few hundred feet below the belly.

The bird and the electronic equipment behind the pilot functioned on electromagnetic impulses to and from the earth. Airborne geographical surveys worked by measuring impulse reactions to mineral bodies as deep as 1,000 feet below the surface mantle. A company representative told me this "input" helped them to discover a gigantic mine at Timmins. Questor Surveys, he added, proudly held world rights to the system.

The pilot's job consisted of more than flying duties. At the end of a trip, I developed film to send with computer tapes to Toronto, paid crew expenses and carried large amounts of cash. When anyone ran short of spending money, I acted as their banker. Whenever they asked for cash, they signed a green voucher. After a week on the job, I trusted my workmates completely and rarely bothered asking for signatures. This naive trust later became a source of trouble.

The company didn't worry about cloudless skies. Ironically, most of the work went on during winter, since warm-weather atmospheric disturbances affected the sensitive equipment. It became a Questor joke that if a thunderstorm occurred in Calgary, we in Northern Ontario didn't fly for days. Consequently, summers became the quiet times—the opposite of aerial photography.

A pilot, navigator, and equipment operator made up the airborne crew. The navigator sat beside the pilot to help keep the Trislander on track by interpreting photomosaics, or high-altitude air photos, glued together in strips. Behind the navigator, the equipment operator manipulated the analogue chart recorders, ran 35-mm, continuous-strip cameras, and changed film. Frequent adjustments and breakdowns kept him busy as the airplane surveyed at 120 knots.

At Timmins, I met the crew. Although the chief pilot and most of the Questor's staff seemed anxious to do their best, some who traveled with the airplane came across as peculiar.

The navigator, a physically huge, immature young man, had worked in Moosonee as a cargo loader. Someone told me later that he had held a shotgun to his base manager's head. The gentle equipment operator kept to himself and didn't get along with the navigator.

After several days of non-stop flying in 30 below weather, the crew decided to visit a local bar in Kapuskasing. The navigator began arguing with the equipment operator and a battle broke out in the streets of the pulp and paper town. Hardly conducive to harmonious working relationships, I thought, but the chief pilot didn't dismiss the navigator. Training another would take too much time, he said.

Most contracts turned out to be short-term, so boredom rarely affected the team. It seemed that we landed in one community, did the job in a few days, and moved somewhere else. In a few months, the triple-engine Trislander took me to several provinces, but never near Quebec City.

With an assignment completed above the flat terrain near Kapuskasing and Hearst, we went to Thunder Bay on the north shore of Lake Superior. We planned to survey plots west of the city, not far from a community called Shebandowan. Reports indicated poor conditions for a direct flight from Kapuskasing to Thunder Bay. Flying to Wawa looked like a good idea, since it would put us closer to the contract area.

Another Questor airplane, called a Short SC-7 Skyvan, had already been working from the mining town of Wawa for two weeks. A more powerful airplane, the square-shaped "Shoebox," as its crew dubbed it, handled hilly terrain far better than the sluggish Trislander. The Irish-built Skyvan, pilots said, flew like a Mack truck with wings.

After several days, ceilings lifted above Lake Superior's north shore and we decided to try for Thunder Bay. Snow-clearing facilities at Wawa's unpaved runway didn't exist, so several inches of snow covered the surface. The mechanic drove the company truck from one end of the runway to the other for nearly an hour to create a take-off path. I walked the airstrip's length and decided it would be adequate, if barely, for the Trislander.

With wings cleaned of snow and three successful engine starts, I stopped at the end of the runway. Gently easing in all throttles, we slowly accelerated. If we didn't leave the ground by a preselected point, we would abort and try later.

Sluggishly, we reached lift-off speed. As an extra safety margin, I kept the control wheel slightly aft. A few extra knots above our minimum control speed would be like money in the safety bank. The trees and boulders at the runway's end didn't strike me as a pleasant place to end a career, should an engine quit.

The airspeed indicator needle crept fifteen knots past the

normal target speed. With the control wheel further back now, the ungainly Trislander lifted into the air. The boulders and spruce tops passed beneath by a wide margin.

Later, the mechanic told me he thought the airplane ran off the end of the runway. From the gas pumps, he couldn't see anything but a blustering, white snow cloud. When he didn't hear the crunch, he knew we had made it. He climbed into his company truck and drove to Thunder Bay.

The flight became an exercise in map reading, until we recognized a hill called the Sleeping Giant, east of Thunder Bay. As we taxied in after a routine landing an Air Canada DC-9 pilot saw the Trislander and remarked over the radio, "If I were that ugly, I'd only fly at night." After putting the airplane to bed, we checked into a hotel and planned an early-morning survey.

That evening, the crew gathered in the dining room. The navigator quickly drank himself silly and, as usual, became an instant expert in aviation. His hours in the right seat of the Trislander, he told me, negated any need for flight instruction. No question, he said, he far outranked our company pilots when it came to expertise in flying airplanes. Now, in the hotel dining room, he slobbered something about almost "helping me out" back in Wawa.

"Man, I thought we weren't going to make it," he said, downing another beer. "Me, I was just about ready to feather those engines for you, man."

I couldn't believe anyone could be so stupid. No one but the pilot touched the controls of an airplane. Try as I could, I couldn't come up with any way to understand this imbecile's train of thought. Just as brain surgeons wouldn't expect janitors to remove handfuls of gray matter, I couldn't imagine a passenger grabbing the controls of my airplane.

Feathering implies rotating a propeller blade into wind to reduce drag—standard procedure when an engine quits. A flight instructor once compared it to turning a pie plate sideways after trying to force it through the air flat side out. If the navigator had pulled the propeller levers to feather, the Trislander would have ended in a twisted mass of flesh and metal. Accident investigators like to summarize their reports with "pilot error." In this case, no one would have known about this moron's action on that take-off run.

I discussed the incident with the chief pilot. He agreed the navigator had long ago reached a dangerous stage. Nevertheless, he retained him. Years later, I maintained an interest in aerial survey and watched accident reports. Having never come across anything in which blockheads had taken control from qualified pilots, I concluded the navigator had left aviation.

Another contract took us from Thunder Bay across Lake Winnipeg, and on to Flin Flon, Manitoba, where we began surveying lines close to the airport. At one point, as I returned for fuel, it took some time to locate the runways in relation to the town. Circling over Flin Flon, I withdrew the instrument-approach plate and studied it. Minutes later, I flew the indicated heading and landed. Soon, the navigator spread a rumor that we had been lost—unlikely, since the community's mine smoked beneath the Trislander's wings.

When replacement pilot Roger Croker arrived, he accepted my remaining cash and green voucher slips. We confirmed our matching totals as a crosscheck, and he became the banker. I boarded the first Quebec City-bound airliner. Normally, I didn't hear from anyone until reporting for duty thirty days later.

Once, the chief pilot called in less than a week, asking what happened to several hundred dollars expense money. Strange, I thought, the accounts balanced when I left the job site. He explained how the mechanic disclaimed accepting cash from me. He certainly did, as did everyone else on the team, but I had stopped asking for signatures on the petty-cash vouchers. The chief pilot accepted my explanation and what transpired between him and the dishonest mechanic I never knew.

Before the end of my thirty-day leave, head office called again to request an early return to work because another pilot became ill. The chief pilot added that the time had arrived to upgrade from the piston-engine Trislander to Questor's turbine-powered Short Skyvan. We had talked about the change weeks before.

The type check on the Short Skyvan would take two days. Eagerly anticipating an opportunity to fly one of the rarest airplanes in Canada, I arrived at Toronto's international airport. Unfortunately, the technicians had removed all radios from the instrument panel. Colored wires hung from empty holes, panels leaned against the seats, and hundreds of screws, bolts, and safety clips lay scattered everywhere.

"She ain't leavin' this place today," said one mechanic. "Probably tomorrow."

The next day, with check list memorized, I was about to leave my hotel room when the telephone rang. No checkout today, the chief pilot said, but he asked that I attend a meeting. Perhaps the company had an overseas assignment, I thought. After all, nothing other than the petty-cash voucher incident had taken place, and my production record had been excellent.

Ushered into a room containing a huge desk and tiers of cardboard map tubes, I waited. Soon, the chief pilot appeared. Moments later, Questor Surveys' operations manager walked in. They closed the door and sat on chairs facing me. Worried now, I said nothing.

"It's Diller," the chief pilot announced. He referred to the mechanic who traveled with the Trislander crew—the same one guilty of embezzling Questor money. The company had accepted an geophysical contract in Rhinelander, Wisconsin, which required a pilot and mechanic experienced on the Trislander. Bitter over having his thievery exposed, the mechanic flatly refused to accompany any operation with me as pilot. Knowing Questor had more pilots than mechanics, especially ones familiar with Britten-Norman Trislanders, I knew what was coming next.

"'If Grant goes, I don't,' is what he said, Bob, and we're sorry, but we need him," the operations manager explained. "We don't feel you're to blame but there's nothing we can do. That airplane's got to be on the job."

Damn. One of the best flying jobs in my career ended. Never a believer in burning bridges, I left the office.

Disillusioned with air survey, I turned to flying a corporate twin-engine turboprop for Browndale, Inc. in Toronto. After two months of autopilot flights, it was obvious this type of flying would never suit me. I missed dipping a wing to moose munching on forested hill sides or circling caribou herds galloping in the barrenlands.

Resigning didn't seem fair since my employer had sponsored costly training on the Mitsubishi MU-2K in Texas. However, during a Detroit stopover, the owner announced his decision to "remove the financial burden of the airplane." This unexpected turn gave me a chance to pursue my hopes of someday working with Ontario's "Yellow Birds."

For more than eight years, lack of experience and surplus pilots had thwarted attempts to join the famous government air arm. I had nearly given up but decided to try one more time and followed up with a phone call to chief pilot Wally K. Warner.

To my surprise, Warner said, "I was just going to call you."

Hired by what I believed to be the most professional aviation organization in Canada, I made myself ready to report for duty in Sault Ste. Marie on April 12, 1977. Before leaving, another pilot dropped by my home.

A veteran Noorduyn Norseman "driver," he seemed aghast at my decision to accept what he considered a soft government job. Disgustedly he snapped, "Them civil servants can't tell a float pump from a fire hose!"

"You'll never last," he said and drove away.